GO AFTER JESUS:

THE 6 IDENTITIES OF THE CHRIST-FOLLOWER

DR. TIMOTHY BROWN

Published by Dr. Timothy Brown

Cover Design
Muhammad Akram, 99Designs.com

Stock Image
Freepik.com

6 Identity Character Portraits
Daniele Fabbri, Reedsy.com

Editors
General Editor: Kim Faistenhammer
Denise Loock, Lightning Editing Services
Mercy, Fiverr.com

Scripture References

ISBN: 979-8-9998228-0-2

Published by Dr. Timothy Brown, www.DrTimothyBrown.org

Acknowledgements

It takes teamwork to make a dream work! This is especially true when it comes to composing a book. I want to take a moment to acknowledge a few of the people who helped make this dream a reality.

To the love of my life, Lori, your love, support, and encouragement have meant the world to me. Thank you for believing in me, cheering me on, and watching our six children at times when I needed the space to write. You're the best!

To our incredible six children, Keira, Noelle, Gabriel, Lincoln, Grace, and Elijah, I hope that this book helps guide you and support you on your own Christian journey as you **Go After Jesus**!

To my amazing parents, Leon and Janice Brown—thank you for instilling in me a love for Jesus and a deep appreciation for the local church. To my five wonderful siblings—Karen, Jan, Philip, David, and Michael—thank you for your prayers, love, and faithful support throughout the years.

To the faithful members of Radiant Church, thank you for your encouragement over our last decade of ministry. Your prayers, reassurance, and support have meant the world to me. Much of this book was birthed out of our journey together, making our way through the Bible one passage at a time. Pastoring you has been one of the joys of my lifetime.

To my executive assistant, Kim Faistenhammer and office manager Carol O'Connor, thanks for your help with reviewing this book and adding your helpful feedback. Brother Bob Machen, thanks for your input and labor of love!

To all my mentors and friends in the ministry, you have made this journey exciting. I am thankful that because of you, I have not had to **Go After Jesus** all alone.

To Pastor Skip Heitzig, I am forever grateful for your willingness to write the foreword to this book. What a gift. Your humility and heart for God and others are a blessing to the Body of Christ.

To every reader who picks up this book, welcome to the adventure of a lifetime! My prayer is that this book inspires you to **Go After Jesus** today, tomorrow, and for the rest of your earthly pilgrimage.

Above all, to my Lord and Savior Jesus Christ, You are the reason that I write. Every word on every page is dedicated to you and prayerfully surrendered to your Lordship. May you use this book to impact the lives of many who desire to follow you in today's world.

On this journey with you,
Dr. Timothy Brown

Contents

Foreword

I am a pastor. I teach week in and week out to a thriving congregation. It is the joy of my life to watch the Word of God transform people. Besides this, our church has hundreds of small groups that are devoted to breaking down the truths heard from the pulpit and applying them to the personal lives of these devoted disciples. We also have "specialty" groups that meet, targeted to help people overcome addictions, recover from divorce or the loss of a spouse, become a responsible citizen, and even become a wise entrepreneur.

Why so much activity and variety? For one essential goal: maturity! We want to make mature disciples. Paul advanced this idea to the New Testament church at Colossae. "He is the one we proclaim, admonishing and teaching everyone with all wisdom, so that we may present everyone fully mature in Christ" (Col. 1:28 NIV). Such a lofty goal! Is that even possible in our fragmented and diversely opinionated culture? Well, I can assure you, it is, and you've come to the right book for help.

The COVID pandemic of 2020 brought monumental changes to the world, our country, and the American church landscape. Suddenly, no one came to church. Everything was online. Everyone became disconnected. We quickly discovered an upside to this with the massive increase in online church involvement. Christians became consumers of sermon media. You could sit in your living room and watch the country's greatest preachers while sipping your oat milk latte!

But with the growth of our online community, something else was growing: my concern for these computer congregants' spiritual maturity. Was church now becoming just another spectator sport rather than a community of participants? That same question can also be asked of all brick-and-mortar churches as well. Is there a way to transform spectators into participants? Dr. Timothy Brown's new book, **Go After Jesus,** offers a clear pathway to accomplishing this noble goal.

Think of this book as a ticket, a ticket that admits the holder into an adventure-laden path of following the living Christ. As you begin to view your identity through six different lenses, Seeker, Disciple, Friend, Fisherman, Soldier, and Lover, you will discover an excitement for God by going after Jesus freshly and dynamically.

Go on then, off to your adventure!

Pastor Skip Heitzig
Senior Pastor of Calvary Church, Albuquerque, New Mexico

Go After Jesus

A Fresh Approach to Following Jesus

(A Preface)

"I would give my life completely to Jesus, but Christians don't seem to have any fun." Those were the thoughts that ran through my mind as a preteen. I became a Christian at the early age of five, but as a preteen, I had not yet reached the point of complete surrender.

The sneaky and sinister lie that held me back was that my life would be quite dull and boring if I decided to follow Jesus with reckless abandon. "Don't fully devoted followers end up moving to the jungles of Africa and eat bugs, snails, and all kinds of nasty creatures for dinner?"

I found out that I was quite wrong about giving my life fully to Jesus. Since I finally made this decision, my life has been anything but boring. Over the last 3 decades, my life has been one that is flooded with adventure, creativity, and purpose.

When I was 14 years old, I gave my life to God as a blank check and told God this: "God, my life is yours completely. I'll go wherever you call me to go. I'll do whatever you call me to do: Anywhere, anyplace, anytime, and at any cost."

Little did I know that after I decided to go all in for Jesus, He would call me to preach at the age of fifteen. Everything since then has been all because of grace, I didn't deserve this . . . and I didn't earn this, but God has been so good to me. Here's a snapshot of God's grace and goodness in my life:

- My walk with Jesus is stronger today than ever before, and it just keeps getting better with time. The more I know about Jesus, the more I love Him.

- I married the love of my life, Lori Brown, and together we have six amazing children (3 boys and 3 girls).

- I have had the joy of leading many special souls to saving faith in Jesus! Did you know that when you lead someone to Christ, you start a party in heaven? (Read Luke 15:10.)

- The Lord has allowed me to serve on staff at nine different churches for almost three decades. It's a beautiful thing to behold the Bride of Christ (the church) in all her beauty.

- I have experienced the highs and lows of being a church planter, starting a church from scratch.

- The Lord called me to revitalize a dying church that was about to close its doors, then God intervened to change everything. The church I now pastor is thriving with life as people are deciding to **Go After Jesus**.

- The Lord has opened the door for me to minister to both believers and nonbelievers all around the United States through our radio ministry, "Truth for Transformation with Dr. Timothy Brown."

What is *Go After Jesus* all about?

Go After Jesus is a fresh approach to discipleship. Instead of being based on the "do" this book is based upon the "who." Many books about growing in one's relationship with God often focus on best practices or spiritual disciplines. This book takes a different approach: Your identity (the who) directs how you live your life (the do). When it comes to following Jesus, the do (spiritual disciplines) flow out of the who (identity).

Before you read another word in this book, I want to state this boldly and clearly: The Christian journey is made possible because of the GRACE of God. You were born spiritually dead, but the grace of God didn't leave you that way. Jesus came to you, just as you were, to offer you complete forgiveness, healing, and the promise of a new life in Christ.

"For He made Him who knew no sin to be sin for us, that we might become the righteousness of God in Him" (2 Cor 5:21). Friend, it's all of grace. Grace is God treating you better than what you deserve, because Jesus took what you deserved. Grace is God's unmerited favor in your life. Grace is God shining His glorious light to push back the darkness in and around you.

Grace is God treating you like His very own child, because you have been adopted into His glorious family. You are saved by grace alone, through faith alone, in Christ alone. And guess what? You *continue* in the Christian life through grace alone, through faith alone, in Christ alone. In summary, discipleship flows out of a heart that has been touched and transformed by grace. You are saved by grace, and you are *sanctified* (a big bible word that means set apart for God) by grace.

Why this book? Why now?

I want you to discover the identity and calling of…

- The **Seeker:** I want to **discover** the awe-inspiring truth of who Jesus really is.
- The **Disciple**: I am **determined** to follow Jesus wherever He leads.
- The **Friend**: I **desire** to enjoy the richness of daily, intimate time with Jesus.
- The **Fisherman**: I **aspire** to bring others into the Kingdom of God.
- The **Soldier**: I **aim** to stand boldly for Jesus in life's battles.
- The **Lover**: I **long** to fully devote my mind, heart, and soul to Jesus.

Dr. Timothy Brown's Personal Invitation

This book will take you on a journey, a passionate pursuit of a thriving relationship with Jesus Christ. Whether you are exploring the Christian faith or you have been walking with Jesus for a long time, this book will help your faith grow even stronger. ***Go After Jesus*** is an invitation to the adventure of a lifetime: Following Jesus each day of your life. In this book, you will discover the six identities of what it means to **Go after Jesus** as a 1) Seeker, 2) Disciple, 3) Friend, 4) Fisherman, 5) Soldier, and 6) Lover.

To all apprentices of Jesus who want to know and love Him in deeper and more meaningful ways, welcome! This book will encourage, equip, and empower you for a lifelong pursuit of following Jesus.

I hope that this book inspires and challenges you to **Go After Jesus** every day of your life, starting today.

Here for this exciting journey together,

Dr. Timothy Brown,
Author of ***Go After Jesus.***

P.S. God not only loves you, but He also likes you. Turn the page to dive into the great adventure of following Jesus.

INTRODUCTION

The Most Exciting Adventure of Your Lifetime!

It was a classic case of love at first sight, or should I say, "love at first sound"? A small gathering of young adults huddled around a crackling bonfire in the heart of the Appalachian Mountains of Western North Carolina. Friends, both old and new, enjoyed the heat of the flames and lively conversations. Laughter and joy rang out into the dark night.

While some friends shared the latest happenings in one another's lives, others became acquainted for the first time. This was a night of fun. A night of possibilities. Something magical floated in the air. Then something extraordinarily ordinary happened. A visitor showed up later that night to join the group. This new person captured the attention of one of the young men who stood on the other side of the fire.

He could tell she was not local. Her accent did not have the Appalachian lilt. As he listened to her, he became more intrigued by this new arrival. He made his way over to her and introduced himself. It was so dark that night, he could not fully see what she looked like, but her voice captivated him with its feminine tone and cadence.

After the brief introduction, he could not help but think about the sound of her voice. Later, after the guests went their separate ways, he could not get his mind off that encounter. Her voice was a melody in his mind, like the beautiful sound of a flute. *What does she look like?* He had written down her name so he could look her up on Facebook. Lori Viens. "Interesting last name," he said to himself. *I wonder if she's French.*

The young man couldn't sleep until he matched a face with the voice. He logged onto Facebook and typed her name into the search bar. A long list of Lori's emerged from the query.

He scrolled down until he saw what she looked like. *Wow! She is gorgeous. I will send her a friend request and see what happens from here.*

The pursuit began that spring night in the Appalachian Mountains. Who was the young man, and what was his role in this book? That young man is the author, Timothy. Nice to meet you!

Welcome to the Adventure

Have you ever pursued something or someone that changed your life forever? You may be reading this book because you are interested in knowing Jesus on a deeper level. Maybe a friend gave you this book to read. Maybe you saw the title, **Go After Jesus,** and it piqued your curiosity.

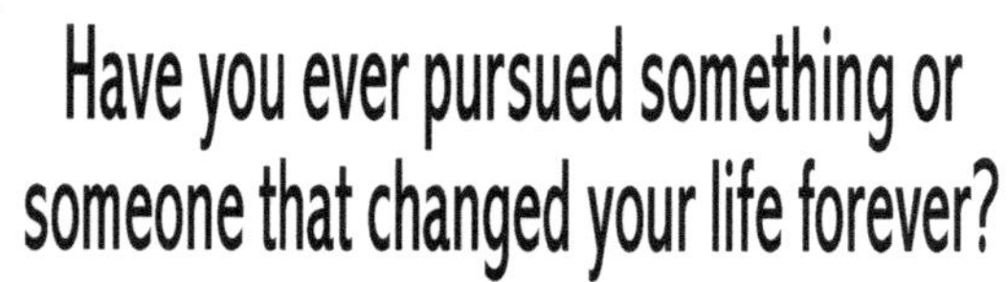
Have you ever pursued something or
someone that changed your life forever?

As you read ***Go After Jesus***, I invite you to take a journey with me- a passionate pursuit of a relationship with Jesus Christ. Some of you have not started this journey yet, and you are simply checking out what this "Jesus thing" is all about. Some of you are new to Christianity, and you picked up this book to grow in your relationship with God. Welcome!

Still others reading this book are already on fire for God and spending time with Him daily. Others have been walking with Jesus for quite a while. You are sharing your faith with the lost and actively making disciples. Some readers are completely devoted to Jesus, to the point where they are willing to lay down their lives for the sake of Jesus and the gospel. Welcome to the lifelong pursuit of knowing, loving, and following Jesus.

To all pilgrims who want to take a journey of knowing and loving Jesus in deeper and more meaningful ways, I welcome you to the adventure of a lifetime. This book will be an encouraging resource for you on your personal pursuit of Jesus. My purpose is to encourage, empower, and equip you for a lifetime of following Him.

In our journey together, we will examine the progressive nature of discipleship. Discipleship is the relational process of knowing Jesus and then following Him in every area of your life. We will examine six core identities of what it means to follow Jesus. Each chapter will also give you practical principles to help you know who you are in Christ.

The Six Identities of Those Who Go After Jesus

The Seeker:	I want to **discover** the awe-inspiring truth of who Jesus really is.
The Disciple:	I am **determined** to follow Jesus wherever He leads.
The Friend:	I **desire** to enjoy the richness of daily, intimate time with Jesus.
The Fisherman:	I **aspire** to bring others into the Kingdom of God.
The Soldier:	I **aim** to stand boldly for Jesus in life's battles.
The Lover:	I **long** to fully devote my mind, heart, and soul to Jesus.

I look forward to joining you on your journey of pursuing Jesus. Let's **Go After Jesus** together,

Dr. Timothy Brown

Part One

The Seeker

I want to discover the awe-inspiring truth of who Jesus really is.

CHAPTER 1

Come and See

"Rabbi . . . where are you staying?"
"Come and see," he said.
John 1:38–39

An Introduction to Go After Jesus

Christians are kind of strange. They're out of touch with culture. They do not look like they're having any fun. Devoted disciples, well, they all seem kind of old. I do not know anyone my age who is following Jesus that I can relate to. Those thoughts ran through my mind as I contemplated what it meant to be a fully devoted follower of Jesus at the age of fourteen.

I discovered Jesus at the age of five, but I had not committed my entire life to Him. I was what you might consider a "Sunday Morning Saint." I went to church on Sundays, and that was pretty much it. Was I correct about Christ-followers who were fully devoted, that they were a little strange? Did they truly have no fun like the rest of us? With these challenging questions circling in my head, I began my journey to truly discover who Jesus is and what it would be like if I decided to fully live my life for something or someone greater than myself.

I was like many typical teenagers, self-absorbed and crazy about girls. I was highly involved in sports, especially basketball, and dreamed that one day I would be the next Michael Jordan and rule the NBA as one of the few white kids who could soar through the sky like him. Despite all these exciting dreams and desires, something was missing in my life.

A Better Plan

Have you ever tried to look happy, but knew deep inside that it was not genuine? Have you ever wondered why you stay so busy and cannot stand to be still? Are you the type of person who is uncomfortable with silence, your music is always playing in the background, and your phone notifications are constantly buzzing? Do you sleep with the phone by your bedside, afraid you might miss an important call? If you answered yes to any of the above questions, I have good news for you. There is more to life than you are presently experiencing.

God has a plan that is far better than you could ever dream or imagine (Ephesians 3:20). Can I take you on a journey, a journey that has the power to change your life forever? In this chapter, we will take a deep dive into who Jesus really is. Whether you are still kicking the tires of Christianity or are already a follower of Christ, join me in looking into what being a Christ-follower is all about.

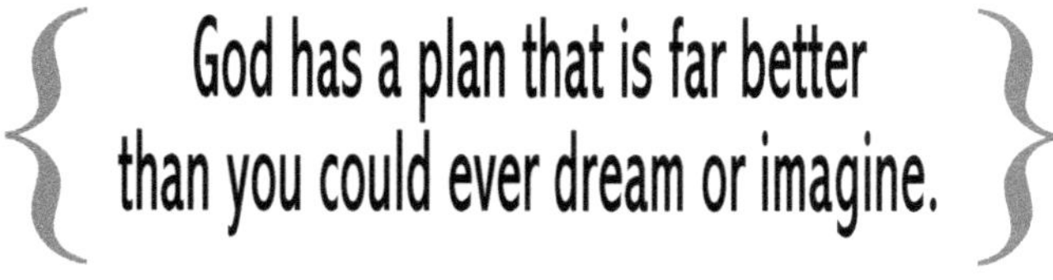
God has a plan that is far better
than you could ever dream or imagine.

Go After Jesus: The Seeker Introduced

I want to take you to the Judean wilderness where a wild man by the name of John the Baptist is preaching. John has been baptizing many people. These people are Seekers, hungry for the truth. They have decided to do a complete 180 and turn their lives over to God. These newly baptized followers listen as John preaches about repentance.

Repentance is not just feeling sorry for the bad things you have done in your life. Repentance involves turning from living your life for yourself and by your rules to living for God and doing things His way.

> Repentance is turning from living for yourself and by your rules to living for God and doing things His way.

John is baptizing so many people that he draws the attention of the religious elite from Jerusalem. The religious leaders ask John this simple but profound question: "Who are you?" They wanted to know if John was proclaiming himself to be the long-awaited Messiah. The Jewish people had been waiting some sixteen hundred years for a promised Messiah who would rescue them from all their enemies. The first-century Jews were more focused on a political Messiah than a spiritual one.

John's response? "I am not the Christ."

The religious leaders were shocked and confused about John's identity. "Well, who are you then? Are you Elijah, who has come back again? Are you the promised prophet?"

John again answered with a simple no. "So, who are you then?"

John's response echoed throughout the desert that day: "I am the voice of one crying in the wilderness, 'Make straight the way of the Lord,'" as the prophet Isaiah had predicted about seven hundred years before (John 1:23 NIV).

John maintained he was not the Christ; he was the forerunner who came to prepare the way for the long-awaited Messiah. John's mission was to clear away every obstacle that might hinder someone from coming to faith in Jesus as their Messiah. So, how can I clear the path for you to come to know, love, and follow Jesus? What are the obstacles in your way? The next chapter will cover three of the top obstacles many people must overcome if they want to decide to follow Jesus fully.

Searching for the Meaning of Life

May I give you some good news . . . I mean, some truly good news? Jesus desires to have a relationship with you. While you have been searching for God, He has been trying to reveal Himself to you. In fact, God's love for you is so great that He loved you even when you did not love Him in return. Paul tells us just how great this love is: "For when we were still without strength, in due time Christ died for the ungodly. For scarcely for a righteous man will one die; yet perhaps for a good man someone would even dare to die. But God demonstrates His own love toward us, in that while we were still sinners, Christ died for us" (Romans 5:6–8).

God's love for you is so great that He loved you even when you did not love Him in return.

Are you searching for the meaning of life? Do you want to know what your future holds? Would you like to have hope in this life and certainty in the next one? The Bible tells us that all your answers can be found in Jesus Christ. Jesus told His disciples He was "the way, the truth, and the life" (John 14:6).

If you are looking to find purpose, look no further; Jesus is the **Way**. In a world where there is so much fake news, how do you know what is real and what is true? Look no further, Jesus is the **Truth**. Are you searching for the meaning of life? Do you want to make a difference in the world? Look to Jesus because He is the **Life**. All true life, all lasting life, and all life worth living is found in a genuine relationship with Jesus Christ.

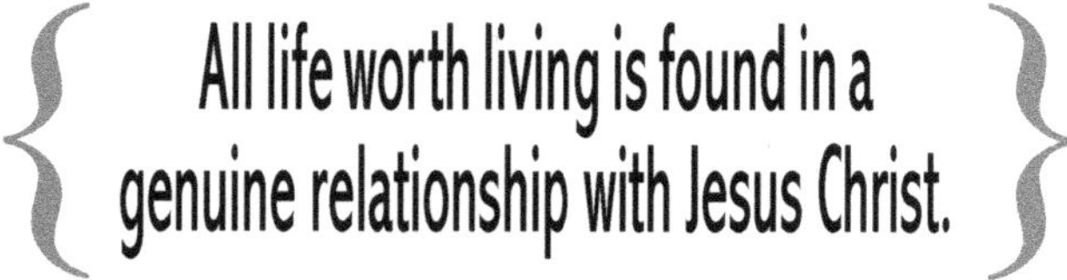
All life worth living is found in a
genuine relationship with Jesus Christ.

God's Wonderful Plan for Your Life!

The prophet Jeremiah gave this encouraging message to a group of people who had lost their way: "For I know the plans I have for you," declares the Lord, "plans to prosper you and not to harm you, plans to give you hope and a future" (Jeremiah 29:11 NIV). The Jews were captives in Babylon. They missed home, and they found it difficult to see anything to live for. They struggled with despair, since life was so hard and different for them in this strange land.

Can you relate? Is life hard for you right now? Do you need some hope so you can cope with all that is coming your way? Here is some amazing news: Jesus has a plan for you, too! He has a future planned for your life and a destiny beyond your wildest imagination. Ephesians 3:20 says God desires to do something that is "exceedingly abundantly above all that we ask or think, according to the power that works in us."

Take this journey with me—a pursuit of knowing, loving, and following Jesus. I know you have questions you want answered. You may wonder, if God wants the best for me, why does life seem so unfair and difficult at times? We will walk through this together. In chapter two, I will address your questions as you begin to discover who Jesus really is.

CHAPTER 1 RECAP

Go After Jesus Principle #1

Jesus desires to have a relationship with you.

Read: John 1:29–51

Key Takeaways

- There is more to life than what you are presently experiencing. God has a plan that is far better than you could ever dream or imagine (Ephesians 3:20).
- Repentance is not just feeling sorry about your sins. Rather, repentance is an about-face, turning from living your life for yourself and by your rules, to living for God and doing things His way.
- Jesus desires a relationship with you. While you have been searching for God, He has been trying to reveal Himself to you. In fact, God's love for you is so great that He loved you even when you did not love Him in return.

Reflection

- What would it be like to spend a day with Jesus?
- How do you think John the Baptist felt when his disciples left him to follow Jesus?
- What challenges and concerns keep you from fully following Jesus?

Looking Ahead

Chapter 2: The Challenges of Following Jesus, Part 1

CHAPTER 2

The Challenges of Following Jesus PART 1

"Come, follow me." The man agreed, but he said,
"Lord, first let me return home and bury my father."
Luke 9:59 (NLT)

What is Holding You Back?

"I've considered becoming a Christ-follower, but there are just too many things holding me back."

"I would like to follow Jesus, but ______________________."

How would you fill in that blank? For me, I desired to follow Jesus, *but* I also wanted to have fun. Most of those church folk did not seem to live the adventurous life I desired. Can you relate? What obstacles are staring you in the face right now that are keeping you from surrendering your life and following Jesus? Let's look at some of the challenges seekers often face. In this chapter, we will cover the first three of the seven top challenges many people have to overcome before following Jesus.

Challenge #1 My Past
"You Don't Know What I've Done."

One weapon the enemy, Satan, loves to wield against us is **guilt**. So many Christ-followers struggle with past sins. Have you ever noticed that even though you have confessed and repented of your wrongs, the dark clouds of guilt and shame seem to hover over your day?

So, how do you overcome guilt from the past?

The answer lies in understanding forgiveness. If you have trusted Jesus as your Savior and have confessed your sins to Him, Jesus takes away not only your sin but also your guilt. The apostle John says it this way: "If we confess our sins, He is faithful and just to forgive us our sins and to cleanse us from all unrighteousness" (1 John 1:9).

**If you have trusted in Jesus as your Savior . . .
Jesus takes away not only your sin but also your guilt.**

If Jesus took away all your sins by forgiving and cleansing you, you do not have to hold on to guilt anymore. You are totally forgiven, cleansed, and made righteous before a holy God! So, the next time Satan reminds you of your past, remind yourself that your past has been forgiven. Paul says that when you become a new creation in Christ, God sees you as holy, blameless, and above reproach (Colossians 1:22). To be holy means that you are set apart for God and His purposes. To be blameless means that Satan's accusations against you have no merit in God's heavenly courtroom because Jesus paid the debt for all your sins (past, present, and future). To be above reproach means that not only has God completely forgiven us, but He has also given us Christ's righteousness. This is all good news for those who follow Christ.

Challenge #2 My Doubts
"I'm Not Sure If Jesus Is Really God."

The second trap Satan uses against you is ***doubt***. Doubt is uncertainty about something. You do not know whether something is true or not. You do not have enough certainty to place your complete trust in something or someone. Here is how the enemy uses the tool of doubt in your life: *He tempts you to question God's Word.* This has been Satan's sinister scheme from day one. Go back to the Garden of Eden in Genesis 3. Satan tempted Eve by causing her to question God's Word: "Has God indeed said, 'You shall not eat of every tree of the garden'?" (Genesis 3:1). Satan attempted to cast doubt in Eve's mind concerning what God said. Well, guess what? Satan is still using the same bag of tricks in your life today.

Satan often keeps you from God's best by keeping you from God's Word. If Satan can cause you to doubt any of God's truth, he has led you into a lie. If he can lead you into a lie, he can lead you into sin. If Satan can lead you into sin, he can construct a stronghold in your life. Once you are under a stronghold, you will feel bound by the darkness of doubt. So, do not let doubt keep you from the life God intends for you.

Overcoming Doubt

How do you overcome the deception of doubt? The aged apostle John gives us the answer in the book of Revelation: "Then they overcame him by the blood of the Lamb and by the word of their testimony, and they did not love their lives to the death" (Revelation 12:11). If you want victory over doubt, you need to experience *complete forgiveness* and *complete victory.*

{ If you want victory over doubt, you need to experience complete forgiveness and complete victory. }

True forgiveness is experienced when you accept *what* Jesus did for you on the cross. Two possible options could grant you access to heaven. ***Option 1: Never make a mistake.*** If you can live a perfect life and never sin, not even one time, you will be accepted into heaven because of your perfection. Since God is perfect and holy, only those without any faults can enter His presence. Would you qualify for this option? ***Option 2: You can be forgiven by Jesus.*** Jesus came to our place, planet Earth, to die on the cross in our place so that He could take us one day to His place, heaven. The way to receive this option is by asking Jesus to forgive you and accepting Him as your Savior. Guess what? Jesus is not only willing to do this, but He is ready to do this for you right now. Keep reading. It is about to get good!

Examine the two options: Option 1, live a perfect life. Option 2, accept forgiveness by accepting Jesus as your Savior. Hmm . . . this is a tough one. Not really. No one, including yourself, is perfect.

No One Is Perfect, Now What?

The apostle Paul says we have all failed when it comes to living a perfect life. "For all have sinned and fall short of the glory of God" (Romans 3:23). Face it . . . None of us are anywhere near perfect. If we want to live without guilt, we need to find another alternative, because living a perfect life is not humanly possible.

What about the second option: *accepting forgiveness in Christ*? How does one go about this? How can we get rid of our guilt and shame? If someone must be perfect to get into heaven, how in the world will any of us make it? The Bible goes on to state, "For the wages of sin is death, but the gift of God is eternal life in Christ Jesus our Lord" (Romans 6:23). Do you want the bad news or the good news first?

We will get the bad news over with. You and I have failed when it comes to living a perfect life. We have sinned in our thoughts, we have blown it with our words and actions, and most of us mess up daily. The verse we just read says that the outcome, or the wages, of our sin is *death*. This death is twofold: *physical* and *spiritual*.

The sad reality is that we are all dying. A sober thought, I know. As soon as we are born into this world, our life span becomes one day less every day that we live on planet Earth. We may not think much about this fact until we hit forty, maybe fifty or beyond. We know we are all dying physically, but did you know that was *not* part of God's original plan? God designed Adam and Eve to live forever, but they ate the forbidden fruit, and as a result, sin and death came into the world and affected us all (see Genesis 3).

Even worse than physical death is *spiritual death*. What is spiritual death? After one's body dies, if that person has not accepted Jesus as Lord and Savior, they go to a place called hell. Spiritual death is living forever outside of the loving presence of God. The sad reality is that hell was not even made for people. It was created as a place of judgment for the devil and his fallen angels (Matthew 25:41).

If God is so loving, why do some people end up in hell? You may be asking this question: "Why would a loving God send any of His creations to hell?" That does not seem loving at all. Great question. The answer is this: God does not want you to go to hell.

This is why He made the greatest sacrifice in the history of the world when He sent His Son, Jesus, to Earth to die for your sin and my sin, so we would not end up in hell.

The price for our sins was fully paid when Jesus died on the cross and defeated death by rising on the third day. Here's the heart of the Father: "The Lord is not slack concerning *His* promise, as some count slackness, but is longsuffering toward us, not willing that any should perish but that all should come to repentance" (2 Peter 3:9). God does not want anyone to perish. He desires everyone to come to a saving faith through a relationship with Jesus Christ. So do not let doubt keep you from a living, saving faith in Jesus.

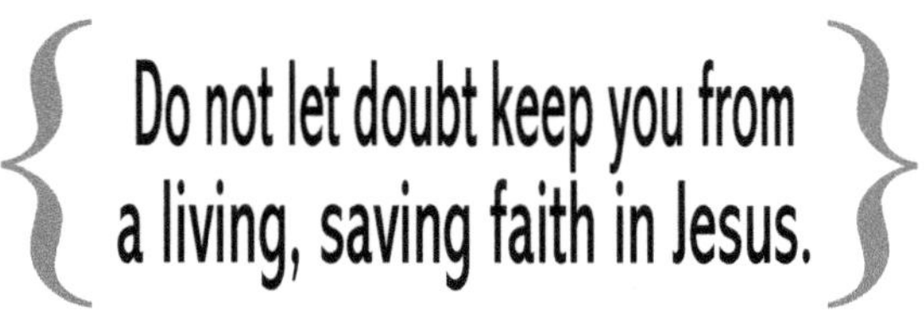
Do not let doubt keep you from
a living, saving faith in Jesus.

You can overcome your doubt by taking that first step of faith and placing your trust in Jesus. Ask Jesus to save you. Ask Jesus to reveal Himself to you. Talk to God about your doubts; He can handle them. In time, the deception of doubt can be transformed into the glorious light of faith. I will cover the plan of salvation in more depth in the next chapter.

Challenge #3 My Feelings
"No One Really Understands Me."

How many times have you allowed your feelings to lead you? What major life decisions were made simply because you had a "gut feeling"? Picture this: You spend time with your best friend every day. You laugh with this friend. You cry with this friend. You go places together. Your friend advises you on every major decision. But then you find out something, your best friend has been lying to you almost every day. How would you respond? Would you trust your friend to advise you going forward?

Your feelings often lie to you. They often tell you things that are not true, like "I do not think God loves me." Your feelings often suggest you do things that are not best for you: "I do not want to read my Bible today because I do not feel like it"; "I do not feel like going to church today";

"I do not want to do *anything* today because I feel too tired"; "I know I should pray, but I feel like I have so much to do."

What is the purpose of your feelings? God gave them to you to be *gauges*, not *guides*. They report to you, but they are not meant to dictate your decisions. Author Jon Bloom says it well: "But because our emotions are wired into our fallen natures as well as into our regenerated natures, sin and Satan have access to them and will use them to try and manipulate us to act faithlessly. That's why our emotional responses to temptation can seem like imperatives (you must do . . .) rather than indicatives (here's what you're being told). Just remember, that's deceit."[1]

God gave you feelings to be gauges, not guides.

Therefore, do not let your feelings keep you from following Jesus. Your faith is based on the facts of the Word of God, not your constantly changing feelings. Paul says that faith comes by feelings, right? No, faith comes by hearing the Word of God (Romans 10:17). Your feelings are a gift from God to help you experience life; He never intended them to direct your life. Feelings such as depression or sadness alert you to something that needs to be addressed, but these feelings are not meant to guide your life. Feelings help you experience life in the moment, but feelings are not meant to be your guides for the future.[2]

CHAPTER 2 RECAP

Go After Jesus Principle #2

Do not let your past mistakes, your present doubts,
or your fleeting feelings keep you from following Jesus.
Read: 1 John 1:5-10

Key Takeaways

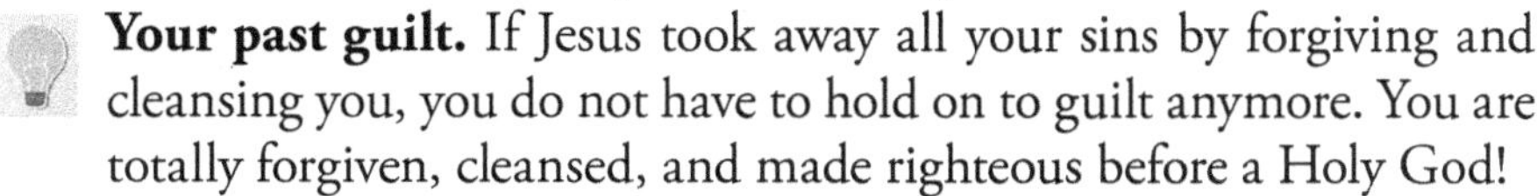

Your past guilt. If Jesus took away all your sins by forgiving and cleansing you, you do not have to hold on to guilt anymore. You are totally forgiven, cleansed, and made righteous before a Holy God!

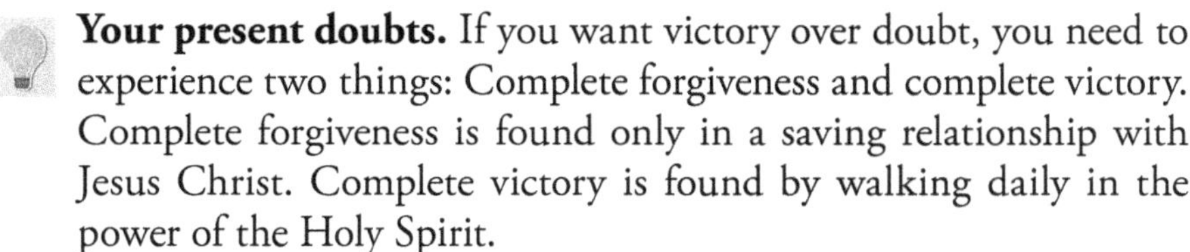

Your present doubts. If you want victory over doubt, you need to experience two things: Complete forgiveness and complete victory. Complete forgiveness is found only in a saving relationship with Jesus Christ. Complete victory is found by walking daily in the power of the Holy Spirit.

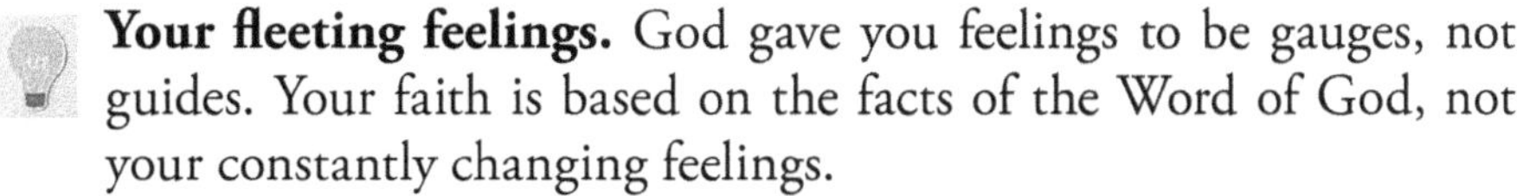

Your fleeting feelings. God gave you feelings to be gauges, not guides. Your faith is based on the facts of the Word of God, not your constantly changing feelings.

Reflection

What guilt over sin are you hanging on to that Jesus has already forgiven?

What doubts are keeping you from embracing complete forgiveness?

In what circumstances are you most likely to be led by feelings?

Looking Ahead

Chapter 3: The Challenges of Following Jesus, Part 2

CHAPTER 3

The Challenges of Following Jesus PART 2

Then He said to them all,
"If anyone desires to come after Me, let him deny himself,
and take up his cross daily, and follow Me."
Luke 9:23

"I think I'll become a Christian when I'm older. I have too much life to live right now." In the last chapter, we addressed the first three challenges people must overcome to become genuine followers of Jesus.

Now we will look at the other four challenges.

Challenge #4 My Lifestyle
"I Don't Want to Give Up ______. "

When you look at Christ-followers, it may seem like all they do is go to church, read their Bibles, and pray. Boring! But did you know that faithful Christ-followers will enjoy life more than those who do not follow Him?

Those who are not pursuing Jesus may seem to be happy, but they are not fully enjoying life because they are only *two-thirds* alive. They are alive physically, and their personalities are alive (body and soul), but they are dead spiritually. In Ephesians 2:1-3, Paul tells us that before a person experiences a saving faith in Jesus, they are spiritually dead. This means that the unsaved person can only experience two-thirds of life because they are not alive spiritually.

Those who are not pursuing Jesus are only two-thirds alive.

Therefore, do not believe Satan's lie that if you decide to follow Jesus, you will not have any fun. The opposite is true. Christ-followers will have more authentic, more abundant lives because they can experience the joys of life fully alive; body, soul, and spirit. Do not live your life partially alive, live it fully alive! If you decide not to follow Jesus, at best, you can only be two-thirds alive because your spirit is still not activated. Only when you give your life to Christ fully, without reservation, can you begin to experience life fully alive.

Let me give you an example: Sally meets a guy who takes her breath away. Henry is the total package. He is good-looking, he has a successful career, and he is also very intelligent. However, there is one catch. Sally is a Christ-follower, and Henry considers himself New Age. The problem? If Sally decides to date and marry Henry, she can never fully experience the type of relationship that connects on all levels, physical, intellectual, and spiritual. Likewise, anyone who has not yet given themselves to Jesus is not living a life that is fully alive.

Challenge #5 The Time Myth

"I'll Become a Christ-follower Later."

One of the biggest excuses for not following Jesus is "I'll follow Jesus *later*." Procrastination is dangerous when it comes to your spiritual life for several reasons.

First, you do not know what will happen tomorrow. Today could be your last day on Earth. The person who delays the decision to follow Christ is gambling on their eternity, and gambling on your forever is dangerous.

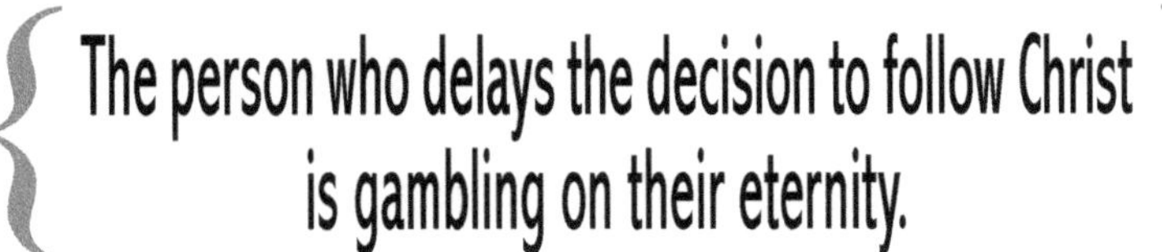
The person who delays the decision to follow Christ
is gambling on their eternity.

Second, it is not a good idea to delay following Jesus because you do not know where your heart will be in the future. What if you have enough faith to believe today, but tomorrow your faith is not as strong? What if your excitement for God and His Word grows cold over time?

This can happen to anyone. That's why it is not a good idea to say, "I'll follow Jesus when I get older. I just want to live my life now and come to Jesus before I die." Often, someone thinks they will follow Christ once they are married and have children, and at that point, they will join a church and come to Jesus. However, you do not know what the state of your heart will be in the future. It may grow colder toward Jesus over time. In addition, though God calls us to Him, He may not continue to knock or call us to Him if we turn away and ignore His voice.

A young man named Julian grew up in the third century. Julian had every opportunity to follow Christ from a young age. He was raised in a Christian home. He also received a Christian education. Julian had so much potential and opportunity in his life that he even ascended to the Roman Imperial throne. After receiving this newfound power, Julian decided to renounce Christianity and instead pursue Roman pagan philosophies. His rejection of Christianity was so great that he even sought to restore Roman paganism to the empire and to suppress Christianity. Julian's story is one of a heart that grew cold over time.[3]

Another reason you should not delay following Jesus is that you have an amazing God given destiny that you do not want to waste. God has an incredible plan for your life, a plan to prosper you, a plan that is overflowing with living hope, and a plan that involves a bright future (Jeremiah 29:11). Do not waste your destiny by delaying your decision to follow Jesus. God has people He wants you to reach, places He wants you to go, and lives He wants you to impact. Your destiny is too bright and your potential in Christ too great to waste by delaying your decision to follow Jesus.

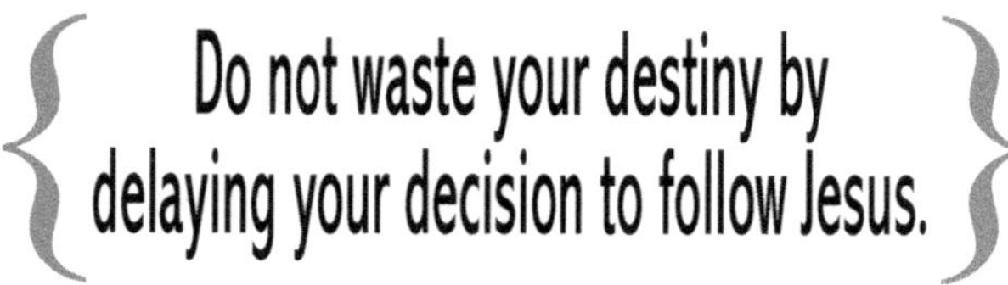
Do not waste your destiny by
delaying your decision to follow Jesus.

Challenge #6 Other Christ-followers

"I know Too Many Hypocrites"

"I would check out going to church, but I know too many hypocrites who go there." How many times have you said or heard this statement? As a Pastor, can I tell you something shocking?

I agree with you. The church is full of hypocrites! Let me explain. A hypocrite is someone who says one thing and does another. The word *hypocrite* ultimately came into English from the Greek word *hypokrites*, which means 'an actor' or 'a stage player.' [4] Therefore, if a churchgoer knows he or she should act one way, but does not, you could call them a hypocrite.

Here's the bottom line: Unless you are perfect, your actions are not *always* going to line up with your beliefs. This is called being human. If your level of knowledge surpasses your level of obedience, you are not living up to what you know to be true. I like to call this the hypocrite gap: the space between what you know to do and what you do.

> **The hypocrite gap: the space between what you know to do and what you do.**

If your reason for not going to church is that it's full of hypocrites, you could not go anywhere else, either. Why? Everywhere you go, people are not living out what they know to be true or right. There are hypocrites at the gym. How many people at the gym exercise as often as they know they should? There are hypocrites at the grocery store. How many shoppers are buying items they know they should not, like bags of chips or candy?

Therefore, do not allow hypocrites to keep you out of church; there is always room for one more. You are welcome anytime. The church is not a showcase for perfect people. Rather, the church is a place of grace where people find forgiveness, love, mercy, hope, and a future through a living relationship with Jesus Christ. Please do not allow shallow excuses to keep you from the life God has for you.

> **There is always room for one more hypocrite in church. You are welcome anytime.**

Challenge #7 The Christian Culture
"Do I Have to Join a Certain Political Party to Follow Jesus?"

Do all Christ-followers belong to a certain political party? If you listen to some evangelical preachers out there, the answer almost seems to be yes. The reality of following Jesus is that you *only* have to say yes to Him and no one else. Salvation is not found in any political party, candidate, or cause. Salvation is a gift that does not require human effort or cause. Paul tells us "For by grace you have been saved through faith, and that not of yourselves; *it is* the gift of God, not of works, lest anyone should boast" (Ephesians 2:8–9).

Following Jesus means you place complete trust in Him and not in anyone or anything else. The only thing that can change the human heart is the grace of God, which is found in the person of Jesus Christ. Only the gospel message has the power to change the world, not any political party. Salvation is placing your faith in Jesus alone, not in anyone else. Granted, following Jesus will inform how you live, how you make decisions, and yes, how you vote.

> **Following Jesus means you place complete trust in Him and not in anyone else.**

Therefore, while I encourage you to take a stand for what is right, and this means voting in alignment with biblical values, I want to make this clear: You are called to follow Jesus, nothing more, nothing less. Thus, to answer your question, you do not have to be part of a certain political party to follow Jesus. You are saved by grace alone, through faith alone, in Christ alone. Do not let the distractions of this world keep you from following the only One who is able to give you true and lasting life.

Your Move: The Opportunity of a Lifetime

Together, we have embarked on this journey to **Go After Jesus.**

Let's look at who Jesus is. Jesus is who He said He is. He is "the way, the truth, and the life" (John 14:6). Jesus came to earth to die in our place, so one day he could take us to His place in heaven. As we have discussed, salvation is a gift that we accept by placing our complete and total faith in Jesus Christ, His perfect life, His death in our place, and His victorious resurrection on the third day.

Recap of the Top Seven Obstacles to Following Jesus.

In the last two chapters, we have talked about the top seven obstacles that often keep people from following Jesus. Which obstacle do you identify with? Are you ashamed of your past? Are you reluctant to give up a certain sin or lifestyle? Whatever the reason, are you ready to respond to God's call to follow Him? Do you want to know Jesus personally and follow Him passionately?

The Gospel Explained

How to Become a Follower of Jesus

If you said "yes" to following Jesus, I want to lead you in your next step on this journey, deciding to **Go After Jesus** passionately. This next part in the journey may be painful. As you look inside yourself, *slow down*. Do not rush through the next section. The story of the Bible can be summarized in three words: *creation, devastation, and restoration.*

Creation

What God made was good!

The Bible says God created a perfect world for us to live in. Adam and Eve thrived in that perfect paradise. The first couple enjoyed a perfect relationship with God in a pristine world. Originally, there was no death or decay. Adam and Eve's relationship with God, each other, and creation was in a state of beauty and perfection. Unfortunately, the story did not continue in a perfect paradise.

Devastation

How things went from perfect to broken.

After creation came *devastation.* Adam and Eve lived the dream until their dream became a nightmare. Into this perfect world crept a sinister intruder who had a plan to ruin everything for this couple and all their descendants. In the Garden of Eden lurked an enemy of God with an evil plot to destroy God's created paradise.

Satan questioned God's Word and God's goodness.

Satan was the intruder's name, and deception was his game. Satan questioned God's Word: "Did God really say?" He also questioned God's goodness: "Isn't God holding back on you, keeping you from eating from the tree of the knowledge of good and evil? If you eat from it, you will be more like God, knowing both good and evil."

Eve found herself in a tantalizing conversation with this undercover enemy. She took the bait. She ate the forbidden fruit. She then invited Adam to join her in this rebellion against God. Adam then willingly and knowingly did what he knew God told him not to do, eat the fruit from that forbidden tree.

The moment Adam ate the forbidden fruit, the world was forever changed. Sin infected humanity. Death tainted all creation. In a moment, the world went from a perfect creation to a corrupted one. According to the Bible, the result of the fall is death, physical death as well as spiritual death.

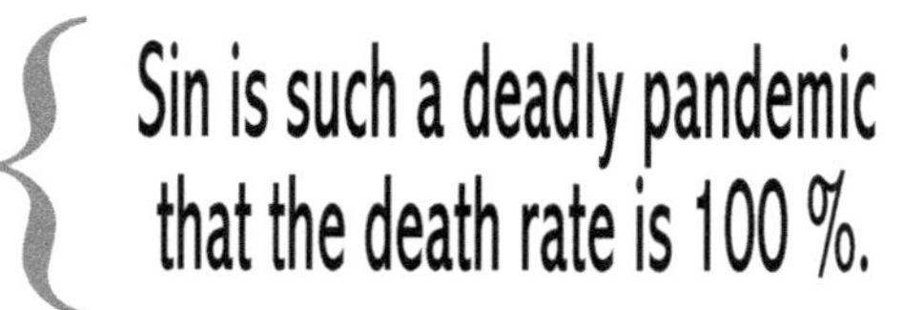
Sin is such a deadly pandemic
that the death rate is 100 %.

Sin is such a deadly pandemic that the death rate is 100%. Even if you live to be one hundred years old, this is still a short life compared to eternity. The Bible tells us "For all have sinned and fall short of the glory of God"

(Romans 3:23). The result, or the wages of our sin, is tragically, physical death (Romans 6:23).

Spiritual death is also a sad reality for us. Not only do the days of our lives fade fast, but now we are born spiritually dead. The Bible says we are dead in our trespasses and sins (Ephesians 2:1).

What does spiritual death look like? Spiritual death means that we are not able to experience a meaningful, loving relationship with God. When we are born, our spirit is not functioning the way God intended it to work. Instead of His Spirit living and guiding us within, we stumble around in spiritual darkness. Thankfully, Adam and Eve's story, and our story, do not have a tragic ending. *Hope was on the way.*

Restoration
There Is Hope!

Creation. Devastation. Where did we go from here?

Do not fear! *Restoration* was the way. The loving Creator's heart was broken as He looked on His creation that had turned into devastation. The perfect world God fashioned had been corrupted by Satan, who thought he had ruined God's perfect plans. Satan thought he had gained the upper hand on God, but he was wrong.

How did God fix this epic problem? He chose to do what only He could do. He sent His Son, Jesus, into the world to do something God had never done before: die. Why did Jesus have to die on our behalf? Was there no other solution?

David gives us the answer in the book of Psalms: "Against You, You only, have I sinned, And done *this* evil in Your sight" (Psalm 51:4). When we sin, we not only sin against others, we ultimately sin against God. God is also the only one who will judge us for what we have done, good and bad. Could God have sent an angel to die for us? No. What about a prophet or a spiritual giant who lived an upright life? No again. None of these alternatives is God.

The answer is simple and straightforward. Since we have sinned against God, only He can make it right. An angel could not make it right because we have not sinned against an angel. A righteous man, such as Moses, could not have died for us because our sin is against God, and only He can forgive us.

> Since we have sinned against God, only He can make it right.

The Good News
Jesus Is the Answer!

There is one major problem with God having to die for our sins. God cannot die. He is eternal, and nothing can destroy Him. How could our cosmic dilemma be solved? The answer is the Incarnation. God sent His eternal Son to Earth in the form of a man, the God Man. This is what Christmas is all about. God coming to earth in the form of a man, the person of Jesus Christ.

> God sent His eternal Son to Earth in the form of a man, the God-man.

Jesus was 100 percent God, and at the same time 100 percent man. Thus, the epic rescue mission was set in motion. The eternal Son of God took on a human body so He could die for the sins of the world. When Jesus died on the cross, His human body died, but the eternal Son continued to live. The mystery of the Incarnation is that the Son of God left the glories of heaven and humbly stooped to become human on our lowly planet. (See Philippians 2:5–11.) He humbled Himself even more when He gave the ultimate gift and became the sacrifice for our sins on the cross, so we could be forgiven and have a relationship with Him. He paid the debt we could not pay.

Creation. Devastation. Restoration. Where is your place in this epic story of God's amazing love and wonderful grace? Are you ready for the best news of your life? All you must do is receive what Jesus did for you by *faith.* Period. How can you receive this free gift of salvation? Paul gives us the answer: "For by grace you have been saved through faith, and that not of yourselves; it is the gift of God" (Ephesians 2:8). "Okay," you say, "so I'm saved by grace through faith when I accept what Jesus did for me?" Absolutely.

Now that you know the truth of the gospel (the good news about what Jesus did for you), it's time to receive this gift by inviting God into your life. You simply have to call on the name of Jesus and ask Him to forgive you, save you, and give you a new start in life. The Bible says, "That if you confess with your mouth the Lord Jesus and believe in your heart that God has raised Him from the dead, you will be saved. . . . For "whoever calls on the name of the Lord shall be saved" (Romans 10:9–13).

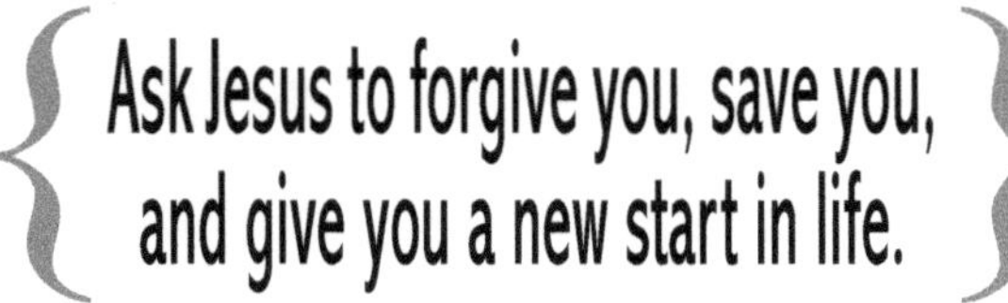
Ask Jesus to forgive you, save you,
and give you a new start in life.

Receiving Jesus as Your Savior

May I have the wonderful privilege of leading you to receive Jesus as your Lord and Savior? If you are willing to give your life to Jesus to be your Lord and Savior, pray something like this:

> **Dear Jesus,**
>
> **I believe the good news that you died for my sins and rose again on the third day. I acknowledge my sin and brokenness. Please forgive me for going my own way. Cleanse me of all my sins. I ask you to come into my life and fill me with your Holy Spirit. Make me a new person. I choose to follow you from this day forward. Thank you for forgiving me and making me a new creation in Christ.**
>
> **Thank You, Jesus, For saving me.**

If you just received Jesus as your Savior and Lord, welcome to the family of God! There is now a party in heaven, angels rejoicing that you are now a child of God and that God has reserved a place in heaven for you. In chapter four, we will begin to unpack what your new life looks like and how to take your next steps.

CHAPTER 3 RECAP

Go After Jesus Principle #3

My desire to follow Jesus should be greater than all the fears keeping me from going after Jesus.
Read: Romans 3:23, 6:23, 10:8–13

Key Takeaways

As a Christ-follower, you can have true and lasting joy because you are fully alive. Those who have not accepted God's gift of salvation are only two-thirds alive.

Do not delay in going after Jesus. You do not know what tomorrow holds, and you may lose interest in the things of God as your heart grows cold toward the gospel. In addition, there is no guarantee that the Lord will draw you unto Himself later.

Do not let anything stand in the way of deciding to follow Christ. Fear of giving up worldly happiness, church hypocrites, political affiliations, and the like should not keep you from the opportunity of a lifetime. Following Jesus means that you place your complete trust in Him and not in anything or anyone else.

Reflection

Do the Christ-followers you know seem boring? Why?

What hypocritical habits do you notice in others but excuse in yourself?

In the epic story of God's amazing love and wonderful grace, are you living in devastation or restoration? Why?

Looking Ahead

Chapter 4: Saved and Still Seeking. Part 1

CHAPTER 4

Saved and Still Seeking PART 1

"Then you will call on Me and go and pray to Me, and I will listen to you. And you will seek Me and find Me, when you search for Me with all your heart. I will be found by you, says the Lord."
Jeremiah 29:12–14

"I told you I loved you when I married you, and that should be enough," said no loving husband ever to his wife. Just like any lasting marriage is built on an ever-growing relationship between husband and wife, your relationship with God is no different. Every Christ-follower is called to continue to be a Seeker. You never stop seeking God. Every single day should be a continual pursuit of your relationship with the Lord.

Avoid thinking of the Seeker only as someone who is not yet a Christ-follower. Think of the Seeker as someone who passionately pursues God over the course of a lifetime. We come to Jesus as a seeker, and we should forever be seekers after the heart of Jesus. Eugene H. Peterson rightly claimed that discipleship is "a long obedience in the same direction."[5] So, how does one make seeking after Jesus a daily practice? Is it possible to keep the fires of holy passion burning in our soul for the long haul?

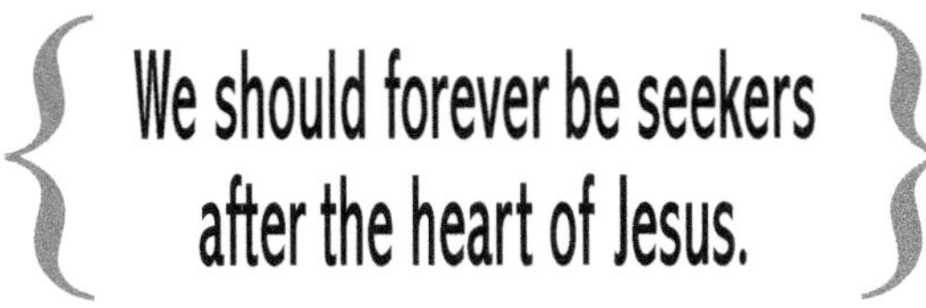
We should forever be seekers
after the heart of Jesus.

The answer is yes, *but*...Yes, we can passionately and persistently pursue Jesus, but that must become a lifestyle. I want to give you the *Seeker's Guide* to becoming a *lifelong* **Seeker**. While it's not rocket science (hard to understand), it is a spiritual discipline (hard to do every day).

The Seeker's Guide to Going After Jesus.

To **Go After Jesus,** begin with the decision to become a lifelong seeker by placing Jesus at the center of your life. In church, you will often hear that you need to put God first in your life. While this statement is true, it is not complete. What is the difference? If Jesus is first, but not at the center of your life, He is simply one of many priorities.

You can put Jesus first in your life on Sunday, but it is often hard to put Jesus first on Friday. Why? For many, Sunday is the Lord's Day when they center their days around worship and rest, so putting Jesus first is not difficult. On Fridays, one can sometimes forget to have their devotional time because they get so caught up in the activities of the weekend.

Placing Jesus at the center of your life is a different matter. When Jesus is at the center of your life, everything revolves around Him. Just like Earth revolves around the sun, so our world should revolve around the Son. What would happen if Earth stopped being in proper alignment in its orbit around the sun?

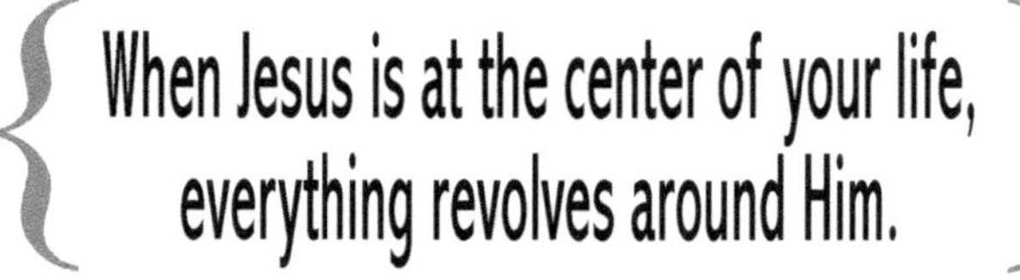
When Jesus is at the center of your life,
everything revolves around Him.

If the Earth were just a little closer to the sun, our world would be destroyed. Our climate would grow hotter, triggering a massive global warming effect. The increase in temperature would cause glaciers to melt, which would cause sea levels to rise, and most of the planet would become flooded. If the Earth moved just a little away from the sun, the Earth would drastically cool, and our planet could potentially freeze.[6] Nobody could survive, much less thrive, on such a planet.

The same can be said about the Christ-follower who tries to live life without Jesus at the center. Jeremiah encouraged the Jewish captives by saying they would one day live again with God at the center of their lives: "Then you will call on Me and go and pray to Me, and I will listen to you. And you shall seek Me and find Me, when you search for Me with all your heart. I will be found by you, says the LORD" (Jeremiah 29:12–14). What about you? Are you still actively seeking Jesus in a passionate pursuit to know, love, and follow Jesus? Did you know that you are as close to God as you desire to be? God tells us to draw near to Him and He will draw near to us (James 4:8). Think of this: The Creator of the Universe, the One who spoke galaxies into being, the God who breathed stars into space, the Lover of humanity who came to earth to live among us is excited about having a meaningful relationship with you!

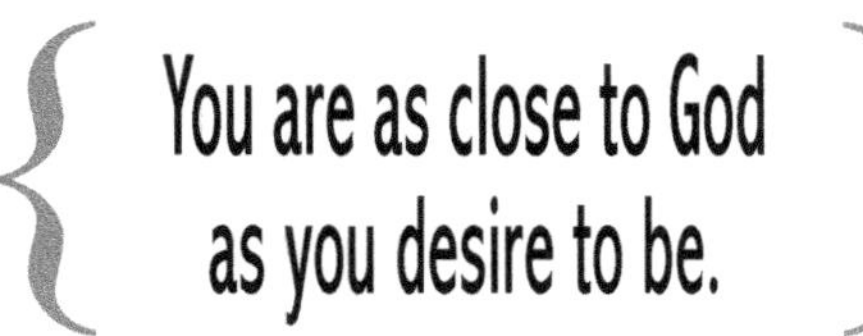
You are as close to God
as you desire to be.

The first identity of every Christ-follower is always to be a ***Seeker***. That sounds good, but how? Let me give you some practical actions that can help you actively seek God every day of your life. First, we need to look to the early church in the book of Acts to see how Christ-followers made it a daily practice to seek after God. Luke gives us this description of the first Christ-followers:

"Then those who gladly received his word were baptized; and that day, about three thousand souls were added *to them*. And they continued steadfastly in the apostles' doctrine and fellowship, in the breaking of bread, and in prayers. Then fear came on every soul, and many wonders and signs were done through the apostles. Now all who believed were together, and had all things in common, and sold their possessions and goods, and divided them among all, as anyone had need. So continuing daily with one accord in the temple, and breaking bread from house to house, they ate their food with gladness and simplicity of heart, praising God and having favor with all the people. And the Lord added to the church daily those who were being saved" (Acts 2:41–47).

Holy Habit #1: Discipleship

Luke highlights five holy habits that characterized the early Christ-followers in their active pursuit of Jesus. The first one is *discipleship.* They "continued steadfastly in the apostles' doctrine." Discipleship is the spiritual discipline of actively studying and applying God's Word to your life. It's *information* that leads to *transformation.* The early church was so hungry to feast on God's Word that they studied the teachings of the apostles daily. They realized the truth was the only thing that could set them free (John 8:32).

{ Develop a desire to feast on God's Word. }

They believed God's Word had the power to change their lives. They believed the Bible was like a guiding light that gave direction and purpose for their daily decisions (Psalm 119:105). The early Christ-followers were inspired, illuminated, and transformed by the truths they were learning from God's Word and the apostles. Their minds were being renewed, and the way they saw the world was radically changed (Romans 12:2).

What are some practical tips or daily habits for seeking God through His Word? The following suggestions will help you develop a daily habit of discipleship.

Set a daily appointment with God and keep it. You make appointments for everything else, your doctor, dentist, coworkers, kids, and spouse. Why not make a daily standing appointment with God? Refuse invitations to do other things during your "God-time" appointment. Tell others you already have plans to spend time with God.

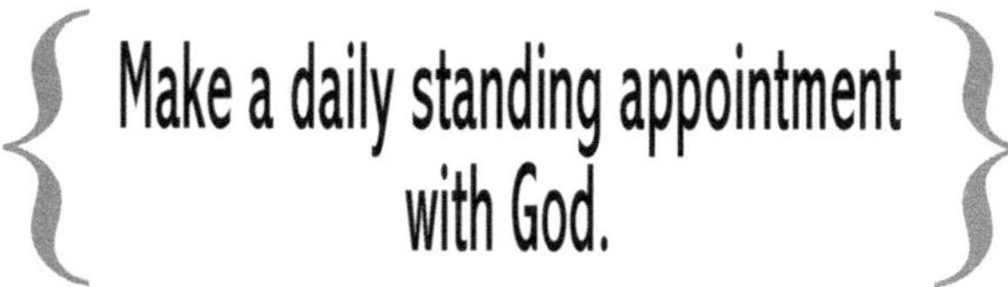
Make a daily standing appointment
with God.

Determine to make your time with God a priority by spending time with God first. Before you leave your home to see the faces of other people, first seek the face of God in prayer. Before you start your daily tasks, bask in the beauty of God's Word. Jumpstart your day with a spiritual feast, meaningful time with God through studying His Word, talking with Him in prayer, and worshiping Him in your heart through thanksgiving and praise.

Matthew 6:33 is an encouraging verse for making God your first and central priority: "But seek first the kingdom of God and His righteousness, and all these things shall be added to you."

{ Study God's Word in a community of faith. }

Get plugged into a Bible study group. Churches use different names for these groups: life groups, growth groups, connect groups, and small groups. In a small group, you will have the opportunity to study God's Word in a community of faith where you not only learn God's Word but also ask questions, learn how to apply the truths, and encourage others in God's Word. You gather in rows (big church), but you connect in circles (small groups).

Treasure God's Word in your heart by memorizing key Scripture verses. God's Word is so lifegiving that you should commit it to memory. Try memorizing verses that will help you in your daily walk with God. Are you struggling with a certain sin issue? Memorize scriptures that deal with that topic. Do you need hope or encouragement? Memorize scriptures that fuel your hope.

Holy Habit #2: Fellowship

The second holy habit is *fellowship*. Notice that the early Christ-followers "continued steadfastly in . . . fellowship . . . breaking bread from house to house, they ate their food with gladness and simplicity of heart" (Acts 2:42, 46). What exactly is fellowship? Fellowship comes from the Greek word *koinonia,* which occurs twenty times in the New Testament.[7] Fellowship involves two or more people working together to further the mission of Jesus and His Kingdom. Fellowship has relational overtones. It is not just you and me working together on a project, but it is also working together in love and harmony, actively advancing God's purposes on the Earth as a team.

Work together in love and harmony, actively advancing God's purposes on Earth as a team.

You do not go as far as your dream; you go as far as your team! It takes teamwork to make the dream work. As a **Seeker**, you are part of something far greater than yourself; you are part of the rule and reign of Jesus through eternity. You are part of a new family called the church. God has created you for community. You matter to God so much that He adopted you into His eternal family, and He values you and your part in the community of faith. (See Romans 8:15.)

What does fellowship look like in the life of a Christ-follower? Fellowship is becoming part of the mission of God in the life of a local church. God has personally designed the local church to be like a spiritual family for your personal growth and development.

Notice that the early Christ-followers shared a common meal together in one another's homes. Following Jesus means that you not only connect with other Christ-followers on Sunday, but you also enjoy authentic and meaningful community throughout the week. When the body of Christ connects to further the mission of Jesus on the Earth, fellowship happens. When Christ-followers gather for corporate worship to lift up the name of Jesus, fellowship happens. When you get plugged into a small group that is meeting for a greater cause, to be on mission with God in your community, you are experiencing the beautiful gift of fellowship.

So, how do I get plugged into this new Christian community? Start by becoming an active, engaged member of a Bible-believing local church. There is no such thing as a spiritual orphan.

You belong to the family of God, and He wants you to become a vital part of a local church.

{ There is no such thing as a spiritual orphan. }

You might think I was crazy if I told you I was a professional athlete but did not play on any team. I just played for myself in my home league. In like manner, a true ***Seeker*** will seek God within the context of a local Christian community. You cannot faithfully serve Jesus if you are not faithful to His church. The author of Hebrews gives us this encouragement: "Let us not neglect our meeting together, as some people do, but encourage one another, especially now that the day of his return is drawing near" (Hebrews 12:25 NLT).

Holy Habit #3: Prayer

The third holy habit is *prayer.* Prayer is talking with God. Prayer involves basking in the presence of God. Prayer occurs both privately in your home and publicly in your local church gatherings. The early Christ-followers had such a thriving relationship with God that their prayer life started at home and continued in their worship services, in both small and large gatherings.

How do you develop a more meaningful prayer life? What does that look like? Most people think of prayer as a monologue, you talking to God, giving God your list of needs and wants. That is part of prayer, but prayer is so much more. Prayer is conversing with God, talking to Him and listening to His still, small voice. Prayer is actively being in God's presence, which means you can be in the spirit of prayer at all times since God is always present (Matthew 28:20).

{ Prayer is conversing with God, talking to Him and listening to His still, small voice. }

Do you remember your first deep connection with someone? You were able to talk with them with ease. You seemed to know what they were thinking and feeling before they uttered a word. You read their body language. You even began to finish their sentences. As you begin to practice prayer, you will develop a deeper spiritual connection with God. You will begin to hear the Spirit speak to you and guide you.

Through your study of God's Word and prayer, you will begin to discern God's voice. God will speak to you daily as you read His Word. Every time you read the Bible, God is speaking to you because the Bible is His Word. Sometimes you will hear that inner voice speak in a still, small voice. (See 1 Kings 19:11-12.) Pay attention to that voice, as The Holy Spirit will be your guide into all truth (John 16:13).

{ Every time you read the Bible, God is speaking to you because the Bible is His Word. }

You possess one of the greatest privileges you can imagine. Access to the throne room of God. The author of Hebrews encourages us to "come boldly to the throne of grace, that we may obtain mercy and find grace to help in time of need" (Hebrews 4:16). We know we should pray, but we often struggle with this spiritual discipline. Even the most seasoned saints sometimes find it difficult to have a thriving prayer life. So, how can we change this? How can we enter boldly into God's throne room in such a way as to find the grace we need every day?

Developing a Prayer Strategy

One tool that has helped guide many Christ-followers is a good prayer strategy, using a helpful method to assist you in developing a rhythm and flow during your prayer time. Let me introduce you to the ***ACTS*** prayer method.[8] Each letter of the acrostic will help lead you through your prayer time. Here's how this prayer strategy works:

A	**= Adoration**	Start your prayer time by telling God how awesome He is.

The Lord's Prayer starts off like this: "Our Father which art in heaven, hallowed be thy name" (Matthew 6:9 KJV). Launch your prayer time with a vertical focus, on God, not yourself. Focusing on God and how amazing He is will set the tone for the rest of your prayer time. Go vertical before you go anywhere else.

C	= Confession	What areas of sin and struggle do you need to confess to God?

It is helpful to begin each day with a clean slate, that is, you do not have any unconfessed sins. Proverbs 28:13 says, "Whoever conceals their sins does not prosper, but the one who confesses and renounces them finds mercy" (NIV). This is amazing news. Jesus will forgive you for any and every wrong you commit, so you should ask for forgiveness daily. As I tell my children, "If you mess up, 'fess up!" Begin each day with a clear conscience so you can have boldness before God in your prayer time.

T	= Thanksgiving	What are you thankful for?

Tell God how grateful you are for His many blessings. Starting each day with a thankful heart will launch your day in a positive (and Christlike) way. Paul encourages us to give thanks in everything because this is God's will for us in Christ Jesus (1 Thessalonians 5:18). Has God been good to you lately? Have you experienced any unexpected blessings? Tell God how thankful you are.

S	= Supplication	Present your requests, desires, and needs to God.

A good practice is to have a prayer list that covers these five categories: family, friends, church, personal, and global needs. This will help you organize your prayer time and also help keep you focused. For example, global needs include praying for our elected officials, world hunger, injustices in our world, the salvation of the lost, and the like.

Let me encourage you to be focused and specific in your prayers. Focused prayer is like a laser beam that shines into the presence of God. As your prayers go up, the provision of God comes down. God already knows what you need before you ask Him, but He wants you to ask. Why does He want us to ask? He has designed prayer as a way for you to have an intimate and growing relationship with Him. Prayer is part of how God cultivates a lively, meaningful relationship with you.

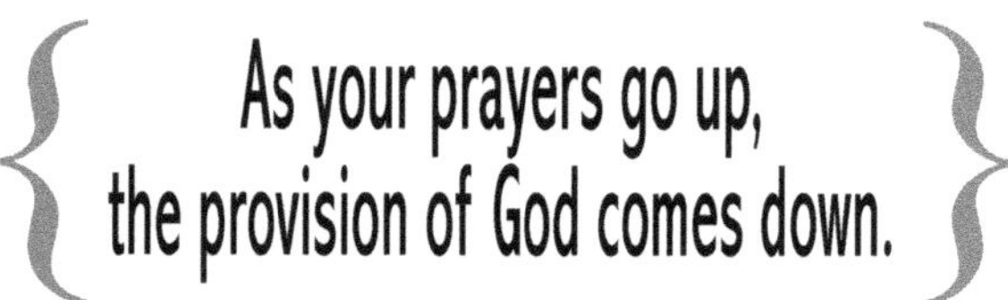
As your prayers go up,
the provision of God comes down.

Practical Prayer Tips

How can you have the amazing prayer life I am describing? Here are a few helpful tips:

- Begin and end each day with prayer.
- Pick a private place where you can minimize distractions.
- Turn off your cell phone notifications and any other potential electronic interruptions.
- Keep a pad next to you. Write down any distracting thoughts that pop up, so you can focus on them later.
- Pray over each meal to thank God for His provision of your daily bread.
- Keep a prayer list or a prayer journal to help your prayers remain focused.
- Start out small and allow your prayer life to grow organically. Some people start out with five to ten minutes of prayer each day. As they want more time with God, some

eventually find themselves praying for an hour or more each morning. The key is to make it a daily practice, even for a few minutes.

CHAPTER 4 RECAP

Go After Jesus Principle #4

Make Jesus the center of your life and become a lifelong Seeker.
Read: Romans 12:1-21

Key Takeaways

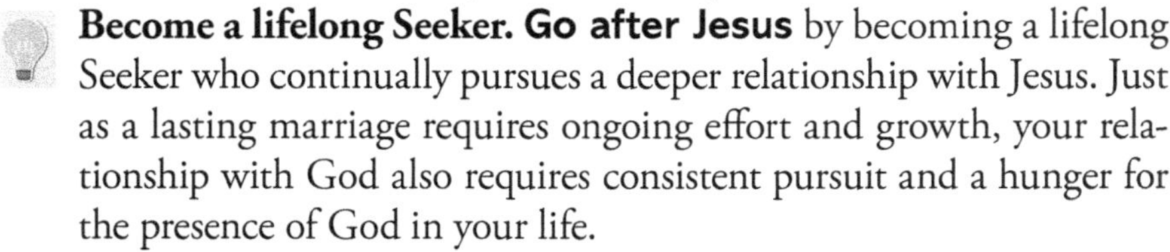

Become a lifelong Seeker. Go after Jesus by becoming a lifelong Seeker who continually pursues a deeper relationship with Jesus. Just as a lasting marriage requires ongoing effort and growth, your relationship with God also requires consistent pursuit and a hunger for the presence of God in your life.

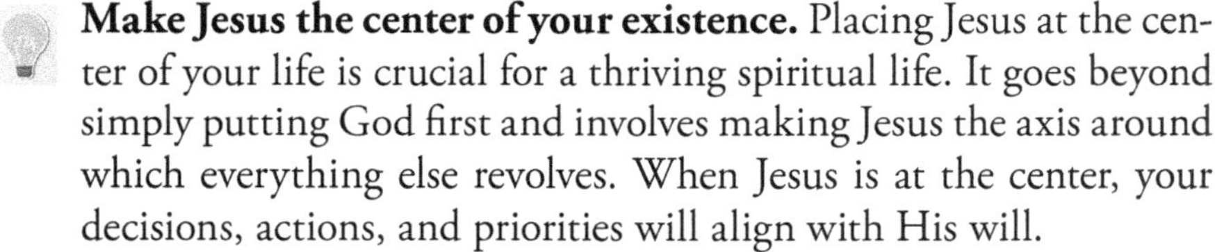

Make Jesus the center of your existence. Placing Jesus at the center of your life is crucial for a thriving spiritual life. It goes beyond simply putting God first and involves making Jesus the axis around which everything else revolves. When Jesus is at the center, your decisions, actions, and priorities will align with His will.

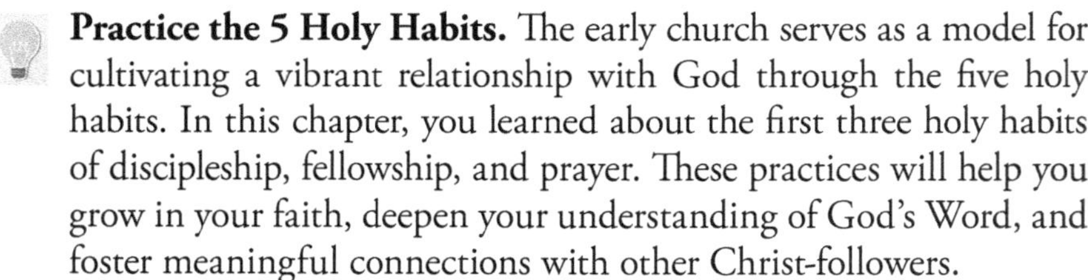

Practice the 5 Holy Habits. The early church serves as a model for cultivating a vibrant relationship with God through the five holy habits. In this chapter, you learned about the first three holy habits of discipleship, fellowship, and prayer. These practices will help you grow in your faith, deepen your understanding of God's Word, and foster meaningful connections with other Christ-followers.

Reflection

What hinders you from spending time with God daily? How could you get rid of that obstacle?

What is your level of involvement in a local church? How could you become more connected?

What prayer tips mentioned in this chapter are you willing to try? What about them appeals to you?

Looking Ahead

Chapter 5: Saved and Still Seeking

CHAPTER 5

Saved and Still Seeking PART 2

"Therefore, do not worry, saying, 'What shall we eat?' or 'What shall we drink?' or 'What shall we wear?' For after all these things the Gentiles seek. For your heavenly Father knows that you need all these things. But seek first the kingdom of God and His righteousness, and all these things shall be added to you. Therefore, do not worry about tomorrow, for tomorrow will worry about its own things. Sufficient for the day is its own trouble."
Matthew 6:31–34

Lori and I have been married for a long time, and guess what? I am still passionately pursuing her. What kind of marriage would we have if I stopped chasing after my bride, if I stopped telling her how beautiful she is . . . if I do not surprise her with flowers anymore . . . if I do not reach for her hand? We would have a lackluster marriage. *We would become roommates instead of soulmates.* We would become acquaintances instead of passionate lovers.

What if I told you that Jesus desires a passionate relationship with you? What if following Jesus became an exciting lifetime adventure instead of just a ho-hum routine during a Sunday worship service? The good news is that you can actively pursue Jesus today, tomorrow, and forever. In the last chapter, we talked about the first three holy habits that will help you pursue Jesus: *discipleship*, *fellowship*, and *prayer*. Now we will look at the other holy habits.

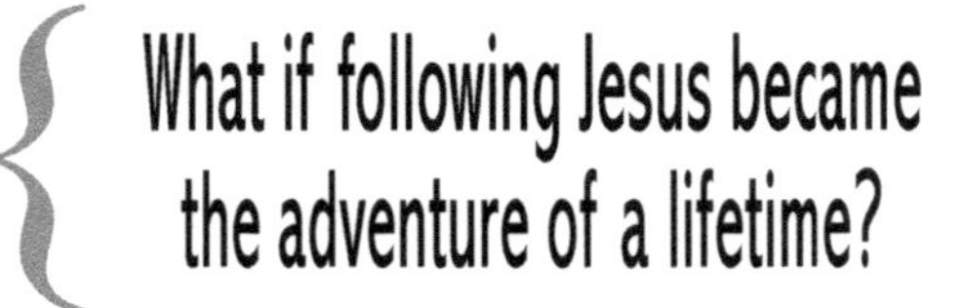

What if following Jesus became
the adventure of a lifetime?

Holy Habit #4: Worship

The fourth holy habit is worship. The first-century Christ-followers were "continuing daily with one accord in the temple, and breaking bread from house to house, they ate their food with gladness and simplicity of heart, praising God and having favor with all the people" (Acts 2:46-47). So, what exactly is worship? John Piper gives us an insightful description: "True worship is valuing or a treasuring of God above all things. True worship is based on a right understanding of God's nature, and it is a right valuing of God's worth." [9]

All true Seekers of Jesus are worshipers. What does a worshiper look like? Jesus gives us the answer in the Gospel of John: "But the hour is coming, and now is, when the true worshipers will worship the Father in spirit and truth; for the Father is seeking such to worship Him. God is Spirit, and those who worship Him must worship in spirit and truth" (John 4:24).

All true Seekers of Jesus are worshipers.

Worship in Spirit. What does it mean to worship God "in spirit and in truth"? To worship God in spirit means deeply connecting with God; to do this, your spirit must be alive. How in the world does this happen? How can we connect with God since we cannot see Him, touch Him, or talk face-to-face with Him? The answer lies with the third Person of the Trinity, the Holy Spirit.

The Holy Spirit gives us the ability to connect with God. Just before Jesus returned to heaven, He gave His disciples this truth: He would not leave us as orphans, but He would come to us through the ministry of the Holy Spirit (John 14:16-18). The amazing news is that when you invite Jesus into your life as your Lord and Savior, something mysteriously wonderful happens. God moves *inside* you. That is right, the Holy Spirit makes your heart His home.

When you invite Jesus into your life as your Lord and Savior, God moves inside you.

The Holy Spirit serves as our Advocate. The Greek Word for advocate is (*parakletos*). As an advocate, the Holy Spirit comes alongside us to support, encourage, and guide us. The Holy Spirit counsels and supports as He dwells within us.[10] When it comes to prayer, the Holy Spirit helps connect you to God. Another amazing truth is that the Holy Spirit is praying for you right now to help with all your struggles (Romans 8:26).

Worship in Truth. We talked about what it means to worship "In spirit," so what does it mean to worship "In truth"? To worship in truth means God only accepts worship based on the truth of who He is. Do you enjoy it when you hear people say things about you that are not true? What about things that are only partially true? Partial truths can turn into major misrepresentations of who a person is, a caricature of who they are.

God only accepts worship based on the truth of who He is.

The same is true of God. God does not like partial truths, half-truths, or any misrepresentation of His character. If you desire to worship God, first learn who God is. How can you know what God is like? The answer is found in the pages of Scripture. God's Word paints a picture of who God is. If you want to get to know the God of the Bible, you need to get to know the Bible itself inside and out.

What is God really like?

God is love. It is impossible to describe who God is adequately, but the Bible gives some amazing insights into His character and nature.

First, God is love (1 John 4:8). What does it mean that God *is* love? Well, because God is love, love is the primary motivator for everything He does and says. Love is the language spoken in heaven. Love is the creative power that made you. Love is the reason you are still alive.

Since God is love, love is the primary motivator for everything He does and says.

You cannot begin to understand who God is if you do not understand what true love is. First John 4:10 says, "This is love: not that we loved God, but that he loved us and sent his Son as an atoning sacrifice for our sins" (NIV). Three important truths about love are given in that verse: Love initiates, love gives, and love sacrifices. As you develop an understanding of what true love is, you have a clearer picture of what God is like. First Corinthians 13 goes into a lot more detail about true love, and we will explore that passage thoroughly in Chapter 19. Here is a simple way to forever change the way you think about God's love for you. Since God is the definition of love, we will replace the word love in the following passage with the name of *Jesus*:

> Jesus is patient, Jesus is kind. Jesus does not envy, Jesus does not boast, and Jesus is not proud. Jesus does not dishonor others, Jesus is not self-seeking, Jesus is not easily angered, and Jesus keeps no record of wrongs. Jesus does not delight in evil but rejoices with the truth. Jesus always protects, always trusts, always hopes, always perseveres. Jesus never fails (1 Corinthians 13:4-8, author's paraphrase of the NIV).

God is holy. Another major attribute of God is holiness. Apostle Peter says it like this: "As He who called you is holy, you also be holy in all *your* conduct, because it is written, 'Be holy, for I am holy'" (1 Peter 1:15-16). What does it mean to be holy? To be holy means to be set apart in a class by yourself. One author summarized holiness as "the natural state of God and the opposite of man's sinful nature. Holiness is the state of perfection, being fully sanctified and set apart."[11]

We live in a world that is mostly devoid of holiness. Our world demands we yield to the world's values and follow the culture's mores and convictions. We live in a society driven by selective outrage. We are pressured to buy into whatever becomes the current cultural agenda. So, how can the follower of Christ stand firm in a world that seems so broken?

{ Go After Jesus = Become More Like Him. }

The answer is found in the daily pursuit of Jesus. A person becomes Holy in two distinct phases. The first phase of holiness is becoming a Christ-follower. This is called *positional* holiness. You are made right with God and become holy in His eyes because you have been forgiven and cleansed by the blood of Jesus.

God now sees you through the lens of the cross, pure, blameless, and above reproach (Philippians 2:15; Colossians 1:22). When you trusted in Jesus as your Savior, God credited Jesus' righteousness to your spiritual account (Romans 4:22). You once were spiritually bankrupt and spiritually dead because of your sin. Now you are right with God and made new in Christ with all His righteousness deposited in your account (Ephesians 2:1-9).

So, you are holy positionally, but what about in your day-to-day life? The second phase of holiness is called *practical* holiness. God wants you to live out practically what you already are positionally. In other words, as you pursue Jesus daily, you become more and more like Him. You are now a child of God because you have been adopted into His family (John 1:12). You are God's masterpiece, and you have been created in Christ to do something amazing for Christ (Ephesians 2:10).

Your stay here on Earth is temporary, because your new permanent citizenship is with God (2 Timothy 1:7). You are now more than a conqueror in Christ (Romans 8:37). To recap, God has made you a brand-new creation, the old life is fading away, and your new life is coming into being (2 Corinthians 5:17). You are made new in Christ so you can become more like Him in your daily walk. You accept Jesus as *Lord*, agreeing to follow His teachings and example.

Thus, the goal of being a Christ-follower is for you to become *practically* (in your daily life), what you already are *positionally* in Christ. Accepting Jesus as your Lord and Savior is only the beginning. Every day becomes a passionate pursuit of Jesus by living out your faith. Your new life, your pursuit of Jesus, changes how you treat people, how you work at your job, and how you view yourself, because your new identity is now in Christ.

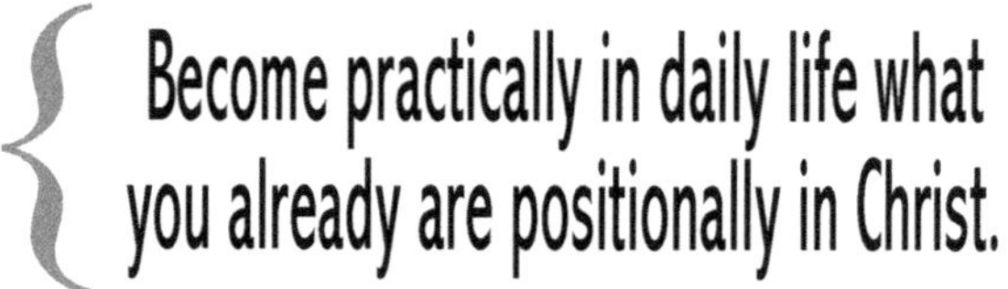
Become practically in daily life what
you already are positionally in Christ.

Holy Habit #5: Ministry

The fifth holy habit is *ministry*. Now that you are growing in discipleship, connected in fellowship, active in prayer, and going vertical in worship, the time has come for you to give back. Ministry is simply doing your part to serve others. Ministry is the outward expression of a heart transformed by the gospel. You use your spiritual gifts and natural talents to help meet the spiritual, physical, or emotional needs of others to build up the body of Christ.

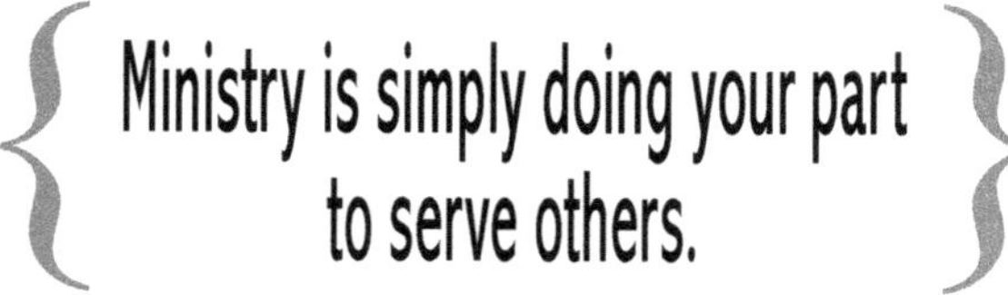
Ministry is simply doing your part
to serve others.

Peter knew a lot about ministry because he watched Jesus minister to others for over three years. Peter gives us this encouragement:

As each one has received a gift, minister it to one another, as good stewards of the manifold grace of God. If anyone speaks, *let him speak* as the oracles of God. If anyone ministers, *let him do it* as with the ability which God supplies, that in all things God may be glorified through Jesus Christ, to whom belong the glory and the dominion forever and ever. Amen. (1 Peter 4:10-11).

Did you know that when you became a Christ-follower, God gave you at least one spiritual gift? It's kind of like this. Have you ever moved into a new neighborhood and received welcome gifts from friendly neighbors? When you accept Jesus, He gives you several welcome gifts. You receive eternal life, you become a member of God's family, you have a home in heaven, your sins are all forgiven, and you receive at least one spiritual gift. A spiritual gift is a special ability or empowerment given by the Holy Spirit to believers in Jesus Christ; intended to be used for the building up of the Church (the body of Christ) and to serve others in love. Some examples include teaching, preaching and hospitality.

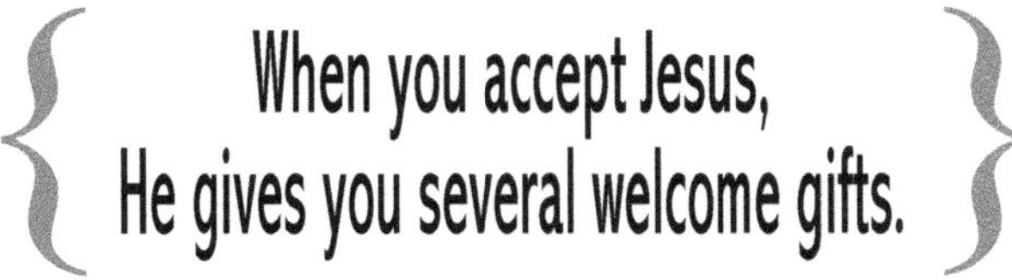
When you accept Jesus,
He gives you several welcome gifts.

How Do You Discover Your Spiritual Gifts?

So, how can you discover your spiritual gifts and start serving in the local church? Great question! The first step is serving in different ministries to determine where you best fit. Maybe you start serving as a greeter or brewing coffee with the hospitality team. Do you sense God's pleasure as you serve in these areas? One key indicator that you have discovered one of your gifts is that you *sense God's divine pleasure.*

Another key indicator is the *response of others.* God will use others to help you discern your gift through their affirmation. When I first started preaching at age fifteen, God used others in the local church to affirm my calling. They said things like, "Timothy, this is your gift. You have a special talent for preaching the Word of God." These words from God's people encouraged me and let me know I was going in the right direction.

Here is a key wisdom principle: You know the will of God by *doing* the will of God. As you serve in different ministries, your main spiritual gifts will rise to the top. An old Southern expression is "The cream will always rise to the top." The same can be said about your spiritual gifts; your top gifts will eventually rise and be noticed by others as you do your part to build up the body of Christ.

You know the will of God by *doing* the will of God.

Another resource that can be helpful is a spiritual gifts test. Many insightful tests ask you questions about your passions and your interests to identify where you are spiritually gifted. Many of these tests ask fifty or more questions and take about fifteen minutes to complete. Here are two good resources for spiritual gifts tests: Lifeway's Spiritual Gifts Survey[12] and Jeff Carver's free spiritual gifts assessment.[13]

What does it look like to **Go After Jesus** in your everyday life?

Are you still passionate about growing in your faith? Do you long for others to know Jesus as their Savior as you do? Are you going after Jesus daily? This passionate pursuit of Him should never end. The longer you live, the more passionate about Jesus you should become. Are you involved in serving in your local church? Use your spiritual gifts to build up the body of Christ. If you're not serving, you're swerving! Serving God and others will help keep you on the right path.

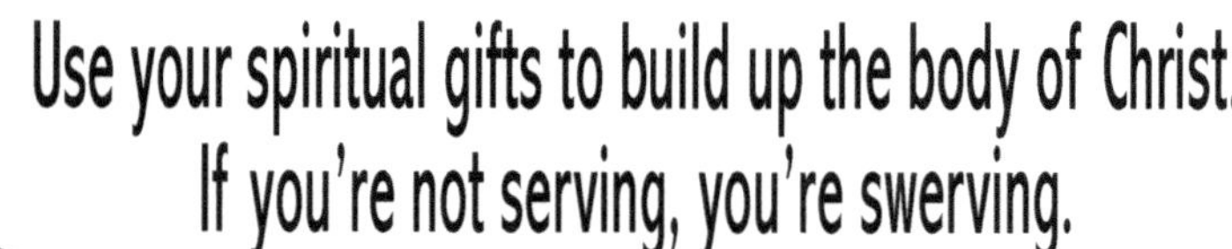
Use your spiritual gifts to build up the body of Christ.
If you're not serving, you're swerving.

Continue forever being a ***Seeker***, never stop. Keep your passion burning brightly for Jesus, don't let your love for Him grow cold. Let your glow show so others may know! Now that we have explored what being a ***Seeker*** of the Savior is like, we will turn our attention to the ***Disciple***. This section will take you deeper as you **Go After Jesus.**

CHAPTER 5 RECAP

Go After Jesus Principle #5

A ***Seeker*** is one who enjoys the lifelong adventure of worshiping God in Spirit and in truth, discovering one's spiritual gifts, and serving others in the local church.

Read: 1 Corinthians 12:4–7, 12–14; 1 Peter 4:10–11

Key Takeaways

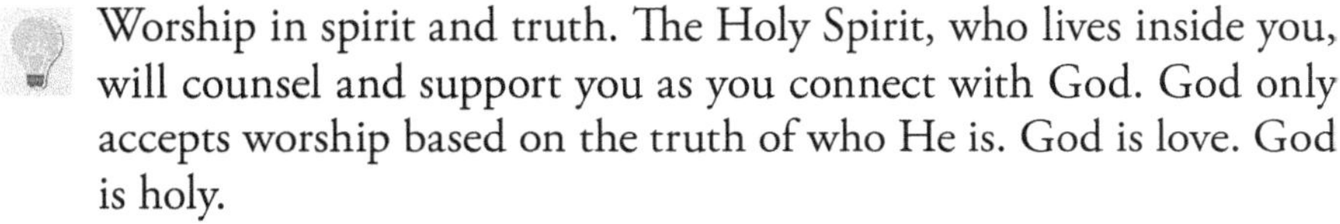

Worship in spirit and truth. The Holy Spirit, who lives inside you, will counsel and support you as you connect with God. God only accepts worship based on the truth of who He is. God is love. God is holy.

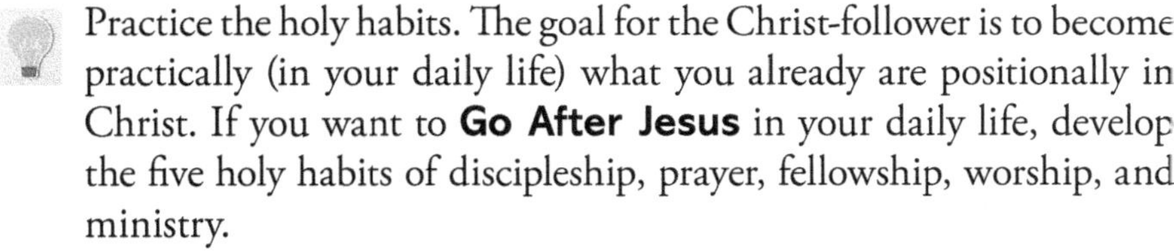

Practice the holy habits. The goal for the Christ-follower is to become practically (in your daily life) what you already are positionally in Christ. If you want to **Go After Jesus** in your daily life, develop the five holy habits of discipleship, prayer, fellowship, worship, and ministry.

Discover and develop your spiritual gifts. God has graciously given you at least one spiritual gift to build up the local church. If you are not serving in a local church, find a Bible-believing church in your area where you can invest your life in serving Christ and loving others.

Reflection

What does your worship life look like? What demonstrates you value (treasure) God above all?

Do you believe that God sees you as holy, pure, blameless, and above reproach? Why?

How are you using your spiritual gift(s) to serve other seekers and Christ-followers?

Looking Ahead

Part 2: The Disciple. Chapter 6: Jesus Enters Your World

Part Two

The Disciple

I am determined to follow Jesus wherever He leads.

The Seeker: I want to ***discover*** the awe-inspiring truth of who Jesus really is.
The Disciple: I am ***determined*** follow Jesus wherever He leads.

CHAPTER 6

Jesus Enters Your World

"And Jesus, walking by the Sea of Galilee, saw two brothers, Simon called Peter, and Andrew his brother, casting a net into the sea; for they were fishermen. Then He said to them, 'Follow Me, and I will make you fishers of men.' They immediately left their nets and followed Him. Going on from there, He saw two other brothers, James the son of Zebedee, and John his brother, in the boat with Zebedee their father, mending their nets. He called them, and immediately they left the boat and their father, and followed Him."
Matthew 4:18–22

Do you remember the first time you fell in love? Where were you? What first captured your attention about that person? What emotions swept through you? My first crush happened early in my life. When I was in third grade, my heart was smitten by a blonde-haired, blue-eyed girl named Gina. This crush lasted over seven years, well into my high school days.

I did everything I could to know her better by *studying* her. I found out what she liked and what she didn't. I eventually became her best friend. Now that I have you thinking about your own first-love story, I want you to think about your relationship with Jesus. After you become a ***Seeker,*** you should eventually decide to *follow* Jesus. The second identity of a Christ-follower is a ***Disciple.***

A disciple is a learner. You begin to study someone until you get to know them. You learn what they like and what they do not like. When you became a Christ-follower by accepting Jesus as your Lord and Savior, you also decided to become a lifelong follower, or a disciple, of Jesus. In this chapter, I will take you back to Jesus' original disciples. As we learn what it was like to follow Jesus then, we will see what it looks like to follow Jesus now.

A Call to the Eternal

Jesus was walking by the Sea of Galilee. This body of water is a freshwater lake that is about thirteen miles long and seven miles wide. It was known for its abundance of fish. Josephus wrote that the Sea of Galilee was "wonderful in its characteristics and in its beauty."[14]

In this scenic area, Jesus spotted his first disciples, Peter and Andrew. These brothers were going about their daily job of catching fish. Jesus captured their interests by talking about fishing. "Follow Me, and I will make you fishers of men" (Matthew 4:19). The essence of Jesus' calling the brothers to follow Him was this: "Hey, do you want to do something similar to what you are doing now but of much greater significance? You're trying to catch fish, but if you follow me, you're going to get a much better catch, people!"

With those words, Jesus captured the hearts and souls of the two brothers. They were doing the ordinary, but Jesus was calling them to the extraordinary. They were experiencing the natural, but Jesus wanted them to taste the supernatural. This is the essence of being a ***Disciple*** of Jesus: He meets you where you are, and He takes you to places you never dreamed possible.

> **The essence of discipleship: Jesus meets you where you are, and He takes you to places you never dreamed possible.**

But the story does not end with Peter and Andrew. As Jesus continued his walk down the Galilean shore, now as a party of three, He saw two more people. Ironically, they had a lot in common with Peter and Andrew.

They, too, were brothers and fishermen. James and John were with their father, Zebedee. They were repairing their nets so they could go on the next fishing trip (Matthew 4:21).

Matthew tells us that the first disciples left everything behind to follow Jesus: Their boats, their fathers, and of course, their fishing careers (Matthew 4:22). Imagine what it must have felt like for the first four disciples to leave everything behind to follow Jesus. Why were they willing to change their entire lifestyle and give up everything to follow this rabbi?

Something about Jesus drew these rugged fishermen to Him. Jesus was different from anyone they had ever met. He was not just calling them *from* something; He was calling them *to* something. They were exchanging their fishing nets for gospel nets. They were trading catching fish for catching followers. They were giving up the temporary for the eternal. They were swapping their day jobs for a heavenly calling that would impact countless lives for eternity, including yours.

A Call to Something Greater

When Jesus calls you from something, it is always because He has something far greater to offer. In the Gospel of Luke, we read about Jesus calling another disciple, Matthew, who was also known as Levi. Matthew was a guy nobody liked because of his occupation. He was a tax collector. People do not like tax collectors now, but first-century Jews despised them. In biblical times, Jewish tax collectors were considered sellouts because they worked for the enemy, Rome. They often collected more money than necessary to line their own pockets and become wealthy, often at the expense of poorer Jews.

{ When Jesus calls you from something, it is always because He has something far greater to offer. }

Luke tells us that while Matthew was sitting at his tax office one day, Jesus simply said, "Follow Me." Matthew then got up and left his lucrative business behind to follow Him (Luke 5:27-28). He was so moved by his encounter with Jesus that he decided to throw a huge party for his tax collector friends. Guess who was the guest of honor? None other than Jesus Himself. This did not go over well with the religious people of Jesus' day (the scribes and Pharisees). They griped and complained about Jesus eating with the "scum of society," sinners. By the way, if you try to reach lost people today, guess who will often still be complaining? You got it, the religious people.

How did Jesus respond to their criticism? Jesus compared Himself to a doctor. Who does a doctor treat? Healthy people, or people who are sick, maybe even dying? You are right, Jesus came to help sick people (sinners) find healing. And the truth is, we are all spiritually sick. We are sinners who need spiritual healing. Matthew understood Jesus' mission, and so did some of his friends (Luke 5:29-32). Do you desire to follow Jesus? Do you want to **Go After Jesus** in your daily life? Just as Jesus called those first disciples *from* something *to* something far greater, He is calling you. He is calling you to follow Him.

A Call to Major Changes

What does this call mean to you? Becoming a Disciple of Jesus may mean you will have to make some major changes in your life:

- **Loss of relationships.** Some friends may not want to be around you or invite you to their gatherings anymore.
- **Criticism.** Those in your family may not understand the new you and push back on the changes you have made.
- **Suffering for your faith.** Once you say "yes" to Jesus, the enemy puts a target on your back. Satan does not like it when one of his own switches sides to **Go After Jesus**.
- **Sacrifice and denial.** Following Jesus means laying aside your agenda in pursuit of a higher, heavenly call, living for God and doing things His way.

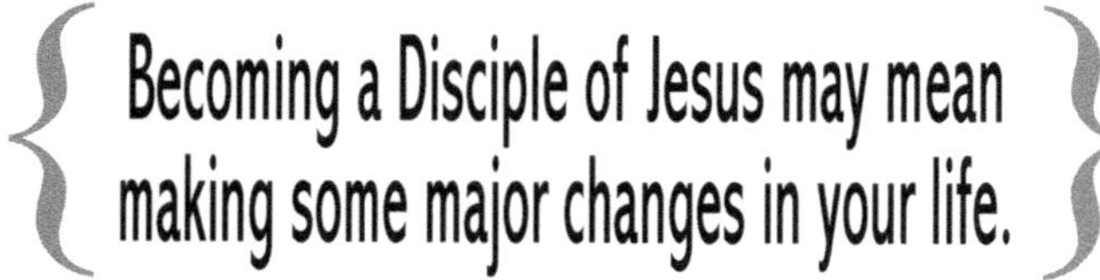
Becoming a Disciple of Jesus may mean
making some major changes in your life.

Have I talked you out of fully surrendering your life to Christ? I hope not. But you should count the cost of being Jesus' disciple. He gives this challenge to those who are contemplating the call to follow Him:

> **"For which of you, intending to build a tower, does not sit down first and count the cost, whether he has enough to finish it, lest, after he has laid the foundation, and is not able to finish, all who see it begin to mock him, saying, 'This man began to build and was not able to finish'? Or what king, going to make war against another king, does not sit down first and consider whether he is able with ten thousand to meet him who comes against him with twenty thousand? Or else, while the other is still a great way off, he sends a delegation and asks conditions of peace. So likewise, whoever of you does not forsake all that he has cannot be My disciple."**
>
> **(Luke 14:28-33)**

If you have counted the cost and are ready to leave behind your nets (your past and present pursuits) and are ready to go all-in on following Jesus, a sweet adventure lies ahead of you. In the next chapter, I am going to lead you to take that step of faith, to fully follow Jesus by contemplating an exciting decision.

CHAPTER 6 RECAP

Go After Jesus Principle #6

When Jesus calls you *from* something, it is always because He is calling you *to* something far greater!

Read: Matthew 4:18-22, Luke 14:28–33

Key Takeaways

- Jesus is calling you to faithfully follow Him. Once Peter, Andrew, James, and John decided to follow Jesus, they became disciples, followers, and students of Him. This is the essence of being a disciple of Jesus: He meets you where you are, and He takes you to places you never dreamed possible.

- What if you must leave something behind? When Jesus calls you from something, it is always because he has something far greater to offer.

- Becoming a disciple of Jesus may mean making major changes in your life. It may also mean loss of relationships, criticism, suffering, sacrifice, and denial. It means you are willing to lay aside your agenda in pursuit of the higher, heavenly call to discipleship.

Reflection

- Think about your first crush. What things did you think, do, and speak about to that person? Does that behavior mirror your love for Jesus in any way? How?

- What first attracted you to Jesus? What has drawn you closer to Him since then?

- What major changes have you made in your life since you decided to follow Jesus?

Looking Ahead

Chapter 7: "Follow Me"

CHAPTER 7

"Follow Me"

"As Jesus passed on from there,
He saw a man named Matthew sitting at the tax office.
And He said to him, 'Follow Me.'
So he arose and followed Him."
Matthew 9:9

The world wept for a sports legend who had died. On the foggy morning of January 26, 2020, an out-of-control helicopter crashed into a California hillside. Eight people were killed in that horrific tragedy. One was NBA star Kobe Bryant. Many people were heartbroken. How could this happen? Why did the pilot take off in such unfavorable weather conditions?[15]

Long before this fatal event, the basketball legend graced the NBA courts for twenty electric years. Kobe was the favorite player for many basketball lovers. How did Kobe become one of the greatest players of all time? Obviously, he practiced a lot. He had one of the best work ethics of any athlete in any sport. But that was not the reason. Kobe copied the basketball moves of the greatest player of all time, Michael Jordan.

Kobe admired Michael and mimicked the way he played until he could perform MJ's moves as well as MJ himself. You could say Kobe was a disciple of Michael Jordan. Kobe followed Michael's career as an admiring kid until he became an NBA player himself and followed in MJ's footsteps, eventually playing like Mike.

Three Truths about Discipleship

When Jesus called His original disciples to follow Him, what did that mean? We can glean several important truths from the disciples' call to follow Jesus.

First, the call to discipleship is *the call to be with Jesus.* In the Gospel of Mark, we learn how Jesus chose His disciples. His group of four initial disciples eventually grew to twelve. One reason Jesus selected these twelve was "that they might be with Him" (Mark 3:14). The call to follow Jesus as His *Disciple* is the call to get to know Jesus on a personal level.

The second truth about discipleship is that Jesus calls us *to impact the lives of others through ministry.* Mark goes on to say that Jesus also chose the Twelve so they might have a ministry of helping others. Jesus sent His first disciples out to preach, to heal sicknesses, to help deliver people from the power of Satan, and to cast out demons (Mark 3:13-19). Following Jesus leads you to find meaning and purpose in your life. Anyone who spends time with Jesus develops a passion for Jesus, which naturally results in a desire to serve others in His name.

To follow Jesus means to find purpose in your life.

A third truth about discipleship is that following Jesus means you are willing to leave your personal preferences and pursuits behind. Jesus said, "If any of you wants to be my follower, *you must give up your own way,* take up your cross, and follow me." (Matthew 16:24 NLT, emphasis added). The passage implies losing "sight of oneself and one's interests."[16] A Disciple chooses to put Jesus' plans and interests ahead of their own.

Jesus captured the attention of His first disciples and offered them the chance of a lifetime: to be with Him, live for Him, and change the world through Him! When Jesus entered the lives of the first disciples, their world was forever changed. Once grace walks into your life, your world can never remain the same.

{ The chance of a lifetime: to be with Jesus, live for him, and change the world through him. }

The World's Way or God's Way?

Speaking of grace, Lori and I named our fifth child ***Grace.*** She is a lovely redhead who lights up our world every day. Not only is she beautiful like her mother, but she is also smart . . . like her mother.

Grace was named after a concept that has forever changed our hearts. By grace, I mean God pouring out His undeserved and unmerited favor on us when Jesus adopted us into His family. When Jesus changed my life, I was graced by His love. I was transformed by His kindness. I was captured by His unending mercy that kept coming my way.

Do you find yourself at a crossroads in your life right now? God is calling out your name; at the same time, the world is trying to pull you toward itself. The problem is that these are two opposite directions. God's way looks like a narrow path headed straight up a steep, rocky mountainside. The world's way seems much easier. The path is wide, the scenery inviting, like walking through a cool forest in the hot summer sun. Why would anyone choose God's way?

People decide to go God's way because it is the best way. The world's way may be fun temporarily, but the fun does not last. Even if you live to be one hundred years old, that is a very short life against the backdrop of eternity. Jesus' way is often hard, but the rewards and the joys of eternity far outweigh the hardest life here on earth.

{ The rewards and the joys of eternity far outweigh the hardships of life on earth. }

Paul gave this encouragement to the church at Corinth	"Therefore we do not lose heart. Though outwardly we are wasting away, yet inwardly we are being renewed day by day. For our light and momentary troubles are achieving for us an eternal glory that far outweighs them all. So we fix our eyes not on what is seen, but on what is unseen, since what is seen is temporary, but what is unseen is eternal" (2 Corinthians 4:16-18 NIV).

Your life is too short to waste. Many people are so busy living the day-to-day, they do not stop to think about the purpose of their lives. What is your purpose? This question has intrigued philosophers for centuries, and they have provided many different answers over the years. Some people have sought to find meaning through various philosophies such as existentialism, hedonism, stoicism, epicureanism, utilitarianism, and religion. Here is a brief rundown of three of them:

- **Existentialism** teaches that freedom and your personal pursuits are the purpose of life.
- **Hedonism:** In hedonism, the purpose of life is to maximize pleasure and minimize pain and suffering.
- **Stoicism:** In Stoicism, the pursuit of reason, virtue, and nature is the ultimate purpose of one's life.

With so many schools of thought, which one is correct? How can anyone know the purpose for the short life we have been given? Only one person knows the answer. The one who changed the entire world. Jesus is the only person who claimed to be God and then proved it by rising from the dead. Jesus is the only person who never made a mistake, never committed even one sin. Jesus is the only person who fulfilled more than 300 prophecies from the Old Testament during his earthly ministry.[17]

Jesus said this about himself:
**"I am the way and the truth and the life.
No one comes to the Father except through Me."**
John 14:6 NIV

Let's get back to the question. What is the purpose of your life? The purpose of your life is to follow Jesus, who is life. As you follow Jesus, you will bring glory to God, which is the ultimate purpose for every person on planet Earth.

{ The purpose of your life is to follow Jesus, Who is life. }

The Most Important Decision of Your Life

Are you ready to follow Jesus as His disciple, starting today? Are you ready to live your life for a greater purpose? I encourage you to become a ***Disciple*** of Jesus. The decision to know, love, and follow Jesus is the most important decision of your life! So, how can you decide to follow Jesus starting today?

If you have counted the cost of discipleship (see Chapter 6) and are ready to take your next step in this exciting adventure of going after Jesus, as a ***Disciple*** (a learner and an apprentice to Jesus), may I have the privilege of leading you through this decision?

Pray this prayer with me.	Jesus, I have counted the cost, and You are worth it! You gave Your whole life for me, so I am going to give my whole life for You. I know You as my Savior … and now I want to surrender my life to follow You as Your Disciple. I choose to follow You, every day, starting today, in this new and exciting adventure of learning from You . . . following You . . . and impacting the world for Your glory. In Your name I pray. Amen.

CHAPTER 7 RECAP

Go After Jesus Principle #7

If you want a true purpose for your life, determine to **Go After Jesus** by following Him wherever He leads.
Read: Luke 9:23-26, 2 Corinthians 4:16-18

Key Takeaways

Captured by grace. Jesus' grace captivated His disciples to such an extent that they were willing to leave everything behind to follow Him with reckless abandon. Jesus offers you the chance of a lifetime, to be with Him, to live for Him, and to change the world through Him.

Total commitment. Following Jesus is not a casual commitment. Count the cost and determine to follow Him wherever He leads.

Purpose for living. Being a Disciple of Jesus adds meaning and purpose to your life. You are not just living for yourself; you are now living for the Kingdom of God. Your life's purpose now has eternal significance!

Reflection

When you were young, who was your hero? How did you mimic that person?

Do you consider following Jesus as the chance of a lifetime? Why?

What is your purpose in life? Try to convey it in one sentence.

Looking Ahead

Chapter 8: "Apprenticing with Jesus"

CHAPTER 8

Apprenticing with Jesus

"Take My yoke upon you and learn from Me,
for I am gentle and lowly in heart,
and you will find rest for your souls."
Matthew 11:29

What would it be like to follow in the footsteps of Jesus?

Let me introduce you to a young lady who sought to do just that. Her name is Jackie Pullinger. Jackie was born in London. As a young woman, she felt called to make a difference. She wanted to make the world a better place and bring glory to God by spreading the good news about Jesus to those who lived far away.

God laid a call on Jackie's heart to reach those in the infamous Walled City of Hong Kong, which was known for its crime, poverty, and drug dens. Jackie had an unusual burden to touch these people who were enslaved to drugs and those who were cast out by society, the marginalized.

In 1966, at age twenty-two, Jackie left her family and friends in London to move to Hong Kong. She had no formal education or training, but she had a call to follow in the footsteps of Jesus, to reach the unreached, and to love those who were unloved. With unwavering determination, Jackie devoted her life to serving the people of the Walled City. She lived among them, she wept with them, and she learned their culture, customs, and language.

For more than five decades, Jackie served the outcasts in Hong Kong. Through her kindness, compassion, and gospel witness, she saw countless lives transformed. Former drug addicts are clean and sober, criminals have turned their lives around, and so many families have been restored. Most important, people have given their lives to Jesus through Jackie's ministry.[18]

Jackie Pullinger's life illustrates what it is like to apprentice with Jesus. Jackie sought to imitate His love, compassion, and care. Jackie poured her life into those who needed it most, walking in the footsteps of Jesus.[19]

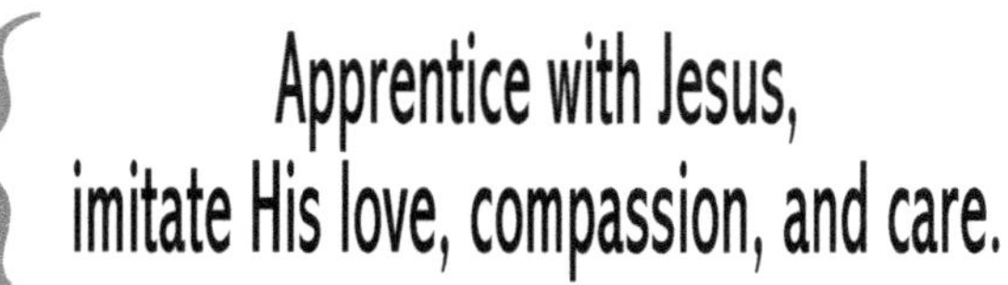
Apprentice with Jesus,
imitate His love, compassion, and care.

What Is an Apprentice?

An apprentice is someone who is learning a trade, craft, or profession under the skilled guidance and watchful eye of an experienced individual who has mastery in that field. Apprenticeship is an age-old method for a novice to gain experience and insight into a specific trade or area of focus. The apprentice learns both theoretical instructions alongside practical training.[20]

So, what does it look like to apprentice with Jesus? In this chapter, I will give you a modern play-by-play of what it means to **Go After Jesus** as His apprentice. You began your journey as a ***Seeker***. You are now a ***Disciple***, and you have determined to follow Jesus wherever He leads. Buckle your seatbelts, and we will discover what an apprenticeship with Jesus looks like.

Time Together. A modern-day apprentice of Jesus follows an ancient practice. If you want to know the way of the Master, you must spend time with Him. Let me take you back to His original twelve apprentices. When you observe their lives, you realize they spent time with Jesus, a lot of time.

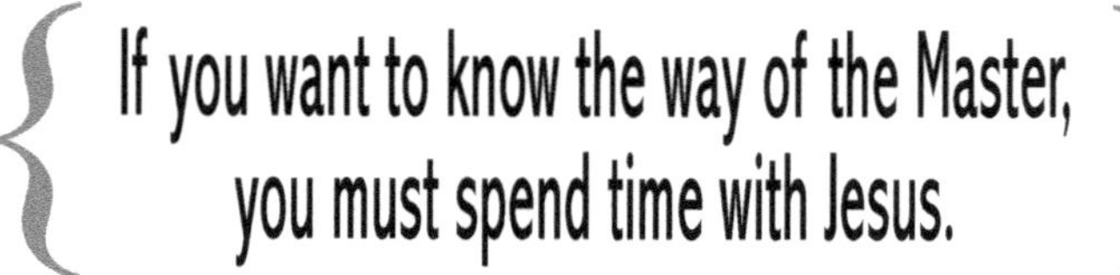
If you want to know the way of the Master,
you must spend time with Jesus.

During Jesus' three-and-a-half years of ministry, the Twelve lived with Jesus. Apart from the times when they were sent out on mission in groups of two and a few other occasions, the disciples spent every waking moment with the Master. They walked with Jesus, talked with Jesus, ate with Jesus, watched Jesus do ministry, and saw how Jesus loved people. How many hours did they spend with Jesus during that time? If you take three years (the timespan of His earthly ministry) and factor in twelve hours a day, guess how many hours this adds up to?

Drum roll.

The disciples would have spent around 13,000 hours with Jesus. How many hours does the average Christ-follower spend with Jesus? Let's focus on the average American Christ-follower for now. Only about 30 percent of American Christ-followers go to church weekly.[21] Say that the average churchgoer attends church twice a month, or about twenty-six times per year. That is around thirty hours a year (rounding up a bit for longer services).

Next, factor in the average Christ-follower's devotional life. Only about half of Americans (55 percent) say they pray every day.[22] So, estimate that the average American Christ-follower spends about fifteen minutes a day with Jesus during their daily devotional time. That adds up to around ninety-one hours a year. So, together with church attendance, the average American Christ-follower spends around 120 hours a year apprenticing with Jesus.

If we round up the number to include time serving the church, special events like Christmas and Easter, and a few hours for fellowship, that equals around 150 hours per year for the average American Christ-follower. How does that compare to the original apprentices? At that rate we would have to spend around eighty-seven years to equal the time the Twelve spent with Jesus in three years!

Maybe you are more devoted than the average Christ-follower. You may serve in your church and invest much more time in your spiritual life. You are reading this book, after all, so you are well on your way to apprenticing with Jesus. But you get the point. If you want to be an apprentice of Jesus, you must be willing to invest your time and, ultimately, your life getting to know Jesus.

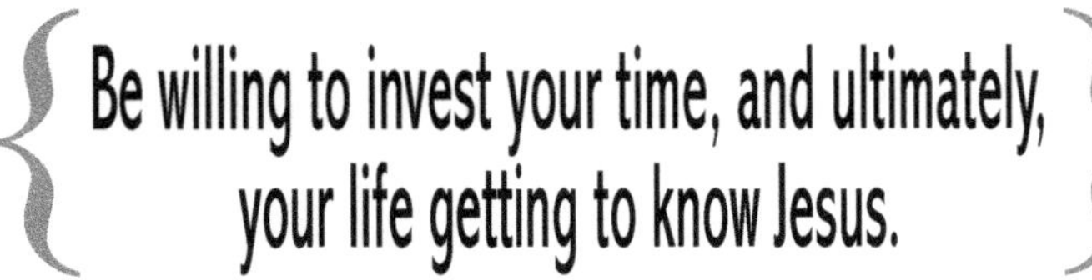
Be willing to invest your time, and ultimately,
your life getting to know Jesus.

"But Timothy, you don't understand," you say. "I'm so busy. I don't have that much time to spend." I understand where you are coming from. I can relate. I have six children who crave my attention, an amazing wife who desires time with me daily, a growing church that wants me at many meetings and events, and the list could go on.

I do not want to burden you with unrealistic expectations. Jesus is probably not going to ask you to quit your job or to give up all these responsibilities so you can spend twelve hours a day with Him. The point is that time with Jesus should be a daily priority if you want to be His apprentice. Here is the good news: You can apprentice with Jesus even if you have a crazy, busy schedule.

Now I will show you how to do this in your everyday, busy life. Here are three apprentice hacks that will help you keep Jesus the focus of each day.

Apprentice Hack #1
Put Jesus First in Your Schedule

This principle seems obvious, of course you should do this. While this principle is a no-brainer, it is often very hard to do every day. One suggestion is to start each day with a special time with Jesus. Even if you begin with just fifteen minutes, you can start your day apprenticing with Jesus. So, what does this look like? For me I start by talking with Jesus in prayer. I keep a prayer list on my phone, people I pray for every day. This keeps me on track and keeps my mind from wandering. As you pray, do not forget to be silent and listen for the Holy Spirit to speak to you through inner prompting in your spirit.

After my prayer time, I continue my time with Jesus by reading the Bible. Every time you read the Bible, you are apprenticing with Jesus by learning what He did and said, and by learning how He spoke through the authors of Scripture. When you read the Bible, you are hearing Jesus speak to you.

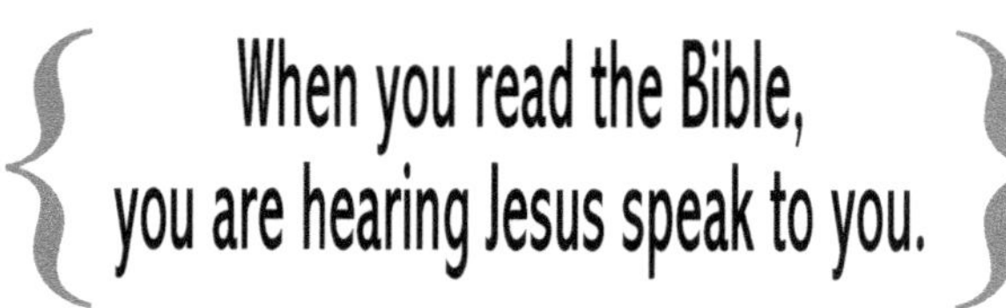
When you read the Bible,
you are hearing Jesus speak to you.

Why do I say that? The apostle Paul tells us this about Scripture: "All Scripture is God-breathed and is useful for teaching, rebuking, correcting and training in righteousness" (2 Timothy 3:16 NIV).

While I was teaching a small group of retired businessmen, one of the retired doctors said to us, "I try to pray, but I've never heard God speak back to me." I am sure many other people feel this way too. This was my response to the doctor's problem of not hearing from God: "Every time you read the Bible, God is speaking to you. All Scripture is God-breathed, so when you read the Scriptures, God is speaking to you."

What do you believe about the Bible? Here is what I truly believe with everything inside of me. I believe every word in God's Word. The Bible is God's very Word. Every time I read the Bible, I hear the voice of God. All Scripture is God-breathed. I get inspired when I read the inspired Scriptures. I am transformed when I allow God's Word to soak into my soul. The Bible stands the test of time. Critics and skeptics come and go, but the Word of God remains faithful and firm forever.

This is why I am challenging you to **Go After Jesus** by getting into the Bible every day. It will provide direction for making the right choices, and when you make a wrong choice, it will redirect you back to where God wants you to be.

I am confident you want your life to matter, that you want to live for a higher purpose. I want this for your life, too. If you allow God's Word to invade your daily routine, it will change you and alter the trajectory of your life. So, start each day hungry for spending time with Jesus in His Word.

Are you ready for the next apprentice hack?

Apprentice Hack #2
Ask Good Questions

As you apprentice with Jesus, you will learn that He asked exceptionally good questions. How many questions do you think Jesus asked during His earthly ministry? If you guessed 100, that is a good guess. But go higher. 200? Try again!

The Gospels record 307 questions Jesus asked. Twelve-year-old Jesus was in the temple asking the teachers of His day questions for three days.

He asked such good questions that they were amazed at His understanding and His answers (Luke 2:41-47). Why did Jesus ask so many questions? He already knew the answers, right?

Jesus did not ask questions because He had no access to the answers; He was God in human form. While the motivation can vary for each situation and person, the main reason He asked 307 questions was that He wanted people to think for themselves. He wanted to teach them how to think in a way that had eternal value. He wanted to spark curiosity, faith, and a profound dependence on the power of God.

Here is a principle that can change your life: If you want to grow in your faith and if you want to **Go After Jesus**, learn how to ask good questions.

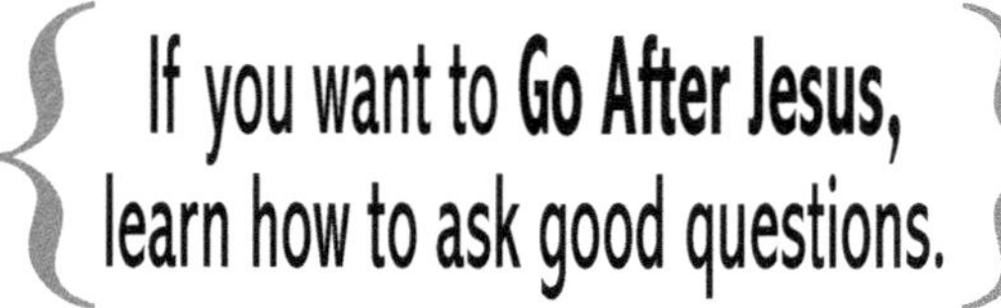
If you want to Go After Jesus,
learn how to ask good questions.

Good questions will not only train you how to think, but they will also help you connect with the heart of the person with whom you are talking. Good questions are also going to help you understand ideas, concepts, and truths you may not have learned otherwise.

If you long to **Go After Jesus**, this next apprentice hack is going to help you follow in His footsteps.

Apprentice Hack #3
Listen to the Father Daily

It may come as no surprise to you that Jesus spent a lot of time talking to and with His Father. Prayer is the conversation that kept Jesus connected to heaven while He was on Earth. Prayer is how Jesus received guidance and encouragement for the daily challenges of His three-and-a-half years of earthly ministry.

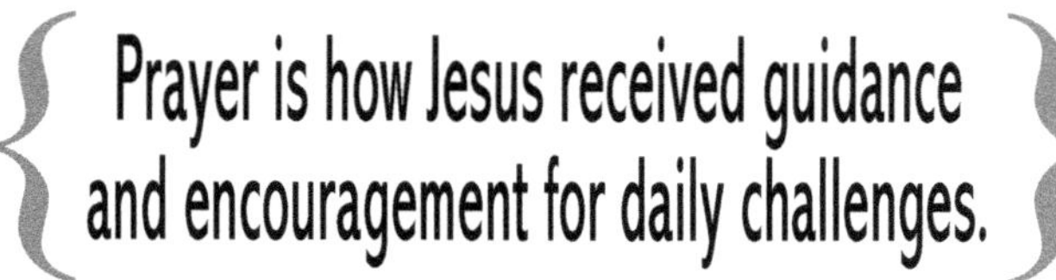
Prayer is how Jesus received guidance
and encouragement for daily challenges.

The Gospel writer Luke tells us that Jesus often withdrew and prayed in the wilderness (Luke 5:16). Matthew tells us that Jesus sent the multitudes away so He could get some time alone to pray on a mountain (Matthew 14:23). Jesus often got up early and prayed long before dawn (Mark 1:35). Every morning Jesus prayed to receive encouragement, guidance, and direction for the upcoming day.

Jesus also prayed for wisdom for key decisions for His ministry. Luke tells us that Jesus spent the entire night in prayer before He selected His twelve disciples (Luke 6:12-13). Once, the disciples privately asked Jesus why they were unsuccessful in casting out a demon. Jesus gave them this powerful insight: Some things can only happen through prayer and fasting. He also challenged them to have "faith as small as a mustard seed" (Matthew 17:14-21).

When little children came to Jesus, He laid hands on them and prayed over them, asking for the Father's blessing on those precious little ones (Matthew 19:13). As Jesus entered His last week on earth, prayer was His source of strength, as He relied on His Father to help Him endure the agonies of the cross. Jesus poured out His heart in the garden of Gethsemane, as He accepted the cup of suffering necessary to fulfill the Father's plan of redemption for humanity. Jesus prayed so intensely in Gethsemane that his "sweat became like great drops of blood falling down to the ground" (Luke 22:44).

I could write an entire book about Jesus' prayer life, but for this chapter, here is the essence of it. Jesus talked with the Father often. He prayed early before His day began. Jesus prayed over food, blessed people, prayed about situations that needed a miracle, and prayed late into the night. Prayer was the communication tool that kept Jesus and the Father in lockstep for Jesus' daily assignments. Prayer was important to Jesus, and it should be important to His apprentices too.

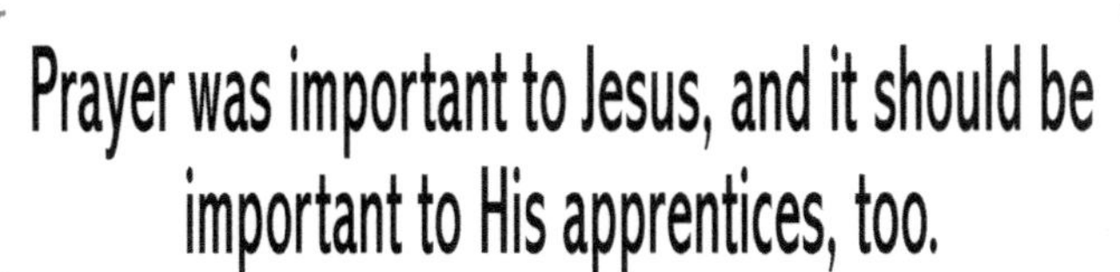
Prayer was important to Jesus, and it should be
important to His apprentices, too.

So, how can you **Go After Jesus** in your daily prayer life? Jesus taught His disciples to pray in what is usually called "The Lord's Prayer." I prefer to call it "The Model Prayer" because Jesus used it to show His apprentices how to pray. Here is the model prayer as recorded in Luke's Gospel.

So, He said to them, "When you pray, say:

When You pray, say:	"Our Father in heaven, Hallowed be your name. Your kingdom come. Your will be done On earth as *it is* in heaven. Give us day by day our daily bread. And forgive us our sins, For we also forgive everyone who is indebted to us. And do not lead us into temptation, But deliver us from the evil one." (Luke 11:2-4)

Nine Powerful Prayer Strategies

How can this prayer serve as a model in your daily time with Jesus? Here are nine prayer strategies that can help you apprentice with Jesus in the way you pray.

Prayer strategy #1

Make prayer a priority in your life. Jesus said, "When you pray." This is not *if* you pray, but *when* you pray. Prayer should be part of your daily schedule, not just on church days. Since Jesus started each morning in prayer, that is a great place to start. Schedule a block of time at the start of every day to be with Jesus. Even ten to fifteen minutes will make a difference in your day.

Prayer strategy #2

Start with God, not yourself. "Our Father in heaven" is the beginning of the model prayer. If you start with God, everything else flows out of that focus. Go vertical with a focus on God before you ever go horizontal with a focus on your needs. Why? If you start with yourself, you will lack perspective, and your prayers can become self-focused very fast. However, when you start with a focus on your heavenly Father, your mindset is changed by the realities of heaven. As a result, your prayers have an eternal focus rather than a temporary here-and-now focus.

Prayer strategy #3

Praise always comes before problem and provision, "Hallowed be Your name." If you are anything like me, it is easy to jump straight to your pressing problems.

"God, I'm in trouble and I need Your help right now!" While God wants to hear all about your problems and deeply cares for every one of them (1 Peter 5:7), He wants you to focus on who He is first. Why? When you focus on who God is, your problems become much smaller. If you begin with your problems, they are magnified; but when you begin with how great and amazing God is, your problems become small and insignificant against the backdrop of God's goodness and grandeur.

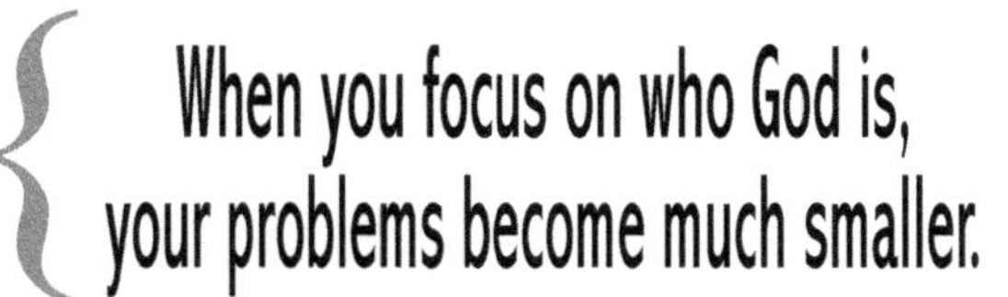
When you focus on who God is,
your problems become much smaller.

Prayer strategy #4

Ask for God's coming Kingdom, "Your Kingdom come." What is God's Kingdom? God's Kingdom is the place where God has rule and reign, where the culture of heaven prevails. You may be saying, "Doesn't God rule everywhere?" Yes, He does. But God allows the enemy, Satan, to have temporary control in some places.

The Bible says Satan is the "god of this world" (2 Corinthians 4:4 NLT). When you pray for God's Kingdom to come, you are asking for the culture of heaven to invade the places where God has placed you: Your family, your neighborhood, your job, your church, and even the grocery store. What would happen if the places where God has placed you became places of grace where people could sense something special was happening? When you pray, ask God to let the culture of heaven invade every space and place you are in.

Ask God to let the culture of heaven invade every space and place you are in.

Prayer strategy #5

Seek to walk in God's plan for your day, "Your will be done on earth as it is in heaven." This prayer flows out of a request for God's Kingdom to come. When heaven's Kingdom invades Earth's kingdom, the actions of heaven will start to happen here on Earth. When God rules your heart, you begin to live out the purpose and plans of heaven here on Earth. So, as you pray, ask God to use your hands to heal, your voice to speak truth, and your feet to travel, bringing people good news and hope. Become a channel of heaven's activities here on Earth as you live out your day today.

Prayer strategy #6

God will meet your needs, but not your vanities, "Give us day by day our daily bread." You may have heard the story about a rich man who had promised his son an annual allowance. Every year on the same day, the son showed up to receive his annual blessing, which would take care of all his needs for the upcoming year. Over time, the son began *only* visiting his father on that one day to receive his money. The father then changed the arrangement, so the son received just enough money for one day's needs at a time. This changed their entire relationship since the father and son met every day, and as a result, their relationship became strong again.[23]

Showing up every day to connect with your Father is a simple aspect of this prayer strategy. Keep showing up. Keep connecting with your heavenly Father every morning, and do not stop there. Let prayer become part of what you do throughout the day. Scripture tells us to "pray continually" (1 Thessalonians 5:17 NIV). Asking God for your daily bread means you can trust God's provision for each day. God does not promise to provide for your needs in advance, but you can ask Him to give you everything you need for that day. As you ask God to meet your needs, you will experience His gracious provision.

Ask God daily to meet your needs and experience His gracious provision.

Prayer strategy #7

Make confession and repentance part of your daily prayers, "And forgive us our sins." Why should I ask for forgiveness as part of my daily prayers? Forgiveness is a daily need for most of us. On any given day, we find ourselves missing God's standard of right living in what we say, in what we do, and in our attitudes. Our heavenly Father desires a thriving relationship with us, but active, unconfessed sin will hinder our fellowship with Him.

When we asked Jesus to save us, He forgave us and took away all our sins. So why do we need to ask for forgiveness if we are already forgiven? Even though all our sins have been taken away and nailed to the cross of Christ (Colossians 2:14), we still need to confess our sins daily. Why?

Jesus gave us a good illustration of this when He washed His twelve disciples' feet. Peter initially refused to let Jesus wash His feet because he felt unworthy. Jesus rebuked Peter for his false humility and told him that if Peter did not allow Him to wash his feet, then Peter would have no part with Him. Peter then responded, "Okay then, not just my feet, but go ahead and wash my hands and my head also!" But Jesus said that those who have had a bath only need to wash their feet because they are already clean (John 13:1–17).

This story illustrates what happens to those who accept Jesus as Savior. They have been made clean through the cleansing power of His blood. Yet when Christ-followers sin, they need to be refreshed and renewed, just like a traveler needs the dust washed off his feet. A daily prayer habit reminds you of the need to live a holy life and to walk in complete fellowship with the Father, not letting sin get in the way of your relationship.

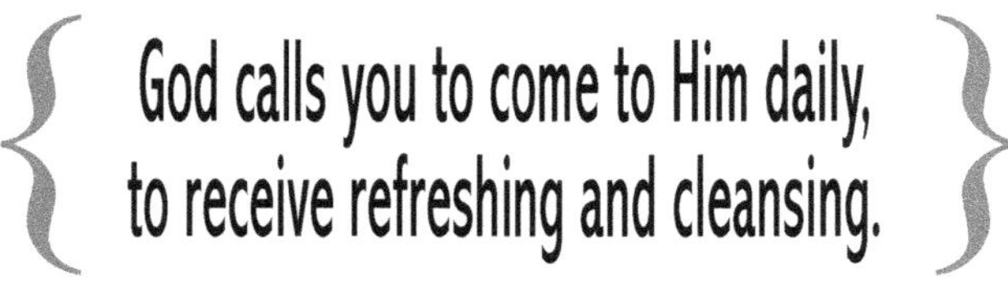
God calls you to come to Him daily,
to receive refreshing and cleansing.

Jesus forgave you when you accepted Him into your life. Now, God calls you to come to Him daily to receive refreshing and cleansing. Confession has another powerful benefit. It turns you away from sin, so sinful habits don't eventually turn into a sinful lifestyle (which is not compatible with following Jesus). Paul told the church at Rome, "Do not let sin control the way you live; do not give in to sinful desires" (Romans 6:12 NLT). As I said in an earlier chapter, when you mess up, it's time to 'fess up!

Maintain Close Communication

Several years ago, a popular Verizon TV commercial featured two people talking on the phone. The Verizon guy had switched to the rival cellular company Sprint. The Verizon guy kept asking the other person, "Can you hear me now?" This was Verizon's creative attempt to encourage people to switch to their company because they believed they would provide a better cellular connection with fewer dropped calls and a wider coverage area.

Did you know there are things in your life that will cause you to drop your close communication with God? One of the top things that produces interference in your prayer life is unconfessed sin. The practice of confessing your sin daily, making things right with Him, will ensure that you do not lose your close connection with God.

When should we confess our sins? That's a good question. We should confess our sins as soon as we realize we have messed up. Do not wait till the end of the day when you are saying your nighttime prayers. Confess your sin as soon as the Holy Spirit brings the sin to your mind. David gives us this good news in Psalm 32: "Then I acknowledged my sin to you and did not cover up my iniquity. I said, 'I will confess my transgressions to the LORD'. And you forgave the guilt of my sin" (v. 5 NIV).

Confession puts you back on the right track in your daily walk with God.

This is such a beautiful promise: If you will simply tell God you are sorry and are willing to do things His way from now on, God will forgive you. Even though you were forever forgiven by Jesus when you accepted Him as Savior, you still need to make sure nothing is presently hindering your relationship with Him. Confession is powerful. It restores your fellowship with your heavenly Father and puts you back on the right track in your daily walk with Him.

My children know that I will always be their loving father. No matter what they say or do or how much they mess up, I will be there for them forever. Even though my relationship with them is secure, my close connection with them is hindered when they decide to disobey me. But something magical happens when they say they are sorry for their disobedience and apologize. Our close connection is restored. Our hearts are united once again.

As you **Go After Jesus**, remember this truth: Jesus wants to be close to you every day. Do not let any sin or struggle keep you from intimacy with your Savior. When Jesus defeated sin and death through His victory on the cross, sin lost its power over the life of every Christ-follower. The Holy Spirit now lives inside you, giving you the power to resist temptation. Do not let sin reign in your life. Daily confession leads to daily victory in your walk with God.

Prayer strategy #8

Recognize that you cannot be right with God if you refuse to be right with others, "For we also forgive everyone who is indebted to us." God wants your relationship with Him to thrive, but there is something you need to know: You cannot be right with God if you hold on to unforgiveness toward others. God has forgiven you, and He expects you to forgive others. If Jesus has forgiven you for all the wrongs you have done to Him, the only reasonable reaction is for you to forgive those who have sinned against you.

{ God has not put a cap on His forgiveness for us; do not put a limit on forgiving others. }

The disciple Peter once asked Jesus how many times he was required to forgive. The highest number he could think of was seven times. The standard in Peter's day was to forgive a person three times, so Peter doubled that number and added one extra time for good measure. Jesus then said something that shocked Peter and the other eleven disciples: "Not seven times, but seventy-seven times" (Matthew 18:22 NIV). Jesus was conveying the principle that forgiveness is unlimited. God has not put a cap on His forgiveness toward us, so we should not put a limit on forgiving others. Jesus then illustrates this principle by telling a parable about a man who owed his king an exorbitant amount of money that today would equal millions of dollars. When the king told the man to pay off his debt or face being sold as a slave (along with all his family) until the debt was paid off; the man threw himself on the ground, begging for the king's mercy and grace. The king responded in storybook fashion by saying that the man's entire multi-million-dollar debt was forgiven, and he was free to go. He was given a new chance at life.

The story does not have a happy ending, though. The forgiven man did the unthinkable. He found someone who owed him several thousand dollars, much less than his debt to the king. He grabbed the man, put him in a choke hold, and demanded immediate payment or else. The debtor also begged for mercy and pleaded for more time to pay off the debt. How did the newly forgiven man respond?

Instead of responding in like kind, forgiving the man as he had been forgiven, the creditor had the debtor thrown into prison until the debt could be paid in full, not a penny less. Soon, word traveled to the king. The king was furious. He could not believe the man whom he had forgiven for a multi-million-dollar debt could not forgive a debt of so much less (Matthew 18:23-35).

This parable beautifully paints the picture that God has forgiven us of a debt that is far greater than the debt anyone will ever owe us. We have sinned against God far more than anyone could ever sin against us. Since we have been forgiven, we need to forgive others. *The forgiven forgive.* Do not allow unforgiveness to turn into bitterness. That will create a wedge between not only you and the other person, but also between you and God.

Prayer strategy #9

Be aware of your own weaknesses and ask for God's help in overcoming temptation and evil, "And lead us not into temptation but deliver us from the evil one." The best offense is a good defense. As you **Go After Jesus**, realize that you are prone to fall short of God's righteous standards (Romans 3:23). This will help you rely on the Father's strength and grace to overcome the temptations that will come your way every day.

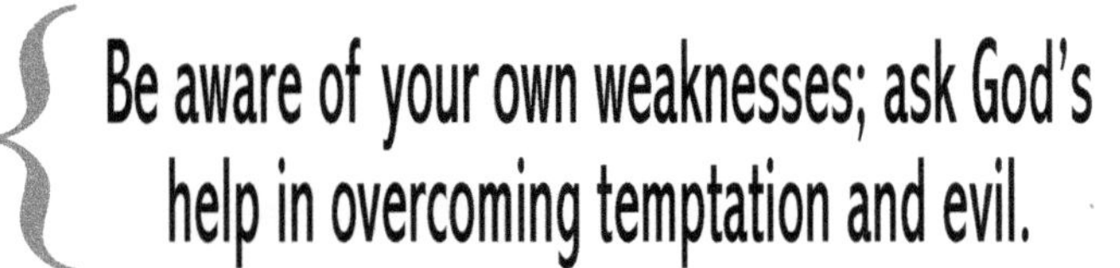
Be aware of your own weaknesses; ask God's
help in overcoming temptation and evil.

When you ask God to help you avoid daily temptations during prayer, it puts your heart in a humble place before Him. In essence, you are saying, "God, you know me. You realize that I'm going to be tempted to make mistakes today. And God … apart from Your help, I'm likely to fall short. So please help me. I'm so weak, I don't want any temptation to come my way. So please help me to be strong for You."

In the story about Job, we discover that prior to his severe testing, Job had been protected by God. Satan told God that the reason Job loved and obeyed Him was that He had placed a hedge of protection around Job and his family. As a result, Job was blessed with a large family and many possessions (Job 1:10). Satan tried to attack Job, but he was hindered by the hedge.

When you ask God for daily deliverance from your own sinful tendencies, you are asking God to surround you and protect you from sin and from unnecessary trials. As you depend on God's daily grace, you will discover this beautiful truth: God is already there, waiting to encourage you. He longs to help you in your times of need.

He understands your daily struggles. Jesus was tempted in every area, yet He was victorious (Hebrews 4:15). You, too, can live in God's victory as you **Go After Jesus** in your daily prayer time.

CHAPTER 8 RECAP

Go After Jesus Principle #8

An apprentice of Jesus spends quality time with Him in prayer and Bible study.

Read: Matthew 17:14-21, Luke 11:2–4

Key Takeaways

Apprentice with Jesus. Start each day by spending time with Jesus. Read your Bible, ask God good questions, listen to Him, and converse with Him in prayer.

Develop a prayer strategy. Prayer was important to Jesus, and it should be important to you. Follow the model prayer in Luke 11:2-4, and make prayer a daily priority. Lead with praise for who God is, ask for God's Kingdom, seek God's plan, ask for God's daily provision, confess any sins, forgive others, and ask for deliverance from sin and temptation.

Establish priorities. Seek to walk in God's plan for your day. As you ask God for your needs daily, you will experience His gracious daily provision. The practice of confessing your sin to God promptly and making things right with Him will ensure that you do not lose your close connection to God.

Questions

How much time do you devote to reading God's Word and talking to Him each day? What could you do to increase that time?

How would you describe your prayers? Do you only present God with a list of your needs, or do you incorporate repentance, praise, and thanksgiving too?

How would your day change if you consistently asked God to put a hedge of protection around you?

Looking Ahead

Part 3: The Friend Chapter 9: Jesus, Your Forever Friend

Part Three

The Friend

I desire to enjoy the richness of daily, intimate time with Jesus.

The Seeker: I want to ***discover*** the awe-inspiring truth of who Jesus really is.
The Disciple: I am ***determined*** to follow Jesus wherever He leads.
The Friend: I ***desire*** to enjoy the richness of daily, intimate time with Jesus.

CHAPTER 9

Jesus, Your Forever Friend

"No longer do I call you servants . . .
but I have called you friends"
John 15:15

In fourth grade, I was on top of the world. I had more friends than ever, and even formed my own club called "The Nike Gang." My club was composed of roughly half of my fourth-grade classmates. We were the athletic ones in the class (or at least we thought we were). Most of us wore Nike shoes, and many of us were fervent fans of Michael Jordan, the best basketball player on the planet in the 1990s. We developed secret passwords and a special club culture. We also had a secretary who kept track of all our secrets and ensured our rival club did not find out about them.

All was going well until . . . until our secretary, Beth, became a traitor and gave all our secrets to the rival club. While her disloyalty seems insignificant now, back then, my nine-year-old heart was devastated. She was a trusted friend, and she betrayed my trust. That sad day, I learned two important lessons: (1) People will let you down, and (2) Some friends are not true friends. People can be your friend one day, and the next day they aren't.

Can you relate? How many times have people you considered friends turned their backs on you or walked away from your friendship? How many times has your heart been broken either by a friend or by a romantic partner? In this world of uncertainty and change, who can you really trust? Most of us had hurtful betrayals of some kind when we were growing up, and unfortunately, many of us suffer heartbreak in our adult life, too. If such betrayal became the norm, we would continually struggle with trust issues because every person has the potential to hurt us in the end.

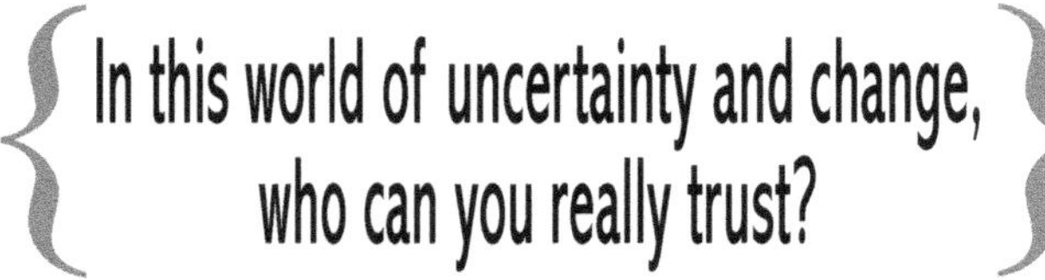
In this world of uncertainty and change,
who can you really trust?

But betrayal is not the end of the story for any of us. There is a better way. As you **Go After Jesus**, you make this discovery: Jesus is your forever friend who will never let you down. He will never turn His back on you, and He will never leave you alone. He promises to always be with you, "to the very end of the age" (Matthew 28:20 NIV). In this chapter, we will discover what it means to develop a close and intimate friendship with Jesus.

As you continue in your quest to **Go After Jesus**, your identity in Christ is developing. You started as a spiritual ***Seeker***, then you became a ***Disciple***. Now you are entering into a deeper relationship with your Savior: you are a ***Friend*** of Jesus.

Abiding: A Deep and Lasting Relationship

What does it look like to be friends with Jesus? In John 15, Jesus gives us a picture of what friendship with Him looks like. It starts with abiding in Christ. "Abide in Me, and I in you. As the branch cannot bear fruit of itself, unless it abides in the vine, neither can you, unless you abide in Me" (John 15:4). To **Go After Jesus**, you are called to develop a deep and lasting relationship with God. I will explain how friendship with Jesus is not only possible, but leads to an abundant life.

Friendship with God begins
with abiding in Christ.

Author and theologian J. I. Packer gives us this powerful insight into the word *abide*, as it pertains to your relationship with Jesus:

> "*Abide* is an old English word for "remain," "stay steady," and "keep your position." What it means to abide in Christ, that is, always to be resting on him, anchored to him, fixed in him, drawing from him, continually connected and in touch with him, is a pervasive theme in chapters 14–17. There is no more precious lesson to learn, no more enriching link and bond to cherish, no more vital connection to keep snug and tight, so that it never loosens, than this. Abiding in Christ brings peace, joy and love, answers to prayer, and fruitfulness in service. The abiding life is the abundant life. As you go after Jesus, you develop a deep connection with Christ, a connection that will help keep your faith steady even under pressure, a connection that will produce lasting communication between you and God, and a connection that will keep your soul anchored to the realities of your new life in Christ. What an amazing truth, you can now abide in Christ!" [24]

Abiding: The Word of God Lives in You

What does it look like to "abide in Christ"? Jesus lays out what it looks like in John 15. First, abiding in Christ means the Word of God lives within you. Jesus gave His disciples this truth: "If you abide in Me, and My words abide in you, you will ask what you desire, and it shall be done for you" (John 15:7). To have Christ live in you means Christ's Word (the Bible) lives in you. When you know the truth, the truth not only changes you, but also sets you free to live the kind of abundant life that is yours in Christ. (See John 8:32). This is also why a Christian must memorize Scripture, so they can easily bring it to mind as they go about their day. Memorizing scripture also helps individuals discern God's will and make wise decisions by providing a framework for understanding and applying biblical principles.

We have already laid the foundation for the holy habit of Bible study. As you study God's Word daily, something amazing happens: Whenever you get into the Word, the Word gets into you. As the Word permeates your mind, something mysterious happens inside you. The living Word produces new life on the inside that begins to show on the outside. Abiding in Christ is not a passive activity; it is a purposeful walk with Jesus. It is spending quality time daily with the person you love most and the one you are now living for.

{ Abiding in Christ is not a passive activity; it is a daily walk with Jesus. }

Corrie ten Boom and her sister Betsie found themselves in a difficult situation that tested their faith to the core. These two sisters were prisoners in a German concentration camp called Ravensbrück during World War II. In *The Hiding Place*, Corrie talks about a time when Betsie was seriously ill and did not know if she would survive. One day, Corrie found her sister quoting this passage from the Bible to find renewed courage: "Rejoice always, pray without ceasing, in everything give thanks; for this is the will of God in Christ Jesus for you" (1 Thessalonians 5:16-18).

Betsie's ability to find courage and renewed strength during a time of great weakness gave Corrie strength and encouragement that helped see her through the dark days in the concentration camp. Tragically, Betsie did not survive the harsh conditions of Ravensbrück, but the Lord spared Corrie's life. On December 28, 1944, Corrie was released from Ravensbrück and then lived her remaining days telling others about her faith. Countless lives have been impacted by Corrie's life and ministry.[25] Corrie's story exemplifies abiding in Christ. The promises of God were her source of strength even on the most difficult days.

The same can be true for you. As a friend of Jesus, He will be your constant companion. His Word will guide you through the highs and lows of life. The Holy Spirit will be there to guide each step, assuring you that you are heading in the right direction as you keep in step with the Spirit's guidance (Galatians 5:25).

Abiding: Your Desires Change

The second truth about abiding in Christ is that your prayers will be answered in amazing ways. Jesus said, "If you abide in Me, and My words abide in you, you will ask what you desire, and it shall be done for you" (John 15:7). So, what does this look like in your life? When you begin to read the Bible, every day you will experience something transformative: Your heart's desires will gradually look more like the desires of God.

When your desires are transformed into God's desires for your life, guess what happens? God fulfills the desires of your heart. When your life is transformed by the grace of God, His desires become your desires, and then those God-given desires eventually become reality.

{ When your life is transformed by the grace of God, His desires become your desires. }

Do you desire true happiness? Do you long for a fulfilled life? Well, you now hold in your hands the key to true and lasting fulfillment: **Go After Jesus**. Do this by reading and studying the Bible daily. This allows God to put new desires in your heart that eventually give birth to blessings along the way.

Abiding: Your Life Is Fruitful

The third truth about abiding in Christ is that your life will be fruitful. Not only does God give you new desires and grant them, but He also promises that your life will be fruitful. "By this My Father is glorified, that you bear much fruit; so that you will be My disciples" (John 15:8). As you **Go After Jesus**, something meaningful happens in and through your life: You become fruitful. What does it mean to be fruitful? Fruitfulness means you are making an eternal impact on the lives of others.

{ Fruitfulness means you are making an impact on the lives of others. }

Do you want to make a profound difference in the world? Do you desire to leave it better than when you found it? May your heart resound with a jubilant "yes!" God is all about progress and growth. The Creator loves to make something out of nothing; after all, He spoke the world into existence.

Everything beautiful that we see in our world He created by speaking it into existance. Every pod of dolphins that plays joyfully in the blue oceans, every butterfly that is transformed from a crawling caterpillar and takes flight for the first time, and every snow leopard that prowls on the snow-covered mountains of South Asia is one tiny glimpse of the creative desire of our God. Let this truth soak into your soul: You were created by the Creator to be fruitful for your Creator!

God made you on purpose and with a purpose. This gives your life intrinsic meaning and a powerful purpose. Why are you here, at this time in history? The answer is this: Jesus gave you new life, so your life could give life to others by doing what I call God-works, God working through you to impact others for His glory. You are not saved *by* God-works; you are saved to *do* God-works. Paul phrased it like this: "For we are His workmanship, created in Christ Jesus for good works, which God prepared beforehand that we should walk in them" (Ephesians 2:10).

As you **Go After Jesus**, the natural by-product will be fruit, abundant fruit! The fruit you produce may look different than the fruit I produce. Some of you may be called to remain unmarried like Paul, and use your life to serve in your local church. Or God may be calling you to serve your family in such a way that your children are shot out like gospel arrows into the world to make an eternal difference in the lives of others. Others are called to serve God as Christ-honoring entrepreneurs, having an eternal impact on the lives of your employees and customers. No matter what your calling is, the result will be that you will leave the world better than when you found it, as Christ works through you.

CHAPTER 9 RECAP

Go After Jesus Principle #9

Jesus is my forever friend who will never leave me.
Read: John 15:1- 8

Key Takeaways

Abiding in Christ is a lifelong, dynamic relationship. Just as branches are lifeless apart from the vine, so are you without Christ. You cannot bear any lasting fruit apart from a living and lasting relationship with Jesus.

Your heart's desires will be transformed the longer you stay connected to Christ. His desires will become your desires. The key to contentment in daily life is to continually draw closer to Christ as you abide in Him.

Fruitfulness is the by-product of faithfulness. As you live for Jesus daily, something amazing transpires: You begin to bear fruit. You have an eternal impact on the lives of others. God's goal for your life is that you will bear fruit, more fruit, and eventually much fruit (John 15:1-8).

Reflection

What qualities do you most value in a friend?

What are your deepest desires? How do you think they align with God's desires?

Who has made an eternal impact on your life? In what ways are you making an eternal impact on the lives of others?

Looking Ahead

Chapter 10: Delighting in Jesus

CHAPTER 10

Delighting in Jesus

"Delight yourself also in the Lord,
And He shall give you the desires of your heart."
Psalm 37:4

What if I told you I was more in love with my wife, Lori, today than when I first met her 15 years ago. At the beginning of this book, I introduced you to our love story. What is the secret that makes my love for Lori grow stronger as the years roll by? The more I know about her, the more there is to love about her. As we walk through life together, through both the amazing experiences of joy and the low valleys of disappointment, we continue to grow closer together.

Whoever said "love is blind" did not know what they were talking about. Lasting love is not blind. It is based on a deliberate choice, with eyes wide open, not shut. Real love is based on truth and endurance. The mind-bending truth about love is this: Knowledge and experience make love grow deeper and stronger with time. This truth is not only applicable to a significant other, like a spouse or a child, but the same applies to our relationship with God.

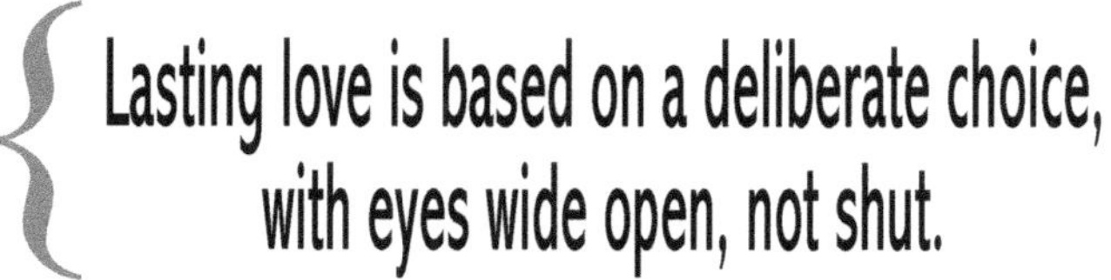
Lasting love is based on a deliberate choice,
with eyes wide open, not shut.

As you **Go After Jesus** as a ***Friend***, you develop a deep desire to enjoy the richness of daily, intimate time with Him. What does it look like to

Go After Jesus with delight each day? In this chapter, we will continue to build on the foundation of what it looks like to be a ***Friend*** of Jesus.

We laid the foundation of the holy habits: spending time in God's Word, talking with God daily, connecting with community weekly, serving God in your church (ministry), and worship. In this chapter, you will discover what it looks like to delight in God practically. Five action principles will transform your relationship with Jesus.

Principle One:
Unconditional Love

Think of this: The Creator, the one who crafted you, the one who creatively knit you together in your mother's womb, the one who hung the stars in the sky, the one who is holding the world together, is the same one who wants to be close friends with you! The first principle of delighting in Jesus is to bask in His unconditional love. If you want to be close to Jesus, embrace the fact that Jesus truly does love you with an unconditional, everlasting, and experiential love.

{ Jesus truly does love you with an unconditional, everlasting, and experiential love. }

In the last chapter, we explored several truths from John 15:1-8. In this chapter, we will explore John 15:9-17. In verse 9, Jesus gives this beautiful promise: "As the Father loved Me, I also have loved you; abide in My love." If you want to delight in Jesus, realize how much Jesus truly loves you. "Jesus Loves Me" is not just a children's song; it is a captivating fact that will change you if you embrace it. How can you experience this love for yourself? You may believe Jesus truly loves others, but can you accept that He loves you? To experience the love of Jesus in personal and practical ways, look at how Jesus showed His love for you. The apostle John found evidence of God's love when he looked at the sacrificial death of Christ on our behalf: "This is how God showed his love among us: He sent his one and only Son into the world that we might live through him" (1 John 4:9 NIV).

If you want to be assured of God's love for you and delight in it, look no further than the cross. John 3:16 is one of the most famous verses in the Bible because it illustrates this great love: God loves you so much that He sent the greatest gift in the cosmos, His own Son, so you could have true life, everlasting life, once you receive this gift of love. God not only loves you, He also likes you. As Max Lucado wrote in *God Thinks You're Wonderful,* "If [God] had a wallet, your photo would be in it. If he had a refrigerator, your picture would be on it. He sends you flowers every spring and a sunrise every morning. … Face it, friend. He's crazy about you!"[26] Embracing, receiving, and experiencing Jesus' unconditional love is the first step in delighting in Him as your friend.

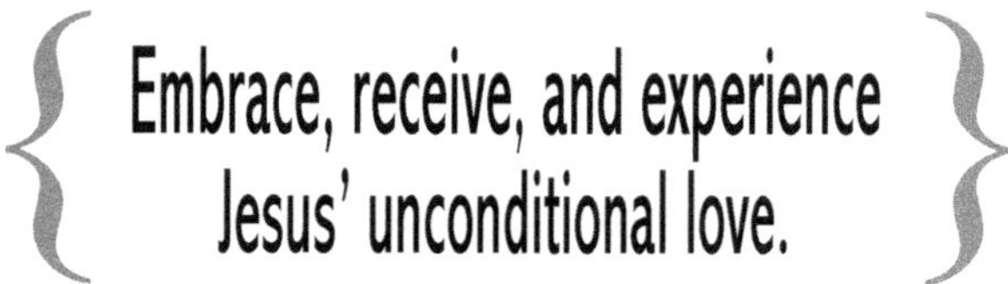
Embrace, receive, and experience
Jesus' unconditional love.

Principle 2:
Living Out His Unconditional Love

After you have truly experienced the love of God, the second action step, as one who delights in Jesus, is to live out the love of God by living for God. Jesus continues His teaching in John 15 with this amazing promise: "If you keep My commandments, you will abide in My love, just as I have kept My Father's commandments and abide in His love" (John 15:10). The way to experience the love of God is to live it out. As an adopted member of His family, God loves you unconditionally, but you cannot fully experience this love until you begin to live it out in your daily walk with God.

So, how are you doing with living for Jesus in your everyday life? If you are like most Christ-followers, your walk with Jesus is filled with a lot of ups and downs. On good days, you are walking in loving obedience to God and His Word, but on other days, you find yourself doing the things you do not want to do and struggling to do the things you know you need to do. Paul fought this battle too. In Romans 7:13-25, he claimed the struggle was so real that he kept doing the things he hated (sin) and struggled to do what was right (keeping God's commandments).

For a glimpse of what delighting in Jesus looks like, study the life of Abraham. Abraham first encountered God when He called him to leave his homeland in the land of the Chaldeans to go to an unknown place. What did Abraham do? He left the known for the unknown. He left the *comfortable* for the *uncomfortable*. Why? He *believed* God and took God at His Word by obeying God's command to go. James gives us this recap of Abraham's first steps of obeying God: "And so it happened just as the Scriptures say: 'Abraham believed God, and God counted him as righteous because of his faith.' He was even called the friend of God" (James 2:23 NLT).

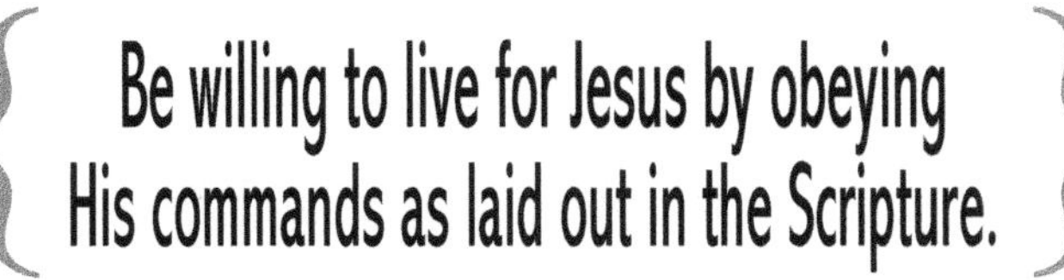
Be willing to live for Jesus by obeying
His commands as laid out in the Scripture.

If you want to delight in Jesus, be willing to live for Jesus by obeying His commands as laid out in the Scriptures. You also obey Jesus when you respond to the Holy Spirit's guidance in your life. As you **Go After Jesus**, you will discover that Jesus is leading and guiding you today just as He guided His disciples during His earthly ministry. How is this possible since Jesus is in heaven? He leads, guides, encourages, and directs you through the ministry of the Holy Spirit. Paul gives us this instruction: "Since we are living by the Spirit, let us follow the Spirit's leading in every part of our lives" (Galatians 5:25 NLT).

Principle 3:
Letting the Joy of the Lord Strengthen You

You have embraced the love of Jesus and decided to live for Him by obeying His Word. Now it is time to implement the third action step of delighting in Jesus: Let the joy of the Lord be your strength. What exactly is joy? How does joy differ from happiness? Joy and happiness are vastly different. Happiness is based on circumstances. According to *Merriam-Webster's Dictionary,* happiness is "a state favored by luck or fortune."[27]

You feel all is well with the world, and you are enjoying the events and circumstances around you. In other words, happiness is something that happens to you when life is going well for you. When all is not going well, happiness typically disappears.

While happiness is based on your present circumstances, joy is *not* circumstantial. Joy is *relational.* Happiness concerns that which is *external*, but joy concerns that which is *internal.* Happiness can be taken away from you, but joy is a constant gift available to every Christ-follower. Joy is part of the fruit of the Holy Spirit, which is one fruit with nine amazing flavors (Galatians 5:22-23).

What's the definition of joy? It is an inner state of contentment, not based on your circumstances but solely on your connection to Christ.

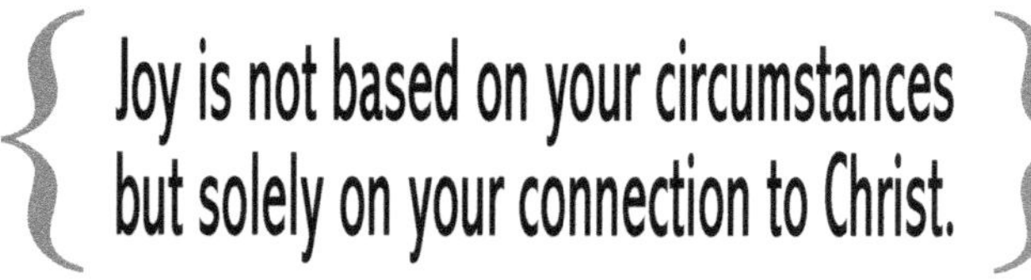
Joy is not based on your circumstances
but solely on your connection to Christ.

Joy is an inner tranquility, a peace of mind and soul. It reflects one's identity as a son or daughter of the Creator of the Universe. One author summarized the difference between happiness and joy this way: "Happiness is a reaction to something great. Joy is the product of someone great."[28]

Kiddie Pool or Adult Pool?

Do you remember going to a swimming pool when you were five years old? Where I went swimming, there were two pools side by side. One pool was for teenagers and adults, those who could swim on their own. Adjacent to that pool was the kiddie pool, a much smaller pool built for those who could not swim on their own. Do you see the analogy?

The kiddie pool is fun for small kids. They play with little boats that battle in their imaginary ocean, and they simply splash around, doing what kids do best: having fun in the sun. All goes well until it does *not* go well. One of a parent's worst nightmares in the kiddie pool is when something that looks like a Baby Ruth candy bar begins to float on the surface of the pool. Then a parent or a lifeguard screams, "Everybody out of the kiddie pool!" What happened? For those of you who have never experienced this, the brown object was not a candy bar. One of the children had an accident in the pool, so everyone had to get out of the pool so it could be cleaned. Then the fun could resume.

Here is the difference between happiness and joy: Happiness is the kiddie pool where everyone is having fun *until* the circumstances change, and they are not having fun anymore. In a moment, both the kids and their parents go from happiness to disgust and stress!

Joy, on the other hand, is like the deep end of the adult pool. Your feet do not touch the bottom in the deep end; even so, you can keep swimming in the deep waters. Happiness is good, but joy is far better. You are happy only when good things come your way, but joy remains as long as you remain connected to Christ.

> **No one can take away the joy Jesus gives you.**

In John 16, Jesus is preparing His disciples for His death and imminent departure. As a result of this conversation, the disciples became sad, for they deeply desired Jesus to stay with them forever. Then Jesus gives them a promise: "Now you have sorrow; but I will see you again and your heart will rejoice, and your joy no one will take from you" (John 16:22). Savor the last part of that verse: No one can take away the joy Jesus gives you.

If Jesus gives His followers a joy that cannot be taken away, how can we experience that joy on a more regular basis? Why are there moments in our lives when we do not feel joyful? Those are great questions. Next, we will explore the reasons we often lack joy in the Lord.

Joy Blockers

Several joy blockers can hinder the experience of joy and block your delight in Jesus. Notice I said joy *blockers*, not joy *stealers*. No one can steal true joy.

The first joy blocker is sin. If you have unconfessed sin in your life, it will hinder your experience of joy. When your joy is being blocked by an active or unconfessed sin in your life, 'fess up! To experience joy again, simply tell God you are sorry, ask for His forgiveness, and then turn away from that sin. David explained it this way in Psalm 51: "Wash away all my iniquity and cleanse me from my sin . . . Create in me a pure heart, O God, and renew a steadfast spirit within me" (vv. 2, 10 NIV).

The second joy blocker is worry. It is impossible to experience joy while you are in a state of worry. Worry means allowing the problems of today to hinder your experience of God's goodness. Worry relates to rumination and anxiety. To ruminate is to meditate on your problems over and over again. To worry is to give problems free rent in your head. Except it is not free rent. Worry will cost you a lot in the end.

Do you, like me, struggle with worry and overthinking situations? Do your problems seem to grow bigger and bigger as the day goes on? There is a solution for your worry: Turn your worries into prayers. Paul gives us this amazing counsel:

Be anxious for nothing	"Be anxious for nothing, but in everything by prayer and supplication with thanksgiving, let your requests be made known to God, and the peace of God, which surpasses all understanding, will guard your hearts and minds through Christ Jesus" (Philippians 4:6–7).

If you are good at worrying, you can become good at praying. Instead of repeating the problem over and over in your mind, tell the problem to God and watch what He does.

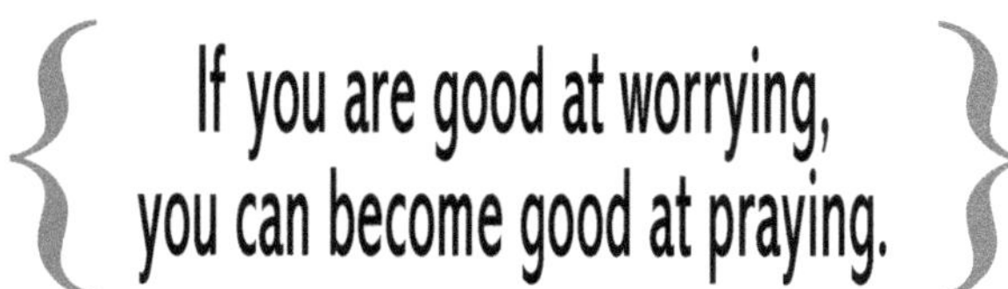
If you are good at worrying,
you can become good at praying.

The third joy blocker is ... people. Yes, that is right. People are not only a source of great happiness, but they can also be a source of great stress. How do they hinder our joy? They often have a significant effect on our well-being. Solomon expressed it well: "As iron sharpens iron, so a man sharpens the countenance of his friend" (Proverbs 27:17).

Just as there are two sides to a blade, friendship is also double-sided. On one side, your friend can be a positive force, challenging you to move forward with your life and your identity in Christ. On the other hand, your friend can influence you in a way that causes you to move away from your purpose and identity in Christ. When a friend is a negative influence, they can hinder your walk with God, and as a result, hinder your experience of the joy of the Lord.

Solomon gives us this friendship advice: "Walk with the wise and become wise; associate with fools and get in trouble" (Proverbs 13:20 NLT). Several modern researchers agree with Solomon: You become like the people you most often associate with. One author and motivational speaker, Jim Rohn, famously stated that "you are the average of the five people you spend the most time with."[29] While this pertains to the law of averages (which has limitations and exceptions), the point is that we are shaped and influenced by those who form our innermost relationship circle.

The apostle Paul also spoke on this topic when he was trying to get the worldly Corinthian Christ-followers to understand the power of negative influences: "Do not be misled: 'Bad company corrupts good character'" (1 Corinthians 15:33 NIV). So, while you cannot lose true joy, the wrong kind of friends can become joy blockers, keeping you from experiencing the joy of the Lord in your life. Choose your friends wisely.

Principle 4:
Love Others as Jesus Loves

The fourth way of delighting in Jesus is to love others like Jesus loves you. Jesus continues in John 15: "This is My commandment, that you love one another as I have loved you. Greater love has no one than this, than to lay down one's life for his friends" (John 15:12-13 NKJV). As you **Go After Jesus** and delight in Him, something amazing begins to happen inside you. You go from loving yourself to loving God, and when you start to love God, you cannot help but love others!

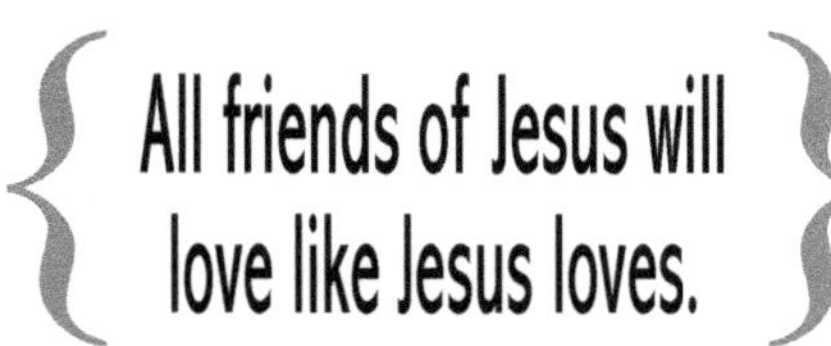

All friends of Jesus will
love like Jesus loves.

Worldly love is like this: I love those who love me. I will take care of people who are kind to me. But if you are not nice or do not give me what I want, you're out of luck.

The kind of love that Jesus calls us to is not like that. It is a supernatural, selfless kind of love. You cannot love like this (at least consistently) if you do not have God in your life. However, once you give your life to Jesus, something special happens. The Holy Spirit moves inside and begins to change you from the inside out, helping you to love and truly care for others. Jesus charged His followers to love the same way He did, even to the point of laying down their lives for them (and not just for "good" people, but also for sinners). A ***Friend*** of Jesus is one who loves like *crazy*, one who is willing to put others ahead of self, even at great personal sacrifice. Do you love others like this? If not, do not be discouraged. As you **Go After Jesus** and delight in Him, you will develop the love Jesus talks about in John 15.

Principle Five:
You Are Best Friends with Jesus

Are you inspired yet? Maybe a little convicted? Me too. The fifth aspect of being friends with Jesus is this: Reframe your entire life around this truth: I am best friends with Jesus. After laying the foundational facts in John 15, Jesus drops this love bomb on the disciples: "You are My friends if you do whatever I command you. No longer do I call you servants, for a servant does not know what his master is doing; but I have called you friends, for all things that I heard from My Father I have made known to you" (John 15:14-15).

Reframe your entire life around this truth, I am best friends with Jesus.

What does it mean to be best friends with Jesus? Think back to your first best friend. I have had only a few friends I considered a "best friend." One of them I met in the eighth grade. His name was Daniel. We went to the same small Christian school. We played basketball together, hung out together and went to the movies together. We shared our deepest secrets, prayed for each other, and simply spent a lot of time in each other's company.

Our friendship was so strong that we went to seminary together after we graduated from high school. DC (his nickname) knew almost everything about me, my strengths and my weaknesses. A best friend is someone with whom you are willing to share your life, your dreams, your struggles, and your future aspirations.

What does it mean to live your life with Jesus as your best friend? First, friendship with Jesus means you spend intimate time with Him on a regular basis. Best friends with Jesus spend time with Him outside of church on Sunday. They long to bask in His presence, soaking in the promises of His Word, and listening to His prompting in prayer. If you want to become best friends with Jesus, do what best friends do: Spend intimate daily time together.

Second, best friends with Jesus do what He tells them to do. Jesus said, "You are my friends if you do whatever I command you" (John 15:14). This is where delighting in your friendship with Jesus looks different than a human friendship. It would be strange if you did whatever your friend wanted you to do; that would be considered creepy at best and codependent at worst. Jesus is different from ordinary friends, though. Jesus is God, Jesus is perfect, and Jesus knows what is best for your life. Your life should revolve around Jesus because He is more than just a best friend. He is your Creator, your Sustainer, and your purpose.

Jesus is more than your best friend.
He is your Creator, Sustainer, and your purpose.

How do you know what Jesus wants you to do so that you can obey Him? The first way is by reading the Bible. The Bible shows you how to live for Jesus by obeying His Word as laid out in the Scriptures. Second, Jesus sent you the Holy Spirit, who will guide you into all truth. As you listen to the Holy Spirit's inner promptings and read God's Word, you will begin to know what Jesus expects of you.

The third aspect of being Jesus' best friend is this: Best friends of Jesus are fruitful. In John 15, Jesus says, "You did not choose Me, but I chose you and appointed you that you should go and bear fruit, and that your fruit should remain, that whatever you ask the Father in My name He may give you" (John 15:16). Jesus gives us a glorious promise: The longer we walk with Him, the more we will start to look like Him, and then we will produce fruit just like Jesus. The life of a Christ-follower is a fruitful life. As you **Go After Jesus** and delight in Him, you will live a life of eternal significance. What does it look like to produce fruit for Jesus? Jesus is talking about spiritual fruit, fruit that lasts forever. Spiritual fruit encompasses anything of eternal value. Two things will live forever: The Word of God and the souls of people. Those who follow Jesus lead others to follow Jesus too.

{ Spiritual fruit encompasses anything of eternal value. }

Fruit also shows in your personal life. Paul asserted that Christ-followers will produce the fruit of the Spirit. Their lives will show these characteristics: Love, joy, peace, longsuffering, kindness, goodness, faithfulness, gentleness, and self-control (Galatians 5:22-23). As you delight in Jesus, your life starts to resemble His: You become more loving, overflowing with joy, more patient, and kindness will radiate through you. Your character will shine by being generous to other people, as well as being a person others can count on (faithful). You will treat others with grace and compassion (gentleness). When Christ is in control, you will also show self-control.

Are you ready to **Go After Jesus** and delight in being best friends with Him? Do you long to develop an intimate relationship with Him? Are you willing to follow God's Word by doing what He says as revealed in the Scriptures? If you replied "yes," then your life will begin to show it. Best friends remember each other.

My prayer is that you will not just want to follow Jesus, but that you will also choose to be very close to Him. So close, that others will say this about you: "There's something different about you. I can see God in you by the way you live your life. I want what you've got."

CHAPTER 10 RECAP

Go After Jesus Principle #10:

When you make Jesus your greatest delight, God begins to fulfill the new desires that He has placed in your heart.
Read: Psalm 37:4, John 15:9–17, Philippians 4:6–7

Key Takeaways

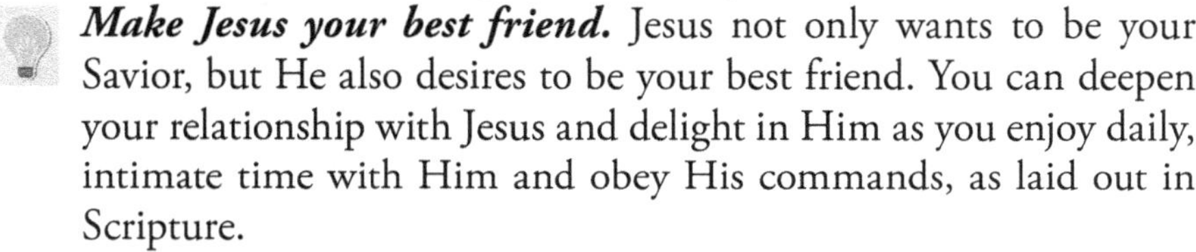

Make Jesus your best friend. Jesus not only wants to be your Savior, but He also desires to be your best friend. You can deepen your relationship with Jesus and delight in Him as you enjoy daily, intimate time with Him and obey His commands, as laid out in Scripture.

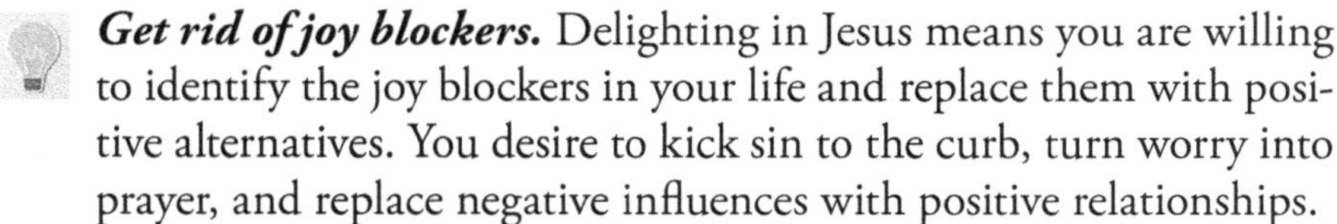

Get rid of joy blockers. Delighting in Jesus means you are willing to identify the joy blockers in your life and replace them with positive alternatives. You desire to kick sin to the curb, turn worry into prayer, and replace negative influences with positive relationships.

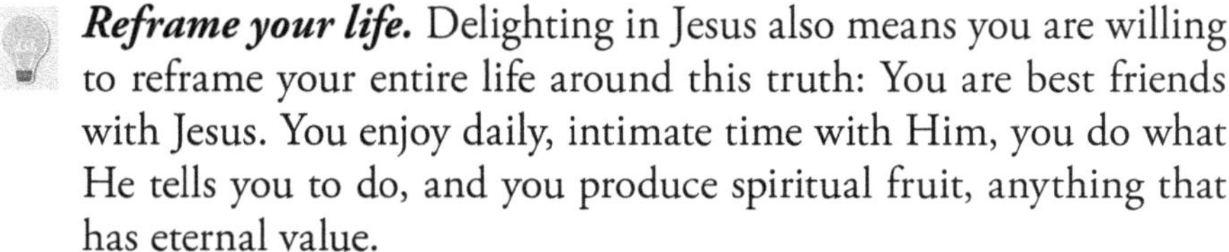

Reframe your life. Delighting in Jesus also means you are willing to reframe your entire life around this truth: You are best friends with Jesus. You enjoy daily, intimate time with Him, you do what He tells you to do, and you produce spiritual fruit, anything that has eternal value.

Reflection

Who is your best friend? How closely does your relationship with Jesus resemble the one with that person?

Do you truly believe Jesus loves you with an unconditional, everlasting, and experiential love? Why?

Which of the joy blockers—sin, worry or other people—do you struggle with most? What could you do to minimize their effect?

Looking Ahead

Chapter 11: The Favor of Friendship

CHAPTER 11

The Favor of Friendship

"No longer do I call you servants, for a servant does not know what his master is doing; but I have called you friends, for all things that I heard from My Father I have made known to you."
John 15:15

He was next in line to be king. Everything seemed to be going in his favor until one day, everything changed. The prince met another young man, and they quickly became best friends. The prince told his friend secrets that only those in the king's inner circle would know. Over time, the prince and his friend grew so close that they agreed to be faithful to each other, no matter what the future brought. Because of his friendship with Prince Jonathan, David was protected from King Saul, who, out of jealousy, wanted to extinguish this bright light in Israel. Jonathan knew something his father, King Saul, also knew: David, not Jonathan, would be the next king of Israel. God had orchestrated the friendship between David and Jonathan to bring about His greater purposes for His chosen people, the children of Israel. Jonathan blessed David with the favor of friendship. David knew the secrets of the king's court and even the secrets of the king's heart because of his relationship with Jonathan. May I share a profound secret with you? When you become close friends with Jesus, you will begin to walk in the favor of friendship. Favor with God is something special. Favor is God's demonstrated delight in me. It is tangible evidence that God's blessing is on my life.[30] Favor is God treating me far better than I deserve because I have a close connection with God's Son, Jesus, who is the Prince of Peace.

Favor is God's demonstrated delight in me.

I have witnessed God's favor in ways that still boggle my mind. God has given me things I did not earn or deserve. God has given me blessings in my life that could only be called miracles. Divine favor is seen when God intervenes in your life, just when you need a breakthrough. God often shows up when you least expect it, and when you need His favor the most.

Now that you are discovering what it looks like to be a ***Friend*** of Jesus, can you experience more of His favor? Is favor even something you can get more of? If so, how? The Bible says Jesus *grew* "in favor" with both God and people (Luke 2:52). How did Jesus grow in favor? To unlock the mystery of favor, we will study a person of high favor from the book of Genesis.

The Flavor of God's Favor

Joseph had favor and lots of it. We meet him in Genesis 37. He is described as a person who was favored by his father Jacob above all his other sons. Because of his father's favor, Joseph was given a coat of many colors as a special gift. This infuriated his ten older brothers because they sensed their father favored Joseph over them.

What did Joseph's older brothers do with their favored brother? They planned to kill him, but at the last minute, they decided to sell him as a slave instead. So, Joseph became a slave in Egypt. But guess what? Joseph's God-given favor continued. We see the flavor of Joseph's favor throughout his life. Instead of ending up in Egypt's slums, Joseph found himself in the prestigious household of Pharaoh's chief bodyguard, Potiphar. Why did Joseph end up in Potiphar's estate instead of working the field of some harsh taskmaster? Joseph was flowing in favor.

Later, Joseph caught the attention of Potiphar's wife, who then made a false accusation about him because he refused to sleep with her. He ended up in prison because of that false accusation. What happened in prison? Joseph was put in charge of all the other prisoners. Why? Because God showered him with favor.

Time passed, and even after Joseph had been in jail for some time, his favor with God continued to grow. Pharaoh had a dream that no one could interpret except . . . You guessed it, Joseph. In gratitude, Pharaoh made Joseph second in command over the entire country. How did Joseph go from being a lowly slave to being the second-most powerful person in the known world at that time? Favor. Nothing more, nothing less. Because of God's favor, Joseph never gave up. God never abandoned Joseph, and he went from the pit to the prison to the palace all because of the favor of God.[31]

> **Joseph went from the pit to the prison to the palace because of the favor of God.**

Can we experience more of God's favor? Yes. In this chapter, I will cover five game-changing facts that will increase the flow of favor in your life.

Five Secrets about Favor

Favor reality #1:
Favor flows from a close connection to Jesus.

What made Joseph different from his brothers? Why did he have favor with God that showed up in every aspect of his life, even during the toughest times? Joseph had a growing, developing, intimate, and thriving relationship with God.

David gives us this insight into the favor that flows from our relationship with God: "Surely, Lord, you bless the righteous; you surround them with your favor as with a shield" (Psalm 5:1 NIV). As you **Go After Jesus** as an intimate ***Friend***, your favored state develops. Favor is not earned or deserved, but it is *relational.* The closer your walk with God, the more the favor of God will flow in and through your life.

Favor reality #2:
Favor separates you from others.

Joseph's story is about being set apart from others. Joseph stood out among his brothers; he stood out in Potiphar's house, he stood out in the prison, and he stood out in the palace. Imagine a radiant star that lights up the night sky. Favor is the star of God's grace on your life. Favor is God's smile that beams joy in a world full of frowns.

When Potiphar saw "that the Lord was with him and that the Lord gave him success in everything he did," he promoted Joseph (Genesis 39:3 NIV). Favor opens the door of opportunity and promotion. The lack of favor closes doors that should be open; it shuts out advancement and promotion. Having God's favor is another way of saying God's hand of blessing is on your life. When God favors you, you achieve goals that would otherwise be out of reach.

How do you activate the favor of God so it will open up opportunities that are currently closed? The more you acknowledge that God is with you, the more you will sense His presence and walk in His favor. If you realize you are already blessed as a Christ-follower, you can begin to walk in that state of blessing. You are not favored by God because you have earned it or you deserve it; no, you are favored by God because you belong to Jesus. When you belong to Jesus, you can choose to walk in His favor that is already present in your life, through the power of the Holy Spirit. The flow of favor increases as you live out the blessings that are already yours in Christ.

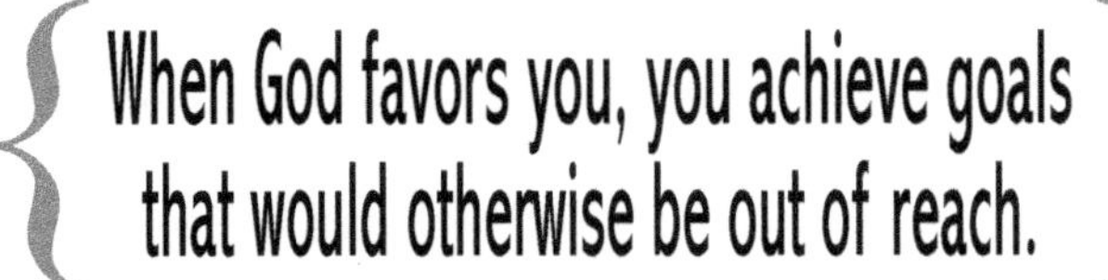
When God favors you, you achieve goals
that would otherwise be out of reach.

Favor reality #3:
The flow of favor increases as Jesus becomes the center of your world.

Many people talk about putting God first in their lives, and that is a good thing, but it is not the best thing. What? No, I am not saying that making God first in your life is a bad thing; I am saying that there's something better.

What is better than God being first in your life? Let's review a concept that we introduced in Chapter 4: Placing God at the center of your life is far better than God being first. Here's why: If God is first in your life today, it's easy for Him to slip to second or third place by the end of the week. When God is *only* first, you are placing Him at the top of a list of priorities.

{ Placing God at the center of your life is far better than God being first. }

When God is on a list of priorities, other things in your life can make their way to the top of that list. Putting God first is easy on a Sunday when you go to church, but it is not always easy when you work all day on Friday and then come home to be with your kids. Before you realize it, the day is over, and you were so busy you forgot to spend time with God. It is now 11:00 p.m. and you are too tired to pray or read your Bible, so you climb into bed and fall asleep. Was God first in your life on this day?

Here is a far better way: Place God at the center of your life. Just like the Earth revolves around the sun, your life should revolve around the Son. If Jesus is first today, your life will still go on even if He is in third place on Friday. But if Jesus is at the center of your life, the entire solar system of your life revolving around Him, guess what happens if Jesus is moved out of the center of your world? You guessed it! Things begin to fall apart when Jesus is no longer the center of your solar system.

Yes, Jesus should be first in your life, but even better, He should be the center of your solar system, your entire life revolving around Him. When Paul urged the Romans to present their bodies as a living sacrifice, he was showing them how to place Jesus at the center of their lives (Romans 12:1). When Paul declared that he was crucified with Christ and that *he* was no longer living but that Christ was living through him, he was illustrating what it was like to have Jesus as the center of your life (Galatians 2:20).

When the life of Jesus is at the center of your life, something amazing happens: The flow of favor spreads throughout your life. With Jesus at the center of it all, you will experience the love of God like never before, you will delight in joy, you will be flowing in the peace of God, and the flow of favor will permeate throughout your life.

Favor will be the flavor of your life!

Favor reality #4:
Generosity increases the flow of favor.

Solomon gave us this wisdom principle: "The generous will themselves be blessed, for they share their food with the poor" (Proverbs 22:9 NIV). If you want to grow in favor, grow in generosity. Generosity is like a spiritual muscle; the more you exercise it, the stronger it grows. You can never outgive God. He will always be more generous than you are. So, give generously. Here is another verse in the book of Proverbs that talks about being generous and experiencing God's blessing: "Whoever is kind to the poor lends to the Lord, and he will reward them for what they have done" (Proverbs 19:17 NIV). So, if you want to grow in favor, grow in generosity. As you give to others out of love, the flow of God's blessing permeates your life.

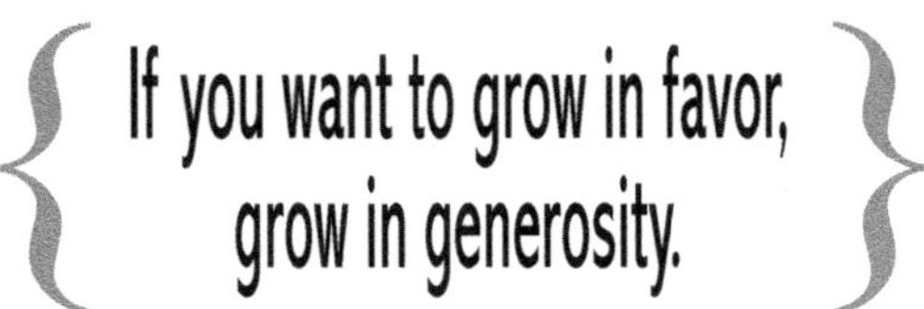
If you want to grow in favor,
grow in generosity.

Paul had a lot to say to the church at Corinth about generosity. He told them: "Remember this: Whoever sows sparingly will also reap sparingly, and whoever sows generously will also reap generously" (2 Corinthians 9:6 NIV). Paul was teaching this principle: God will respond to your level of sacrifice and generosity.

If we are generous, God will be *more than* generous with us. If we are tightfisted with the blessings God has placed in our lives, we cannot expect Him to pour out more blessings. Favor is not something we earn or deserve; it is all grace. Every blessing we have, we did not earn or deserve it. Even the ability to work is a gift from God. If He does not give us life and breath, we cannot do anything.

If we are generous with the gifts of favor God has placed in our hands, God will continue to pour out His blessings and favor in our lives. Generous people live in the favor of God because as they pour their lives into others, God increases the flow of blessings back into their lives. As we give, our capacity for giving increases. We do not give to receive; we give out of a heart of love, and then we witness the flow of favor growing in proportion to our level of generosity.

Favor reality #5:
God pours out favor on the humble.

James gives this promise about the favor of God in your life: "But he gives us more grace". That is why Scripture says: "God opposes the proud but shows favor to the humble" (James 4:6 NIV). Whom does God like to pour out His undeserved favor on? He favors the humble. God likes to lift up the lowly, He likes to bless those who realize their need for His grace, and He likes to smile on those who seek His face. What does it mean to be humble? To understand humility, start with what humility is not. Humility is not thinking less of yourself; it is thinking of yourself less.[32] Humility is not being unaware of your strengths, gifts, and abilities; it is being aware of where they came from and who they are for. Humility is not the person who refuses to accept a compliment. It is not the person who says, "Thank you. It wasn't me; it was *all* God." That's not humility; that's false humility. True humility puts God and others ahead of oneself. Paul gives the church at Philippi this charge:

Paul to the church at Philippi	"Let nothing be done through selfish ambition or conceit, but in lowliness of mind let each esteem others better than himself. Let each of you look out not only for his own interests, but also for the interests of others" (Philippians 2:3–4).

Humility puts the needs of others ahead of your own. It takes the focus off yourself, so you can focus on what is going on with those God has placed in your path. It is getting to the place where you look to God for your daily guidance, wisdom, strength, and support. Humility is full dependence on God in your daily life. It is realizing you are not in control, and that you need God's help every moment of every day.

{ Humility is full dependence on God in your daily life. }

Humility is also power under control. Another word for this is *meekness*. Jesus said the meek are blessed because they will inherit the earth (Matthew 5:5). Humility is having the right and the ability to do something, but choosing *not* to do so out of *love* for another person. For example, somebody hurls an insult at you, and you are tempted to give them a piece of your mind. Humility overlooks an insult instead of replying back with one of your own. So, are you ready to start walking in God's favor in your life? Start practicing the five favor principles and see what happens.

CHAPTER 11 RECAP

Go After Jesus Principle #11

Favor is the fruit of a close connection to Jesus.
The closer you are to Jesus, the more you experience
His favor on your life.
Read: James 4:6, Philippians 2:3–4, Psalm 5:12

Key Takeaways

- ***Favor flows from a close connection to Jesus.*** Like David's friendship with Jonathan, developing an intimate relationship with Jesus will lead to experiencing God's favor in your life.
- ***Favor separates you from others.*** Joseph's story shows that favor sets you apart and opens doors of opportunity and promotion.
- ***The flow of favor increases as you make Jesus the center of your world.*** Placing Jesus at the center of your life is better than making Him a priority; it ensures your life revolves around Him.
- ***Generosity increases the flow of favor.*** Giving to others out of love can increase the flow of God's blessings into your life.
- ***God pours out favor on the humble.*** Humility involves putting God and others ahead of yourself and seeking God's guidance, acknowledging your dependence on Him.

Reflection

- How has God shown favor to you in the past? How is he demonstrating His favor now?
- Who is the humblest person you know? Why?
- What adjustments do you need to make to increase the flow of God's favor in your life?

Looking Ahead

Part 4: The Fisherman. Chapter 12: Changed Forever

Part Four

The Fisherman

I aspire to bring others into the kingdom of God.

The Seeker: I want to ***discover*** the awe-inspiring truth of who Jesus really is.
The Disciple: I am ***determined*** to follow Jesus wherever He leads.
The Friend: I ***desire*** to enjoy the richness of daily, intimate time with Jesus.
The Fisherman: I ***aspire*** to bring others into the Kingdom of God.

CHAPTER 12

Changed Forever

And Jesus said to Simon, "Do not be afraid.
From now on, you will catch men."
Luke 5:10

Al was raised in a family where he was being groomed into a militant Muslim in Saudi Arabia. As a devout Muslim, Al studied the Qur'an and tried to memorize as much as he could. His goal was to memorize the entire Qur'an: all 114 surahs (6,236 verses). By age fifteen, Al had decided to die as a martyr for Allah and was planning to fight alongside his hero, Osama bin Laden.

Al's mother pleaded with him not to go to war, as she did not want her son to give up his life at such a young age. Al struggled with his decision. To remain at home meant he could grow up, get married, and start a family. To die as a martyr meant a guaranteed trip to heaven with a lot of rewards. Thankfully, Al decided not to fight alongside Osama bin Laden.

Instead, Al went to college in Saudi Arabia, then moved to the United States to pursue his graduate education in engineering. Al struggled with his move to the States because he had been taught to hate Christ-followers; they were considered infidels and were to be rejected. This is where the true God stepped in. A Christlike couple befriended Al and invited him to their house for Thanksgiving dinner. Al received love and kindness from this couple, as they prayed over their meal and ate with him. He had never experienced this type of love from his fellow Muslims back home in Saudi Arabia.

God continued to send Christ-followers into Al's life. Their positive impact prompted Al to question his Muslim faith, and he began to investigate Christianity. His spiritual quest led Al to a Bible-believing church, and after listening to the pastor preach on the Gospel of John each Sunday, Al gave his life to Jesus. Today, Al is actively sharing his faith with other Muslims, showing them that Jesus is alive and that they can have a living relationship with Him.[33]

Al's story reminds us of this reality: Jesus is still seeking the lost, and He uses His followers as fishermen. You and I are called not only to follow Jesus, but we are also called to fish for Jesus.

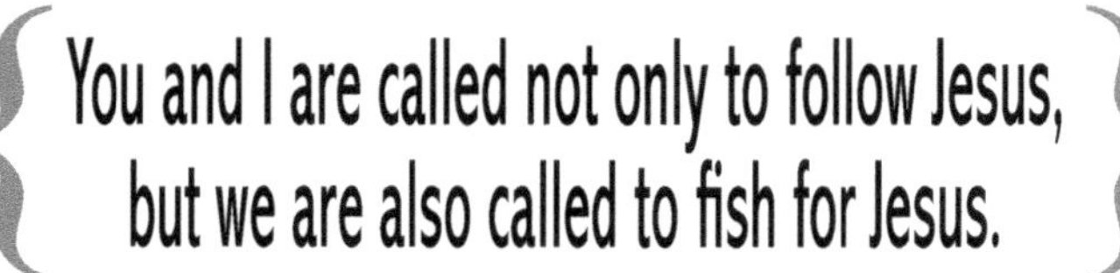
You and I are called not only to follow Jesus,
but we are also called to fish for Jesus.

What does it mean to fish for Jesus? Whom are we fishing for? How can we become effective fishermen? To answer these questions, we will go back in time, almost 2,000 years ago, to the Sea of Galilee.

Fishers of Men

To better understand what it means to fish for Jesus, we will turn to Luke's account of Jesus calling His first disciples:

> "So it was, as the multitude pressed about Him to hear the word of God, that He stood by the Lake of Gennesaret, and saw two boats standing by the lake; but the fishermen had gone from them and were washing *their* nets. Then He got into one of the boats, which was Simon's, and asked him to put out a little from the land. And He sat down and taught the multitudes from the boat. When He ended this teaching, He said to Simon, "Launch out into the deep and let down your nets for a catch."
>
> But Simon replied, "Master, we have fished all night and caught nothing; nevertheless, at Your word I will let down the net." And when they had done this, they caught a great number of fish, and their net was breaking. So they signaled to their partners in the other boat to come and help them. And they came and filled both the boats, so that they began to sink.

> When Simon Peter saw it, he fell down at Jesus' knees, saying, "Depart from me, for I am a sinful man, O Lord!"
>
> For he and all who were with him were astonished at the catch of fish which they had taken; and so also were James and John, the sons of Zebedee, who were partners with Simon. And Jesus said to Simon, "Do not be afraid. From now on, you will catch men." So when they had brought their boats to land, they forsook all and followed Him." (Luke 5:1–11)

As you continue your journey to **Go After Jesus**, you see exciting changes in your life when you progress from ***Seeker*** to ***Disciple*** to ***Friend***. Now He calls you to become a ***Fisherman.*** As a ***Fisherman***, you aspire to bring other people into God's kingdom.

Fishing in Biblical Times

What does it mean to fish for people? First, we will look at what it took to catch fish back then, so we can better understand this analogy. Before he can catch a fish, a fisherman must have the right equipment. Essential equipment in biblical times included a fishing boat and fishing nets. Next, the fisherman had to go to a specific location. In those times, he often fished on a lake or a coastal area.

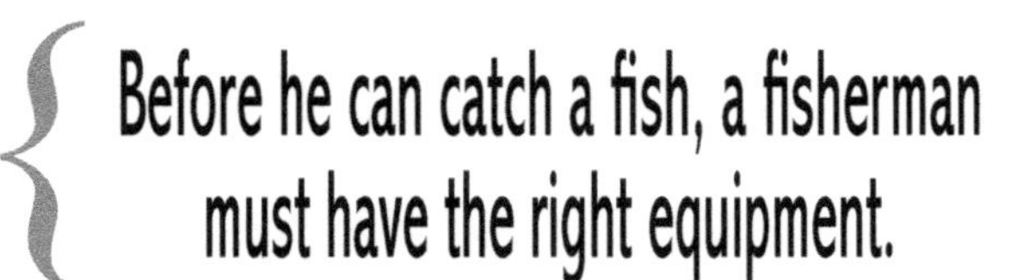
Before he can catch a fish, a fisherman
must have the right equipment.

In biblical times, a fisherman also gathered a fishing crew. Normally, fishing was a communal effort with multiple individuals sharing resources and often working on the same boat or using a fleet of small boats. Next, the crew launched their boat. The best catch of fish often happened in the deep waters, not the shallow waters near the shore. Once the crew reached the deep water, they let down their nets, which were sometimes very large, so that they could catch a multitude of fish.

After the fishing crew let down their nets, they waited patiently. When their nets showed signs of a catch, they hauled in the nets and sorted through the fish. The good fish were stored until they could later be sold at the market or eaten by the fishermen's families.[34] Are there parallels we can draw from this picture of fishing in biblical times that could help us understand what it means to "fish for people"? Over the next three chapters, I will give you a fisherman's guide for catching people for Jesus. In this chapter, we will cover the right equipment, with a focus on how to present the gospel message to others. What does it take to win people to faith in Christ? How can you best present the gospel message to others? What are some helpful scriptures you can use?

The Right Equipment

To catch fish, you need a rod, a reel, and the right bait. To bring people into the Kingdom of God, you need to be equipped with the gospel. The gospel is the good news that Jesus lived the perfect life we were incapable of living. He died in our place and on our behalf, then He rose from the dead on the third day after He was buried. The good news for humanity is this: If you believe in Jesus and receive the gift of salvation that He died on the cross to give you, then you will experience a brand-new life in Christ, all your sins are forgiven, you have eternal life, and you now have a purpose.

So, how can you explain this to someone who does not yet believe in Jesus? Just like a fisherman attracts a fish with bait, you live in a way that gets the attention of others. Your life should be filled with God's light, and people should see that you are different in an attractive fashion.

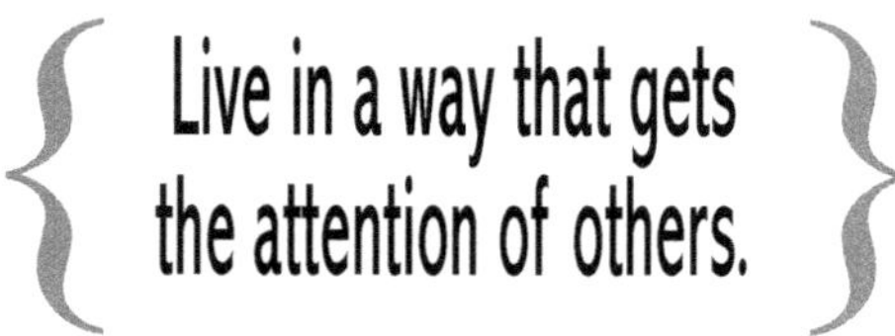
Live in a way that gets
the attention of others.

Your words are infused with grace and love. Others hear a difference in the words you say and the tone you use. Before you present the message of the gospel, your life should line up with the message you proclaim. Your walk should line up with your talk.

The Right Relationship

Next, seek to build a relationship with the person you desire to share Christ with. People want to know you sincerely care for them. Some people are turned off if they sense you are *only* talking with them to share your faith with them. As you **Go After Jesus**, you discover that He spent time with people. Jesus fed people, healed the sick, visited the people's villages, and even went to their homes.

The old saying is true: "People do not care how much you know, until they know how much you care."[35] Connect with someone's heart first as you seek to introduce them to Jesus.

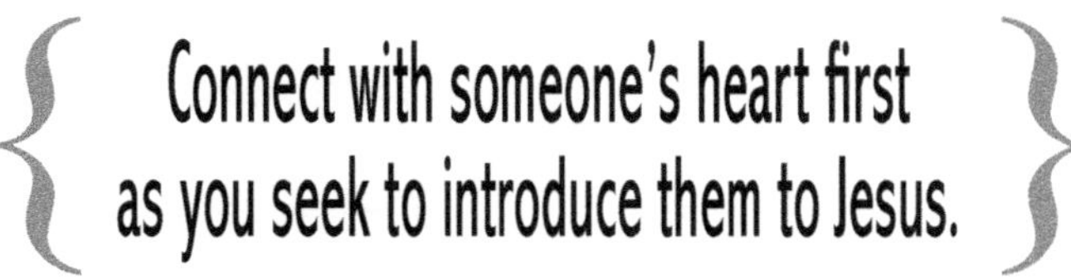
Connect with someone's heart first
as you seek to introduce them to Jesus.

Pastor Dave Ferguson has an excellent strategy for sharing Christ with people in a relational way. He calls it the **B.L.E.S.S.** strategy.[36] Each letter in the Bless acrostic stands for an action that leads you toward sharing the gospel with someone.

B	**= Begin in Prayer**	Pray *before* you go. Ask the Holy Spirit to minister to the person's heart and to prepare the soil of their soul to be receptive to receive Jesus.
L	**= Listen to Them**	Do not just hear them but actively engage in compassionate listening. Listen to their life story and what makes them passionate. Ask them to share both their dreams and their pain. Seek to listen for evidence of God's activity in their lives.

E	**= Eat Together**	Something amazing happens when we break bread together: Open mouths often lead to open hearts. As you share a meal in love, you may realize that God is working in their heart in ways you have not seen. Fellowship is a powerful tool God can use to prepare the soil of someone's soul for the seeds of the gospel.
S	**= Serve their Needs**	You have prayed for this person, you have listened to their heart and dreams, and you have shared a meal together. By implementing the previous steps, you likely noticed some needs in this person's life. Now it is your turn to serve them in love. Be open to opportunities to meet this person's needs.
S	**= Share the Story of how Jesus Changed your Life**	Share the Good News about Jesus with your friend. Your story is always a great way to start. Tell your friend how Jesus has changed your life.

{ Tell your friend how Jesus has changed your life. }

A good way to share your testimony (your story of how you came to Christ) is to use this format:

1) Who were you *before* you met Jesus?
2) How *did* you meet Jesus?
3) How has your life changed since you gave your life to Jesus? As you explain your story of coming to faith in Jesus Christ, watch the other person's expression and allow the Holy Spirit to guide you. Ask if they have any questions about your story.[37]

Share the Gospel Message

Finally, give them the message of salvation. While there are several good methods to help you share the gospel, here is one of the easiest to remember: the ABCs of salvation.

A =Admit to God that you are a sinner and that you need His forgiveness. Start with Romans 3:23: "For all have sinned and fall short of the glory of God." Explain what sin is. Sin is anything we think, say, or do that falls short of God's perfect standard as revealed in the Bible.

Sin separates us from a holy God. Romans 6:23 gives us the reality of our sin, along with God's glorious remedy: "For the wages of sin is death, but the gift of God is eternal life in Christ Jesus our Lord." Sin leads to death, but if you are willing to receive God's forgiveness in Christ, then you will receive eternal life. Guide the person into understanding the gravity of their sin and then point them toward the beautiful promise of forgiveness and eternal life found only in Jesus Christ.

B = Believe in Jesus Christ as God's Son who died in your place and then rose again on the third day. Point the person to God's unconditional love that has been poured out on us in Christ. Although we cannot earn or deserve God's love, we can receive it by faith in Jesus Christ. Explain that salvation is a gift from God. Ephesians 2:8-9 says this: "For by grace you have been saved through faith, and that not of yourselves; *it is* the gift of God, not of works, lest anyone should boast."

C = Confess your faith in Jesus Christ. Ask the person if they would like to receive Jesus as their Lord and Savior. Romans 10:9-10 says, "That if you confess with your mouth the Lord Jesus and believe in your heart that God has raised Him from the dead, you will be saved. For with the heart one believes unto righteousness, and with the mouth confession is made unto salvation." Lead them in a prayer of faith. This is often referred to as "the sinner's prayer," and it goes something like this:

> **Dear Jesus,**
>
> **I want to thank you for Your love for me. I do believe the good news that You died on the cross for my sins and that You rose on the third day. Jesus, I confess my sins to You and ask for Your forgiveness. Please forgive me and take away all of my sins. I invite You into my life to be my Lord and Savior. I surrender my life to You and choose to follow You for the rest of my life. Fill me now with Your Holy Spirit. Thank You, Jesus, for saving me.**
>
> **In Jesus' Name, Amen.**

Suppose the person has just prayed to receive Christ. Congratulations! You have led someone from death to life, from darkness into light. They are now a child of God. Your job now is to help them grow in their faith. We call this discipleship. As a new Christ-follower, they will need to know a few basics like how to study the Bible, how to have an effective prayer life, and how to overcome temptation. This book is a good resource to share, as it will help them to understand their identities in Christ.

Many other resources can help you disciple those you have won to Christ. A few resources that I recommend are the following: Small-Circle one-on-one discipleship:[38] *The Navigators Discipleship Plan,*[39] and the *YouVersion Bible app*[40] has many good daily reading plans. Try to help them find a Bible-believing church to connect with so they can grow spiritually and have a spiritual family to walk alongside them on the journey. Suggest the Gospel of John as a starting point for their daily devotional times.

CHAPTER 12 RECAP

Go After Jesus Principle #12

Followers of Jesus are called to be fishermen for Jesus.
Reached people reach people.
Read: James 4:6, Philippians 2:3–4, Psalm 5:12

Key Takeaways

Equip yourself with the gospel message. Just as a fisherman needs the right equipment, you need to understand and be able to explain Jesus' life, death, and resurrection. A person can only receive forgiveness for sin by accepting what Jesus did for them on the cross.

Seek to build genuine relationships with others. Connect with someone's heart before you try to reach their soul. Learn from the master fisherman, Jesus, who spent time with people and then shared the message of hope with them.

Put the B.L.E.S.S. strategy into practice. This relational approach will help you connect with others so you can share the life-giving message of the gospel with them.

Present the message of salvation. The ABCs of salvation (Admit, Believe, Confess) is one effective, easy-to-remember method you can use to present the gospel to others.

Reflection

Do you feel equipped to share the gospel with someone? Why or why not?

Use the three questions under the final S in the B.L.E.S.S. strategy to put together your story about how Jesus changed your life.

To feel more comfortable sharing the gospel message, practice the ABC method a few times with another Christ-follower.

Looking Ahead

Chapter 13: Location, Location, Location

CHAPTER 13

Location, Location, Location!

When He had stopped speaking, He said to Simon,
"Launch out into the deep and let down your nets for a catch."
Luke 5:4

Samuel Langhorne Clemens became famous for writing books like *The Adventures of Tom Sawyer* and *The Adventures of Huckleberry Finn* under his pen name, Mark Twain. Did you know that Twain (Clemens) was an avid fisherman in real life, not just in his books? Twain loved fishing so much that he even went fishing in the off-season when it was illegal.

On one such trip, Twain was traveling home on a train that passed through Maine. The fishing season had been closed for several weeks, but that did not faze Twain. He went ice fishing and had such a great catch that he decided to bring it home with him. Back on the train, he struck up a conversation with the passenger sitting next to him.

With a mischievous grin, Twain told the stranger about all the fish he had caught. Yes, it was past fishing season, but he could not help himself. The stranger was silent but wore an ominous grin. "So, what do you do?" Twain asked, attempting to fill the awkward moment with his unresponsive listener.

"I am the state game warden," the man said. "And who are you?"

Twain just about swallowed his cigar when the man revealed his occupation. "Well, to be perfectly truthful, warden," he said, "I'm just the biggest liar in the United States!"[41] Twain's wit and humor saved him once again.

Peter's Fishing Location

Do you think Peter was tempted to come up with a fishing tale himself after he fished all night and caught nothing? He was fishing in a familiar location, the Sea of Galilee (also known as the Lake of Gennesaret or the Sea of Tiberias). Located in northern Israel and fed by the Jordan River, the lake's deepest point is only 150 feet. Over 690 feet below sea level, it serves as the main source of water and of commerce for the Galilee region.[42] About this lake, Jewish rabbis said, "Although God has created seven seas, yet He has chosen this one as His special delight."[43]

Peter was a professional fisherman, so he knew a lot about fishing on the Sea of Galilee. He and his fishing buddies, James, Andrew, and John, had caught many fish over the course of their fishing careers. They knew the right strategies, and they had the right equipment. But something was different about the fishing trip we read about in Luke 5: They had worked all night and yet had not caught a single fish (v. 5).

{ Peter and his friends knew the right strategies and had the right equipment. }

Jesus arrived and told them to do something they did not want to do: Try again, boys. "Launch out into the deep water and let down your nets for a catch" (Luke 5:4). Peter was initially resistant; he was weary, ready to hang up his net for the night. But Jesus had another plan for Peter and his fishing buddies: He wanted them to learn to follow His leadership. Peter knew about fishing, but he did not fully grasp that Jesus had created all the fish in the Sea of Galilee, and that if he trusted Jesus, he would witness a miracle.

Peter's response was authentic: "Master, we have toiled all night and caught nothing; nevertheless at Your word I will let down the net" (Luke 5:5). What happened next forever changed Peter's life. When they did what Jesus told them to do, they caught so many fish their nets started to break, and their boat was so full of fish it began to sink. The catch was so large that they had to call for help to drag the catch to the shore.

Peter's response to this miracle is moving: "When Simon Peter saw *it*, he fell down at Jesus' knees, saying, 'Depart from me, for I am a sinful man, O Lord!'" (Luke 5:8). The other fishermen, Andrew, James, and John, were astonished as well. They did not know how to process what they had seen. Jesus reassured them: "Do not be afraid. This is just the beginning. From now on, you are going to catch something far greater than fish; you are going to catch people for me!" (Luke 5:10, paraphrased).

Launch Out into the Deep Waters

What can we learn from this story that will help us to win souls for Christ? First, location, location, location! If you want to have a greater impact, you launch out into the deep waters when others are staying ashore. Jesus wanted the fishermen to go *deeper*. Jesus called his future disciples to go into the deep waters for a catch.

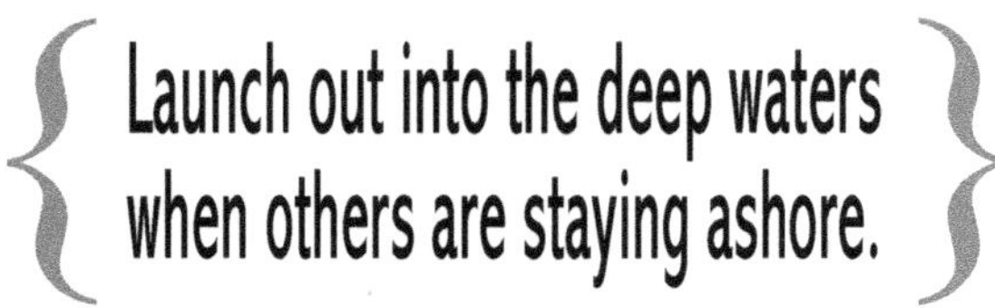
Launch out into the deep waters
when others are staying ashore.

Here is a fishing secret: If you are willing to go deeper in your walk with Jesus, you will have more opportunities to impact lives for Christ. Hanging out on the shoreline is easier and may be more fun. People love to lie out in the sun and relax. There is nothing wrong with a little rest and relaxation. However, if you want to impact more lives with the gospel, you will need to leave the comforts of the shoreline and go into the deep waters. You must be willing to do whatever it takes to save more lives for Christ.

Paul understood this concept of using innovative methods to reach more people. While Paul never changed the message, he was constantly working on different approaches to connect with people so he could share Christ with them.

When Paul preached to the philosophers on Mars Hill (at the Areopagus in Athens), he connected with the leaders by pointing out an altar dedicated to "the unknown god." He told them he knew who this "unknown god" was: Jesus! (See Acts 17:16-34.)

When Paul was trying to reach the Jews, he quoted the Old Testament Scriptures, as this was the best connection point for Jewish people who trusted in the Scriptures. He highlighted passages that pointed to their long-awaited Messiah, which were fulfilled in Jesus.[44] Paul described his approach this way:

> Though I am free and belong to no one, I have made myself a slave to everyone, to win as many as possible. To the Jews, I became like a Jew, to win the Jews. To those under the law, I became like one under the law (though I am not under the law), so as to win those under the law. To those not having the law, I became like one not having the law (though I am not free from God's law but am under Christ's law), so as to win those not having the law. To the weak I became weak, to win the weak. I have become all things to all people so that by all possible means I might save some. I do all this for the sake of the gospel, that I may share in its blessings. (1 Corinthians 9:19-23 NIV)

Paul did whatever it took to reach people as long as it did not compromise his mission or his message.

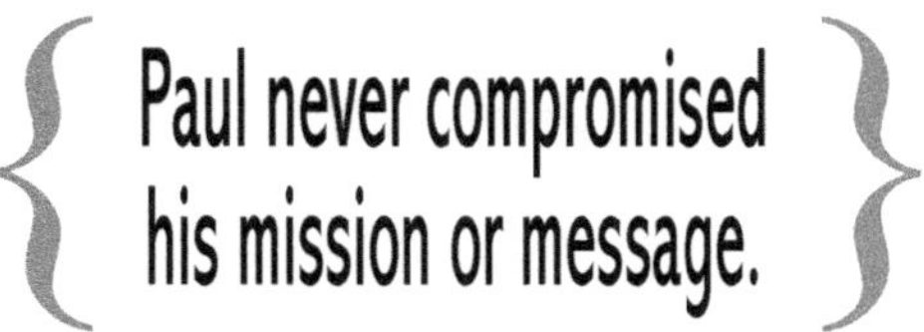
Paul never compromised
his mission or message.

One caveat to this principle: Using creative methods never means compromising the message. Truth never changes, but how we present the truth (the method) must change so people in today's world can understand the truth in their own language and cultural frame of reference.

Principles of Launching into the Deep

As we talk about going deeper to reach more people, here are some principles to ponder:

- If you do what you have always done, you will get what you have always got.
- If you want to have a different result, you need to try a different approach.
- Shallow efforts produce shallow results.
- Launching into the deep multiplies the possibilities.
- Jesus loves you in the shallow waters, but He never leaves you there.
- Every adventure in the deep begins with one more step out of the shallow waters.
- To summarize, when Jesus tells you to do something, He always has a greater purpose in His plan for your life.

Fishing for Greater Impact

We can learn a second truth from this fishing story: If you desire to have a greater impact, you will value God's Word above your own experiences. Notice that Peter's experience did not line up with what Jesus asked him to do.

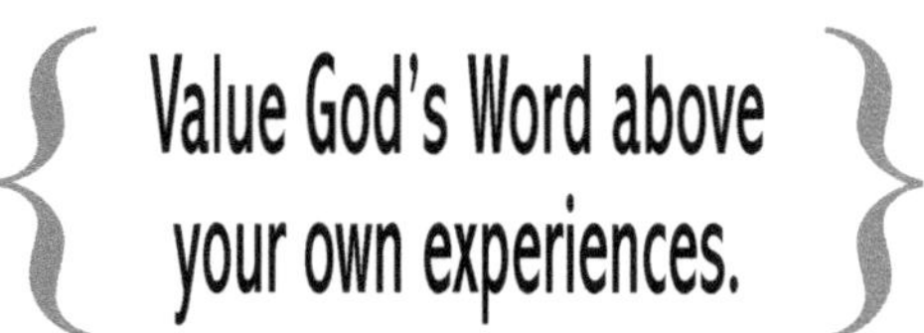
Value God's Word above
your own experiences.

Jesus told Peter to let down his nets in a way that contradicted both Peter's logic and experience. From Peter's vast fishing experience, fishing was more successful at nighttime in the deep waters. If a fisherman did not catch anything at night, the chances of catching any fish during the day were very low.[45]

In this moving story of Jesus' encounter with Peter, the veteran fisherman reached a critical junction in his faith journey: Will the professional fisherman follow the advice of a carpenter? Will the fisherman follow the new teacher everyone is talking about? Look at Peter's response: "Master, we have toiled all night and caught nothing; nevertheless, at Your word I will let down the net" (Luke 5:5). "At Your word", "because You say so", was Peter's response.

Peter faced this crucial decision: Do I go by my experience and logic, or do I follow God's plan? Thankfully, Peter said, "Yes, Lord." What was the outcome? Peter caught more fish than he could have ever dreamed of. This is a picture of the long-term outcome of obedience. When we say, "Yes, Lord, because you say so," we get to see God do what only He can do.

This reminds me of the Bible story of a boy who only had two fish and five loaves of bread. He gave what he had to Jesus and watched the miracle Jesus performed. Jesus fed more than 5,000 people and had twelve baskets of leftovers remaining.[46] To recap, if you want to win your friends and family to Jesus, you will value God's Word above your own logic, experiences, and interests. What happens when you take that leap of faith and seek to share your faith with others? People will respond in various ways. Some will reject the message, not wanting to surrender their lives to Jesus. Others will delay responding: "Let me think about it," or "I'm not ready to decide today." But some will be ready to respond, and you will have the privilege of leading them to faith in Jesus. Remember this truth: You are not responsible for a person's response; you are only responsible for being faithful to share the Good News with those God places in your path. God is the one in the life-changing business.

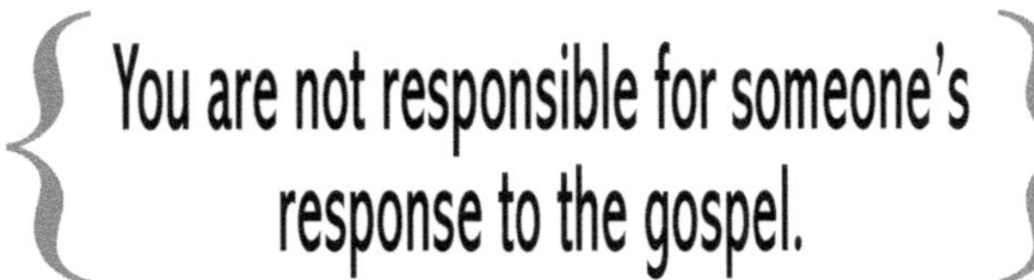

You are not responsible for someone's
response to the gospel.

God Will Change Lives, Yours and Others

This brings us to the third truth we can learn from Peter's fishing story: In His grace, God will forever change the lives of people in your path. In this story, many lives were changed. First, Peter was brought to his knees as he realized his own sinfulness against the backdrop of Jesus' power and purity. Peter's sinfulness met God's graciousness, which produced a change in Peter that brought about his usefulness. Peter's life was forever changed that day, and from then on, Peter became a devoted follower of Jesus.

Others were also impacted by this miracle. The people on shore were astonished at the size of the catch of fish. The Bible does not indicate how many believed in Jesus as a result of this miracle, but several God-stories resulted from it. James and John were present that day. Guess what happened to them after this event? Like Peter, they became fishers of men. This miracle moved Peter, James, and John so powerfully that they left their business (fishing), they forsook all (their former way of life), and they followed Jesus. (See Luke 5:1-11).

When you share Christ with others, you will gain more confidence over time. The key is to be faithful and consistent. God has entrusted you with the greatest message of all time: The Good News that Jesus loves people no matter what they have done and wants to forgive them of every wrong they have ever done or will do. Forgiveness, eternal life, and a new purpose can all be theirs if they are willing to receive what Jesus did for them on the cross with a heart of faith and repentance.

This is the heart of the gospel: We are saved by grace alone, through faith alone, in Christ alone, and this decision changes everything.

CHAPTER 13 RECAP

Go After Jesus Principle #13

If you want the big catch, you must be willing to launch into the deep waters.
Read: John 21:5–6

Key Takeaways

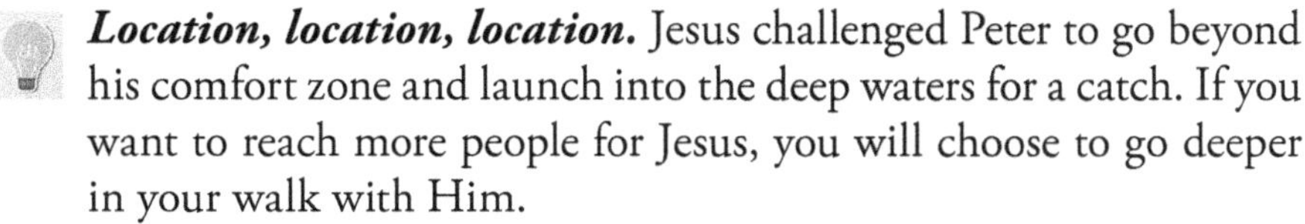

Location, location, location. Jesus challenged Peter to go beyond his comfort zone and launch into the deep waters for a catch. If you want to reach more people for Jesus, you will choose to go deeper in your walk with Him.

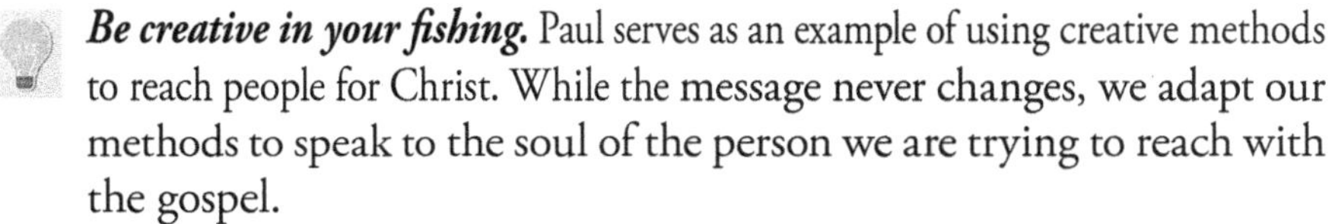

Be creative in your fishing. Paul serves as an example of using creative methods to reach people for Christ. While the message never changes, we adapt our methods to speak to the soul of the person we are trying to reach with the gospel.

Principles of launching into the deep.

- If you want different results, you must be willing to change; doing the same things will yield the same outcomes.
- Shallow efforts produce shallow results, while launching into the deep water multiplies possibilities.
- Jesus loves you in the shallow waters but invites you to venture deeper.

Reflection

Has God ever asked you to do something that seemed illogical? How did you respond?

What, if anything, is holding you back from launching into the deep waters with Jesus?

When are you most likely to trust your experience above God's Word? What might help you put more confidence in God's Word?

Looking Ahead

Chapter 14: The Great Co-Mission

CHAPTER 14

The Great Co-Mission

"And Jesus came and spoke to them, saying, 'All authority has been given to Me in heaven and on earth. Go therefore and make disciples of all the nations, baptizing them in the name of the Father and of the Son and of the Holy Spirit, teaching them to observe all things that I have commanded you; and lo, I am with you always, even to the end of the age.' Amen."
Matthew 28:18-20

A family lived near a harbor that hummed with life. The young son was captivated by the boats zooming in and out of the harbor. One day, he decided to build his own boat using a model kit. He glued the pieces together carefully, doing his best to make sure the pieces of wood lined up correctly. He even glued tiny people to the boat's deck. After his masterpiece was completed, he put his creation in a glass case for safekeeping.

His family became so immersed in the community that they decided to buy a boat and take the family sailing on the weekends to enjoy the beauty and splendor of the sea. They loved sailing at first. Over time though, their love for it diminished, as maintaining the boat required a lot of hard work. After a few months, they only used the boat occasionally.

Eventually, they decided to take the boat out again for a Saturday adventure on the open waters. To their surprise, the boat would not start because the battery was dead. After closer inspection, they noticed barnacles growing on the boat's hull and algae on its sides. They learned that a real boat is only kept in proper shape by being used and maintained.

There is a connection between the little boy's model boat and his parents' boat. The model boat was preserved by being kept safe in the glass case, but the real boat was preserved by being used on a regular basis. "Churches are like the real boat; they are only kept in shape by being used. Churches that are preserved and sparsely used will eventually fall into disrepair. But churches that pour themselves into serving their communities will find energy, passion, and love."[47]

When Jesus was getting ready to leave the world to go back to heaven, He gave His disciples some parting instructions, often called The Great Commission. In this chapter, I will explain every Christ-follower's call to make disciples. As you **Go After Jesus**, your job as a ***Fisherman*** is not to simply make converts; it is also your job to *develop disciples.*

Thinking about your role in bringing others to Christ can become overwhelming at times. You may ask yourself, "How can I help others grow in their faith when I need major spiritual growth myself? I do not know the right words to use. How can I help develop others to be passionate disciples of Jesus?" If these concerns are racing through your mind, that's okay. Here is some good news: You are not in this alone. *Sharing the gospel is not a solo mission; it is a co-mission.*

{ Sharing the gospel is not a solo mission; it is a co-mission. }

When Jesus gave the original challenge to His disciples, He had just defeated death, hell, and the grave. His resurrection paved the way for every Christ-follower to be forgiven and experience new life in Him. Fresh from His victory over the grave, Jesus looked lovingly and intently at His disciples and gave them these parting words: "Go make disciples of all nations." These powerful words showed that He was entrusting the greatest message of all time to His followers. These words were not spoken in a vacuum; some beautiful promises were attached. Several *co-mission codes* will empower you to step out in faith as you seek to reach more people for Jesus.

The Great Co-Mission Codes (Promises)

Code #1:

The Great Co-Mission is empowered by the universal authority of Jesus. You are called to be on mission with God, and you are not in this alone. Jesus' assurance that He has all authority is important in many ways. Here are a few truths that can galvanize your courage to share Christ with others:

- Because you will need *empowering*, Jesus sent the Holy Spirit down from heaven.
- Because you will need *encouragement*, you have the hope of heaven flooding your soul.
- Because you will need *equipping*, Jesus sent down spiritual gifts to build up the body of Christ.
- Because you will need *protection*, Jesus has authority over all angels and can send them out at His command.

Since Jesus has all authority, He can authorize doors to open for you. Are you facing a situation that seems like a closed door? Ask Jesus if this opportunity is His will. If you have peace about moving forward, during your prayer time, ask Jesus to authorize this door to open, in His timing and in His ways.

> **{ Jesus has all authority. He can authorize doors to open so you can share the gospel. }**

Are you sharing the gospel message with someone whose heart is closed? Pray before you share, during sharing, and afterward. Wait with anticipation to see what Jesus will do. Your job is not to save anyone; your job is to deliver the message of hope in a way they can understand and receive.

May I introduce a new word to your vocabulary? Since Jesus has all authority, as you go about doing his will, you are working in His authority.

This means you can walk with *Godfidence*. What is *Godfidence? Godfidence* is being confident in God's work in and through your life. While confidence can lead to pride if it is not kept in check, *Godfidence* leads to a humble yet bold dependence on God to lead, guide, direct, and protect you as you share Christ with those who do not yet know Him.

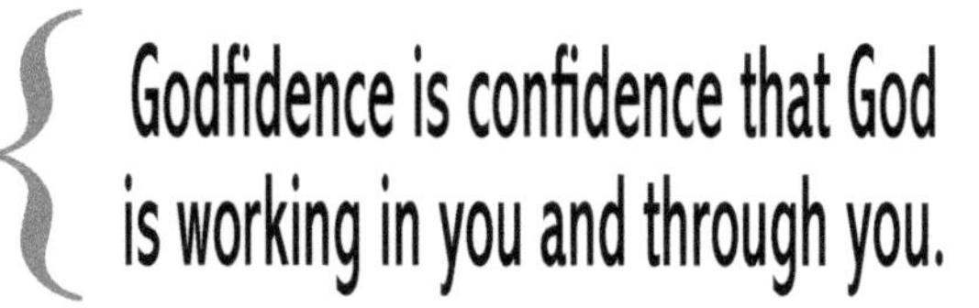

Godfidence is confidence that God
is working in you and through you.

God has a mission to seek and save the lost. He is now commissioning you to join His team, His rescue-mission team, to bring *life* to the *lifeless*, *hope* to the *hopeless*, and *salvation* to the *lost*. All authority in heaven and on earth belongs to Jesus, so be encouraged. You do not engage in this mission all alone. This mission is a co-mission: You and Jesus on a journey to change the world, one life at a time. (This is a good time to say amen!)

Code #2:

The Great Co-Mission is accelerated by missional disciple-making. You are now commissioned by King Jesus, who has all authority in heaven and earth. With this universal authority, you are called to go and make disciples. The main emphasis of the Great Co-Mission is to make disciples. In fact, this is the only imperative command in this commission. The other actions simply support this main idea of disciple-making.

{ The main emphasis of the The Great Co-Mission is to make disciples. }

When it comes to disciple-making, Jesus gives us all the instructions needed for success. Jesus gives us the *who* (everyone), the *what* (make disciples), the *when* (right now!), and the *why* (because Jesus has all authority and He said to do it). What does it mean to be missional? To be missional means actively participating in God's mission to redeem and restore the world. As you **Go After Jesus,** relish this truth: Your life matters for all eternity. Jesus has called you, He has chosen you, and He has empowered you to make an eternal difference in the lives of others. Sadly, for too many Christ-followers, The Great *Co-Mission* has become The Great *Suggestion*, as they will never attempt to win anyone for Christ. Many Christ-followers embrace their identity in Christ as a Seeker, a Disciple, and a Friend, but they never seek to become a Fisherman. According to some studies, 95 percent of all Christ-followers have never won anyone to Christ, 80 percent of Christ-followers do not witness consistently about their faith, and less than 2 percent are active in evangelism.

How should you respond to these startling statistics? If The Great Co-Mission has become The Great Omission in your life, it is time to team up with Jesus for the adventure of a lifetime: A co-mission with Jesus Himself. In the Great Co-Mission, Jesus tells us what to do, make disciples. He tells us where to go, everywhere. He tells us who to reach, everyone from every nation. He tells us what we need to be doing—going (being on mission), baptizing (reaching people with the gospel), and teaching (the fundamentals of Christianity).

Jesus left out just one instruction, "the how."

Why did Jesus omit the specifics of how to do the Great Co-Mission? If Jesus had given an exact method for making disciples, it would have quickly become outdated. Those initial methods would not be optimal in other times and places outside first-century Palestine. Below are some other important reasons Jesus left out the "how" of missional disciple making:

Jesus created you to be creative. The church should be the most creative, innovative organization in the world.

Jesus desires to use your unique personality to impact the world. You will be able to communicate and connect with some people better than anyone else, while your neighbor may be better suited to reach other types of people.

Jesus expects you to make the mission relevant to every nation, people group, and culture, because the gospel is for everyone, from every place and time.

Code #3:

In the Great Co-Mission, Jesus is with you as you go. When you read about changing people's lives for all eternity, it is normal to feel nervous. What if people do not like you? What if they say nasty things in response? What if you lose some friends? What if family members walk out on you because of your faith? All these questions may race through your mind as you step out on the Great Co-Mission with Jesus. May I give you the good news about being on mission with Jesus? Jesus will be there to support and help you every step of the way. Jesus gives us this promise: "I am with you always, *even* to the end of the age" (Matthew 28:20).

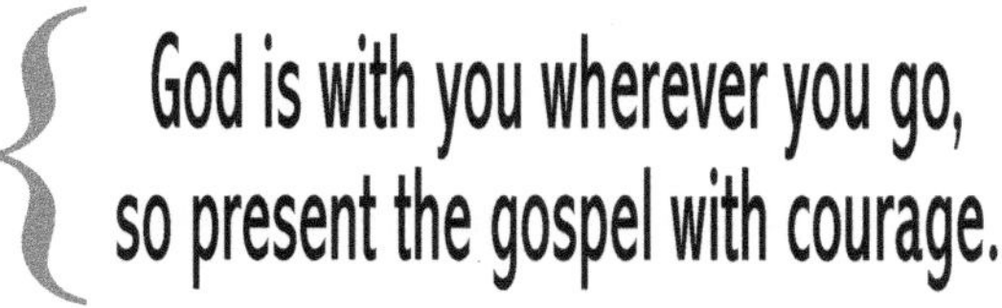

God is with you wherever you go,
so present the gospel with courage.

When you know God is with you wherever you are, you can present the life-giving message of the gospel with courage. What if people reject what you have to say? Remember this: They are not rejecting you; you are just the messenger. They are ultimately rejecting Christ. So, do not take rejection to heart. Instead, continue to pray for Jesus to change that person, so they will eventually open their heart to the message.

The Word of God will never change. The message of the gospel will never change. While the gospel never changes, the methods may need to change so others can understand the Good News in their own culture. The next chapter will outline the challenges to prepare for as you seek to lead people to Jesus. You will need to become a ***Soldier*** of Christ who can stand strong when attacks come your way.

CHAPTER 14 RECAP

Go After Jesus Principle #14

The Great Co-Mission is not a solo endeavor; it's a partnership with Jesus. As you **Go After Jesus**, you will want to share Him with those who do not yet know Him.
Mark 16:15, Luke 24:46-47, Acts 1:8

Key Takeaways

Make the mission of Jesus your mission. God's calling on your life is huge: Impact others for eternity. Embrace your greater purpose of missional disciple-making.

Walk with holy Godfidence. You are now operating in the authority of Jesus as you seek to share the gospel. Trust Jesus to encourage, equip, and empower you for the task of reaching people that are far from God.

Never forget that Jesus is always with you. Seek to overcome every fear and doubt as you live in the promise of God's presence in every step and in every day of your mission.

Reflection

What encourages you about viewing the Great Commission as the Great Co-Mission?

Has Jesus ever opened any doors for you that allowed you to make disciples? (They may be in your neighborhood, church, school, or workplace.)

How would you describe the difference between pride and Godfidence?

Looking Ahead

Part 5: The Soldier
Chapter 15: Prepare for Battle

Part Five

The Soldier

I aim to stand boldly for Jesus in life's battles.

The Seeker: I want to ***discover*** the awe-inspiring truth of who Jesus really is.
The Disciple: I am ***determined*** to follow Jesus wherever He leads.
The Friend: I ***desire*** to enjoy the richness of daily, intimate time with Jesus.
The Fisherman: I ***aspire*** to bring others into the Kingdom of God.
The Soldier: I ***aim*** to stand boldly for Jesus in life's battles.

CHAPTER 15

Prepare for Battle

"You therefore must endure hardship
as a good soldier of Jesus Christ.
No one engaged in warfare entangles himself with the affairs of
this life, that he may please him who enlisted him as a soldier."
2 Timothy 2:3–4

Eight seconds of bravery. But preparing for this moment of heroism required a lifetime of courage.

Florent A. Groberg's family moved to the United States from France when he was twelve years old. After the September 11 terrorist attacks on the Twin Towers and the Pentagon, Groberg resolved to join the US military. To become part of the US Armed Forces, he had to renounce his French citizenship. He was deployed to Kunar Province in Afghanistan. On August 8, 2012, he was assigned to lead a security detail for a high-level meeting with Afghan and American officials when he noticed a suspicious individual walking toward the group. Groberg detected that the person was not a friend but a dangerous enemy. Could this man be a suicide bomber?

As the stranger moved closer to the group, Groberg was confronted with the hardest task he had ever encountered: Risking his life to save the lives of his fellow soldiers. Groberg headed toward the man, attempting to distance the attacker from his men. The bomb detonated and severely injured Groberg, though it did not kill the attacker. Groberg's act of courage protected the lives of those under his care.

Groberg continued to serve until 2015, when he transitioned out of the military. Later in 2015, he was awarded the Medal of Honor for his bravery.[48] What made Groberg so courageous? Why was he willing to risk his life for the sake of his fellow soldiers? He understood what it meant to be a soldier. This chapter explores what it means to be enlisted as a ***Soldier*** for the cause of Jesus Christ.

Brave Like a Soldier

You may not realize it, but when you decided to follow Jesus, a target was put on your back. Anyone who decides to follow Jesus becomes a target for Satan, who is the enemy of everything good and true. As you **Go After Jesus**, your relationship with Him becomes stronger every day you walk with Him: You progress from being a ***Seeker*** to a ***Disciple*** to a ***Friend*** and then to a ***Fisherman***.

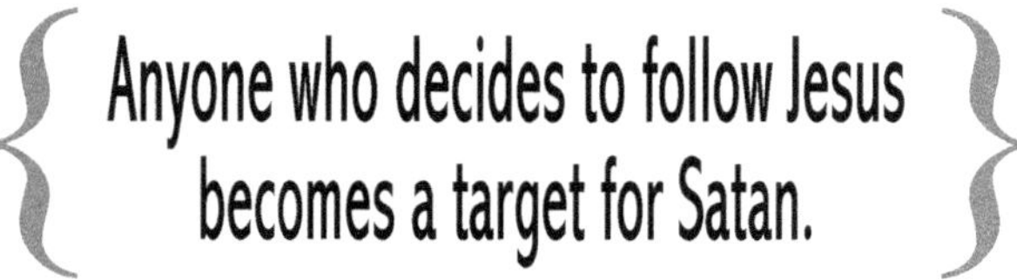

As you **Go After Jesus**, people will be positively impacted through your life, and this will draw Satan's attention. Anytime you win someone to Christ, Satan loses another citizen of his kingdom of darkness, and he does not take losing very well. As you impact the world for Jesus, you will begin to discern the invisible battle that is also going on around you. This spiritual warfare requires spiritual training that will prepare you to stand your ground when the battle intensifies. You are called to be a ***Soldier***.

Soldier Boot Camp

Whenever someone enlists in the army, they are required to go to boot camp. What is boot camp? Boot camp is basic training for a newly enlisted soldier. The purpose is not to break the soldier but to prepare the soldier for active duty. In boot camp, new soldiers learn the importance of physical training, emotional well-being, and discipline that will serve them well as they prepare for the daily rigors of military life. This training takes place *before* the battle. The preparation precedes the conflict.[49]

When you signed up to follow Jesus, you enlisted in His army. The apostle Peter gives us this insight into the spiritual battle raging around us: "Stay alert! Watch out for your great enemy, the devil. He prowls around like a roaring lion, looking for someone to devour" (1 Peter 5:8 NLT). Satan is lurking about, hunting for prey. Like a lion, Satan goes after the vulnerable, the weak, the injured, and those who are separated from the group.

Types of Spiritual Attacks

Since spiritual warfare is real, how can we prepare for these attacks in advance? Spiritual boot camp will prepare you both for the battle already raging around you and battles yet to be fought. Christ-followers will face various types of spiritual attacks as they **Go After Jesus**.

Mental attacks

Satan will mess with your mind and try to get you to question God's goodness, His Word, and His will for your life. For example, soon after Abraham arrived in the land God promised to give him and his descendants, a famine struck. Instead of remaining there, Abraham took his whole family to Egypt, where he got into a lot of trouble by claiming his wife Sarah was his sister (Genesis 12:1-20). Satan likely messed with Abraham's head: "How could staying in this land be God's will for you if there's a famine? A good God wouldn't do this to you. Get out while you can!"

Physical attacks

Satan will wage war on your health, finances, family, and the like. In Job's case, Satan attacked almost everything Job had: His children, business, crops, wealth, and health.[50] But Job's story reminds us that Satan had to get God's permission to attack Job, and this is true for you and me as well. As a child of God, your heavenly Father is actively protecting you.

Any trial God allows to come your way has a greater, more eternal purpose than your current suffering or loss, and every trial can shape and mold your character if you remain faithful to God through it all as Job did.

Spiritual attacks

Anytime Satan can tempt you to doubt God or His Word, this is a spiritual attack. James 1:6 instructs the Christ-follower to pray in faith without doubting, "because the one who doubts is like a wave of the sea, blown and tossed by the wind" (NIV). If Satan can tempt you to doubt God or His Word, he can lure you away from trusting God. If Satan can destroy your trust in God, he can pull you into sin, because "whatever is not from faith is sin" (Romans 14:23).

So, how can you protect your mind against mental attacks? What can you do to prepare your body against upcoming physical attacks? Is there a way to prepare your spirit against spiritual attacks? If you want to overcome the enemy, you must first understand your enemy.

In a war, the opposing sides study each other to discover weaknesses, habits, tendencies, and the like to win. Paul gives us this insight into our enemy: "We are not ignorant of his devices" (2 Corinthians 2:11). The good news is we know what Satan's strategies and schemes are.

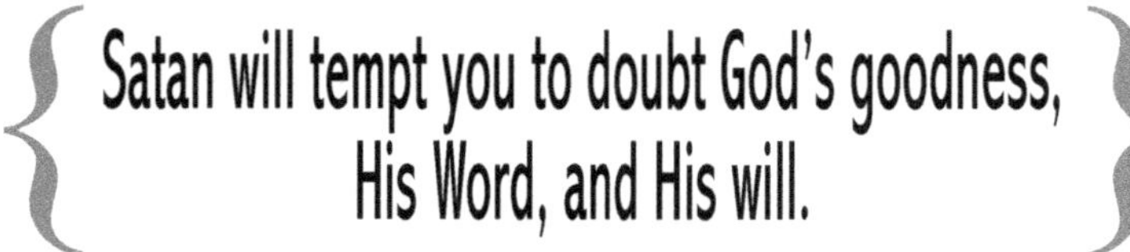
Satan will tempt you to doubt God's goodness,
His Word, and His will.

Satan's Strategies and Schemes

How do we learn our enemy's game plan? Have you heard of film study? In professional sports, often the team with the advantage is the one that spends the most time in the film room. They examine hours and hours of video footage to discover the other team's plays, strategies, and of course, their weaknesses. Christ-followers have several excellent resources for our spiritual warfare film study: Scripture, the experience of others, and our own experience with temptation.

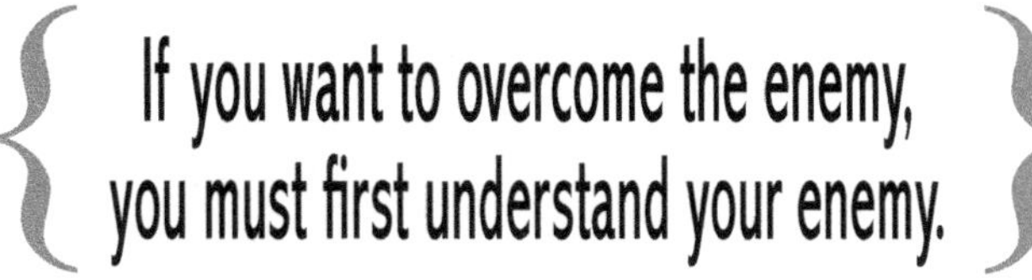
If you want to overcome the enemy,
you must first understand your enemy.

Strategy #1:
Attack after a victory.

What lessons can we learn from the pages of Scripture? First lesson: Satan often likes to attack a Christ-follower after a great spiritual breakthrough or experience.[51] Elijah was attacked after his victory on Mount Carmel, where he defeated 850 false prophets, yet he fled in fear from one evil women, Queen Jezebel. (See 1 Kings 18–19.) Why did he run from one person after standing up to almost one thousand? Satan often likes to strike us after a huge spiritual success. If you have recently experienced a great victory, watch out, because Satan likes to knock you down after God has lifted you up.

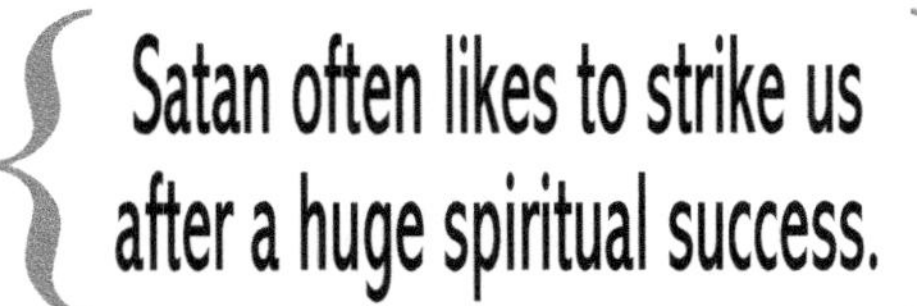
Satan often likes to strike us
after a huge spiritual success.

Strategy #2:
Attack at a new beginning.

Satan also likes to attack you at the beginning of something new and exciting.[52] What happened after God created Adam and Eve? They both were tempted by Satan (Genesis 3). What happened to Abraham after he arrived in the land God promised him? Satan pounced (Genesis 12). What happened right after Jesus was baptized and empowered by the Holy Spirit for the launch of His public ministry? You guessed it. Satan was back at it again (Matthew 4). Looking back over my life and ministry, some of my most intense spiritual attacks came when I launched something new. When I was in my mid-twenties, Lori and I started a new church designed to reach the unchurched. High with excitement, we launched Relate Church with the mission to impact lost lives with the Good News of Jesus. But those years were some of the hardest of my life. I felt attacked on every corner. I was trying to do God's work, and it felt like Satan was coming against me with a forcefulness I did not anticipate. As you **Go After Jesus**, get ready for the battle that comes along with that lifelong commitment.

There are not enough pages in this book to tell you about those difficult days. I was attacked *spiritually*, and people I thought were friends turned into enemies. I discovered a new word during this season: *frenemy*. This person appears to be your friend, but in the end stabs you in the back. I did not expect shots to be fired from my own team.

I was attacked *mentally*, Satan tried to discourage me and get me to quit, more times than I can count. He attempted to sow lies inside my head, tempting me to doubt God's good plan for my life and ministry. Satan also attacked Lori and me *physically* through high levels of stress and anxiety that took a toll on our health and well-being. Ministry is not for the weakhearted. If you sense a call of God on your life, learn how to soldier up (get ready for the battle that is coming).

Strategy #3:
Attack when isolated

Satan often attacks a Christ-follower when he or she is isolated and alone. Remember the metaphor Peter gives us: Satan is like a lion, seeking whom to devour (I Peter 5:8). One trait of a roaming lion is that it picks out the one who is off by himself. Who does Satan go after? The Christ-follower who is discouraged and feels all alone, and the one who is not actively connected to a community of other Christ-followers. Satan loves it when you stop going to church. He has his eye on the prize: You. Beware! As you **Go After Jesus**, do not fall into the trap of isolation by neglecting regular church attendance. Also, do not stay disconnected from other church members by showing up only for a worship service and then bolting for the door before anyone notices you.

Satan likes to go after the Christ-follower who is discouraged and feels all alone.

Signs You're Under Attack

When you passionately **Go After Jesus,** you will fight many spiritual battles against the enemy. Is it possible to recognize an enemy attack when it is first happening so you can be ready and prepared? Absolutely. Recognize the early indicators of a spiritual battle. Next, we will look at some of the top signs signs that you're under spiritual attack.

The first sign of an attack is *discouragement.* Have you ever felt a wave of discouragement wash over you as you do the Lord's work? Maybe you taught your first Bible study lesson and afterward felt a sense of hopelessness. The enemy tells you that you did a poor job and will never be someone God can use. Where do these negative thoughts come from? The apostle John tells us that Satan is the accuser of the brethren (Revelation 12:10). The next time you hear a voice of accusation as you serve the Lord, identify its source: Satan, the Accuser.

Another sign of an attack is a *loss of passion for God.* You were on fire for God and doing well, then your passion sputtered out. How can that happen so quickly? Think about a teenager who goes to summer camp with their student ministry and comes back home fired up for Jesus. Then school starts, and within a few days, the passion for God seems to disappear like a vapor on a sunny summer day. Satan likes to attack us when we are red-hot for Jesus. Recognize this attack on your passion for Him before it quenches your spiritual fire.

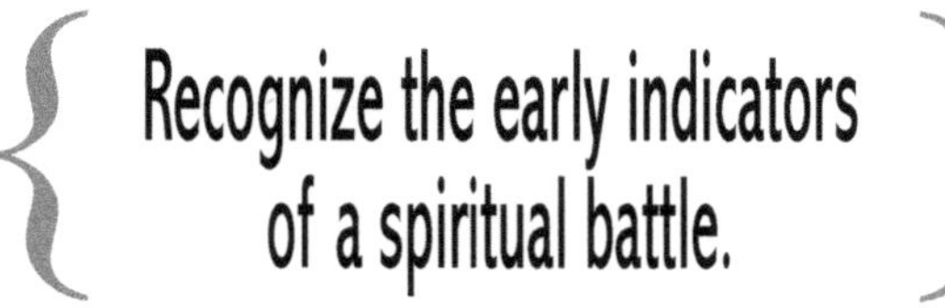
Recognize the early indicators
of a spiritual battle.

You are also under attack when you cannot shake *recurring negative thoughts.* Have you ever had a vile and repulsive thought, but you did not know where it came from? Well, one of the sources of bad thoughts is the enemy, Satan, who likes to shoot darts at our minds. This is why the Bible encourages you to take up the shield of faith to quench those destructive arrows (Ephesians 6:16). If you have recurring negative thoughts, recognize them as the enemy's attack.

An overwhelming sense of guilt is a fourth sign of an attack. You asked God to forgive a particular sin, but the guilt keeps popping up at the most inopportune moments. As the Accuser of the brethren, Satan likes to bring up our past to cripple our confidence in Christ. When Satan reminds you of your past, remember that your past is forgiven, and God does not hold any of your past sins against you. David said, "As far as the east is from the west, so far has He removed our transgressions from us" (Psalm 103:12).

Another sign of an enemy attack is that *your faith suddenly feels weak.* You were going strong for so long, but now you feel spiritually weak. You were on fire for Jesus, telling your lost loved ones and friends about your Savior, but now you just keep quiet. You could not wait for church on Sunday, but now you want to sleep in. If your faith seems weak, realize that Satan may be attacking.

Some Christ-followers report experiencing a deep heaviness and sudden sorrow, a flood of negative emotions that comes out of nowhere, and they do not know why. Satan likes to mess with your emotions. The breastplate of righteousness is the piece of armor that protects your heart (Ephesians 6:14). The next chapter is an in-depth study of the armor of God and how we can use this heavenly resource to overcome Satan's schemes against us.

Other Christ-followers have noted that they know they are under spiritual attack when they have *a strong desire to return to their sinful past.* Satan likes to tempt us with behaviors he knows have caused us to stumble into sin in the past. James gives us the play-by-play of this strategy:

> When tempted, no one should say, "God is tempting me." For God cannot be tempted by evil, nor does he tempt anyone; but each person is tempted when they are dragged away by their own evil desire and enticed. Then, after desire has conceived, it gives birth to sin; and sin, when it is full-grown, gives birth to death. (James 1:13–15 NIV)

The struggle with sin resembles a fish drawn into taking an alluring bait. The problem is the hook attached to the bait will ensnare the fish. The same is true when a Christ-follower gives in to temptation.

{ Satan likes to tempt us with behaviors that have caused us to stumble into sin in the past. }

Another sign of spiritual attack is *chronic physical fatigue when you are doing God's work.* You feel fine before you engage in ministry, but during and after the ministry activities, you feel drained and hopeless. Some Christ-followers identify this as one of the ways Satan attacks us when we are active in the Lord's work.

The list of Satan's schemes could go on forever. I have saved perhaps the most heartbreaking one for last: You experience *betrayal from other Christ-followers.* I wish this last one were not true. I would like to tell you that you will never be hurt by other Christians, but you will. One of the most hurtful of Satan's strategies is when he convinces others to believe lies about you. Satan knows that a house divided against itself will not stand (Matthew 12:25). If Satan can turn another brother or sister against you, you will be in the middle of a great spiritual attack.[53] After reading this list of Satan's strategies and tactics, you may feel discouraged. I understand. But do not give in to fear. Your heavenly Father loves you so much that He has a plan to help you overcome these challenges. The next chapter will show you how to be armed and equipped for every battle by describing the armor of God and how to use it in your everyday life.

CHAPTER 15 RECAP

Go After Jesus Principle #15

As a ***Soldier***, you can stand strong, even during heated spiritual warfare.
Read: 2 Timothy 2:3-4

Key Takeaways

- ***God is preparing you for battle.*** Remember the importance of spiritual boot camp to equip you for the inevitable battles, using the tools of Scripture, prayer, and community support.
- ***Recognize that you are in a spiritual battle.*** Understand that following Jesus makes you a target in a spiritual and often invisible war, where Satan actively works against you.
- ***Recognize the nature of spiritual attacks.*** Learn how to recognize the various forms of spiritual attacks, mental, physical, and spiritual, and how they manifest in your life.

Reflection

- What strategies and schemes has Satan used against you in the past?
- Do you believe you are under spiritual attack now? Why or why not?
- What spiritual warfare study resources do you use regularly?

Looking Ahead

Chapter 16: Armed for Battle

CHAPTER 16

Armed for Battle

"Finally, my brethren, be strong in the Lord and in the power of His might. Put on the whole armor of God, that you may be able to stand against the wiles of the devil."
Ephesians 6:10–11

We were the underdogs, and no one thought we deserved to be at the tournament. The Happy Valley Christian School basketball team found itself competing for a title in the International ACA (Accelerated Christian Education) Basketball Competition. Our Christian school had fifty students, kindergarten through twelfth grade. That is right, just fifty students. How did we muster a basketball team? The rules were not as strict for Christian schools, so we were able to build a team from both middle and high school students.

In our Christian school league, a team was required to compete at the state level to qualify to compete at the international competition, which was hosted in a different state every year. If a team placed first or second in the state, then it was eligible to compete in the big leagues, the ACA International Christian School Competition. Our team had one highly skilled player, a few good players, and the rest, well, they would not have made the basketball team at any other school. So, with big dreams of winning the state championship, we headed to the tournament in our old white school bus, laced up our high-tops, put on our purple jerseys, and pumped ourselves up for the competition. Go Lions! We were ready for whatever came our way … at least we thought we were ready.

The tournament began, and we gave it our all, but the results were less than desirable. We lost most of our games and finished near the bottom of the rankings. Then the unexpected happened. The first and second-place teams decided not to compete for Internationals, and we found a loophole clause in the rulebook. If the first and second-place winners did not compete at the International Competition, the runner-up could represent its state. We qualified, not because we were good but because the other teams were not willing to make the long trip to the International Competition in Flagstaff, Arizona that year (we had to drive all the way from Western North Carolina).

We arrived at the competition along with hundreds of other schools from all around America and even from other countries. We had nothing to lose since we were the biggest underdogs in the competition. So, how did we do? The answer still shocks me. In a single-elimination tournament, we beat the first two teams and made it to the Sweet Sixteen.

Three Principles of Victory

How did we do it? Most would consider our victories miracles, since the worst team in the tournament somehow managed to beat two more talented teams. Here are a few things we did that helped us achieve success, against all odds. *First, we played as a team.* We were not that skilled, so we were forced to rely on one another. The other teams had better players, but we worked as a team better and so we were able to overcome their superior level of talent. Our collective teamwork was greater than their individual talent because of the power of *synergy*. Synergy happens when people work together in a way that multiplies their efforts, producing a greater effect than when one works alone.

> { Collective teamwork is greater than individual talent. }

Second, we truly relied on God's strength. Not that the other teams forgot to ask for God's help, I am sure they did. For us, though, it was a matter of realizing we needed divine intervention to win the battle.

Third, we played passionately. Those tournament games were two of the best games each of us team members played in our entire basketball careers. As I reflect on those victories, I am reminded of this principle: pray as though all depends on God and play as though all depends on you and the team.

The battles on the court were intense. Decades later, I can tell my kids the stories of those exciting victories: "Kids, let me tell you about the time when the last-place team actually won!" In this chapter, I'll give you practical ways you can win spiritual battles. Even when the opposing side seems stronger, you have advantages that will help you achieve victory as you **Go After Jesus**. You will be encouraged, equipped, and empowered for present and future spiritual battles.

The Battle Is Real

If you have walked with Jesus longer than a few weeks, you have discovered this truth: There is an intense spiritual battle going on all around you. Paul instructs his young protégé Timothy with these words: "Join me in suffering, like a good soldier of Christ Jesus. No one serving as a soldier gets entangled in civilian affairs but rather tries to please his commanding officer" (2 Timothy 2:3-4 NIV). The first step is awareness. You cannot be ready for battle if you are not aware of the battle.

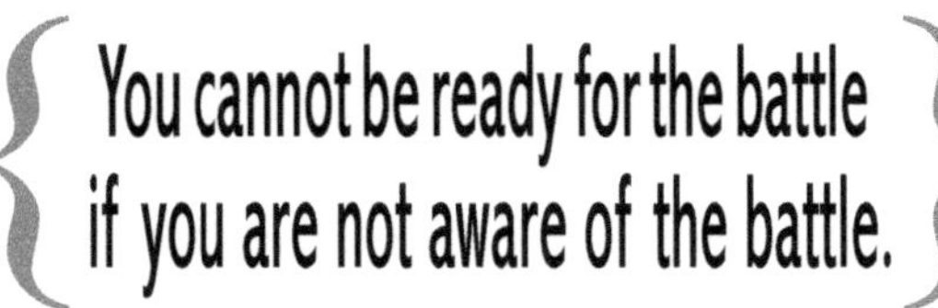
You cannot be ready for the battle
if you are not aware of the battle.

Why is there a battle? In Genesis 3, Satan came in the form of a snake, and like a snake, Satan often sneaks up on us without us even being aware of his sinister presence. Adam and Eve took the bait and gave in to Satan's temptation. The result? Sin infiltrated our world and infected humanity from that day on. A battle is also raging in our world because the enemy of our souls, Satan, has his evil gaze on us and desires to destroy us. Why? One reason is that humans are made in the image of God, and since Satan hates God, he hates and wants to destroy anything that resembles Him.

The Battle Equipment

If this chapter ended with the previous sentence, you would be left with a lot of discouragement and more questions than answers. But here is the rest of the story: God did not leave you without a solution to this ongoing spiritual battle between good and evil. God has graciously provided you with everything you need to be successful in this war. One resource God has provided is spiritual armor that has the power to give you victory even in the most contested battles.

Paul introduces us to the armor of God in Ephesians 6:

> "Finally, my brethren, be strong in the Lord and in the power of His might. Put on the whole armor of God, that you may be able to stand against the wiles of the devil. For we do not wrestle against flesh and blood, but against principalities, against powers, against the rulers of the darkness of this age, against spiritual hosts of wickedness in the heavenly places. Therefore, take up the whole armor of God, that you may be able to withstand in the evil day, and having done all, to stand. Stand therefore, having girded your waist with truth, having put on the breastplate of righteousness, and having shod your feet with the preparation of the gospel of peace; above all, taking the shield of faith with which you will be able to quench all the fiery darts of the wicked one. And take the helmet of salvation, and the sword of the Spirit, which is the word of God; praying always with all prayer and supplication in the Spirit, being watchful to this end with all perseverance and supplication for all the saints, and for me, that utterance may be given to me, that I may open my mouth boldly to make known the mystery of the gospel, for which I am an ambassador in chains; that in it I may speak boldly, as I ought to speak" (v. 10–18).

As you **Go After Jesus**, you need to know how to put on this armor and how to use it effectively. In this section, we will explore the armor of God and how to use it to stand strong in the "evil day." Recognize this paradox: We are weak apart from Christ, but we are powerful with and through Him. Paul tells us to be strong "In the Lord" and "In the power of His might" (v. 10). Satan is far more powerful than we are in our own strength, but Satan is no match for God's power.

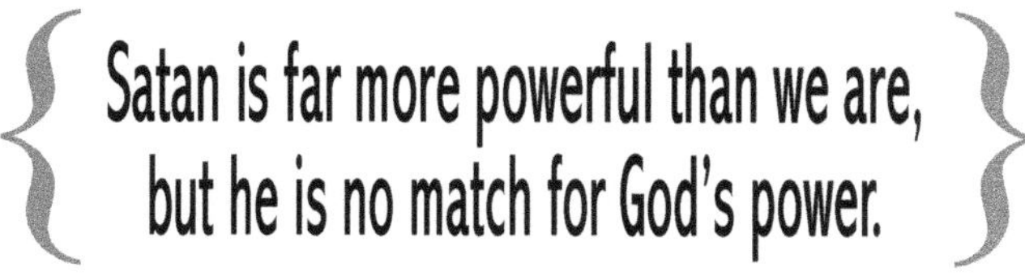
Satan is far more powerful than we are,
but he is no match for God's power.

Understand your objective in your daily spiritual battles: Your goal is to stand strong and not to retreat. Paul gives us our objective: "That you may be able to stand against the wiles of the devil" (v. 11). You may, like me, always want to advance, to move forward in every situation. Although this is a good goal for most situations in life, in a battle, forward progress is not always possible. In an intense contest where all hell is breaking loose against you, your objective is not only to move forward but also to hold your ground, to stand strong, to stay steadfast, and not to go backward.

Paul instructed the church at Corinth to "be steadfast, immovable, always abounding in the work of the Lord" (1 Corinthians 15:58). In a battle, you are called to be *steadfast*, remain committed and loyal to the Lord. You are called to be *immovable*; do not lose any ground to Satan. What about the "abounding" part? As you remain loyal, stable, and hold your ground, you will eventually see fruit as the by-product of your faithfulness. Abounding in the work of the Lord will come, but it often comes after the battle, not in the middle of the war.

Get Suited Up, The Armor of God

God has provided you with all you need to live a victorious life. He provides the full armor, but He does not put it on you; that is your job. God will do the impossible, but He expects you to do the possible. God has done His part; now it is time to learn how to do your part. But how can you put on this invisible spiritual armor?

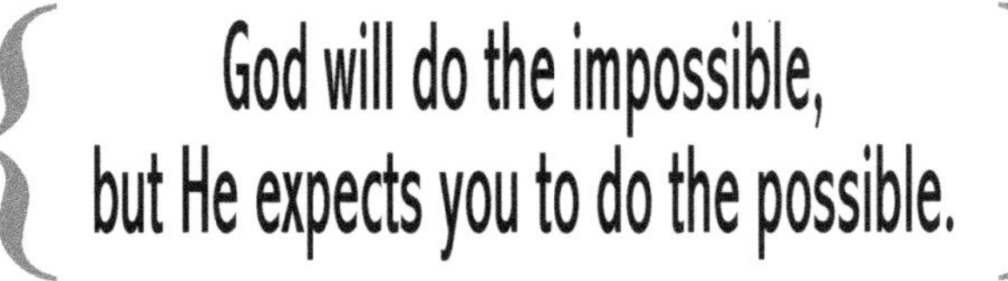
God will do the impossible,
but He expects you to do the possible.

The six pieces of God's armor are divided into two sets. The first three pieces are introduced by the verb *to be*, and the other three are introduced by the verb *to take*. The first set is a state of mind and heart, which we should always manifest; the second set is a group of tools to use on an as-needed basis. Next, I will cover how to put on and wear this armor so you can overcome daily battles against Satan and his evil army.

The Belt of Truth

This piece of armor is mentioned first because it is the first item of clothing a Roman soldier put on as he suited up for a battle. The belt was important for two major reasons. First, the belt connected and held together the whole suit of armor. Without the belt, the rest of the armor was vulnerable during an attack. With the belt, the armor was held securely together.

The second aspect of the belt's importance was that it allowed the soldier to move freely. When a soldier wanted to run, he could tuck his long tunic into his belt to move faster (they wore long robes back in the day). Speed was essential in battle because the soldier had to advance quickly to engage an enemy or to avoid an enemy attack.

How do you put on the belt of truth? You make the Word of God a daily part of your life. God's Word is *truth*. The psalmist says, "The entirety of Your word is truth, and every one of Your righteous judgments endures forever" (Psalm 119:160).

Jesus prayed for His followers to be sanctified by the truth, and He said this about God's Word: "Your word is truth" (John 17:17). The book of Proverbs tells us that every single word of God is pure, which means that you can trust God's Word to always be right on target (Proverbs 30:5).

When you read and apply God's Word to your life,
you are putting on the belt of truth.

When you read and apply God's Word to your life, you are putting on the belt of truth. As you live out the Word of God in your daily decisions, you are wearing the belt of truth. It is not just about knowing the *truth*; it is about *acting on that truth* daily. What happens when you go through a season of not allowing Scripture to shape your life? Your belt sags, and you become vulnerable to the enemy's attacks. In everyday life, what happens when your pants are loose, and you do not have a belt on? Do not go there!

The Breastplate of Righteousness

This piece of armor covered the vital organs of a soldier's chest. "The breastplate of Roman times went completely around the body, so that the back of a warrior was also protected. The breastplate was made of hard leather or metal."[54]

Spiritually, the breastplate of righteousness is both *positional* and *practical*. When you accepted Jesus into your life as your Savior, God did something that changed everything in your life. He took away your sin and exchanged it for the righteousness of Christ. The moment you became a Christ-follower, you became righteous. God now considers you holy, blameless, and without fault (Colossians 1:22). This is called *positional* righteousness because this is now your righteous standing in Christ.

Paul gives us the essence of this divine exchange: "He made Him who knew no sin *to be* sin for us, that we might become the righteousness of God in Him" (2 Corinthians 5:21).

The goal of following Jesus is to become *practically* what you are *positionally*. In other words, as you **Go After Jesus**, you are becoming more like Jesus in your everyday life (this is called sanctification), since now you are in Christ.

The Gospel Shoes of Peace

Why are the right shoes needed? "A Roman soldier's feet were shod with hard, studded shoes."[55] Small nails acted like cleats, and these cleated shoes gave them firm footing during a battle, so they did not lose ground when the enemy launched a stealth attack. The gospel is the Good News that you are in the right relationship with God through faith in Jesus Christ. Knowing that God is for you even when the enemy is against you gives you peace even amid the battle. It also gives you a firm footing when the enemy attempts to push you back. It allows you to stand firm even when everyone else around you is falling.

One time, a little girl met with her pastor to talk about getting baptized. The pastor was not sure the little girl was ready, so he asked her why she wanted to be baptized. She responded that she wanted to get baptized because she had asked Jesus into her heart. The pastor tested her with one more question: "Well, suppose that tomorrow the devil knocked on the door of your heart and asked to come in. What would you do?" She said, "I would let Jesus answer the door!" The pastor said, "Okay, you are ready because you know what it means to have Jesus in your life."[56] The gospel shoes of peace give you a firm footing when the devil comes in for an attack.

The gospel shoes of peace give you a firm footing when the devil comes in for an attack.

The studded nails at the bottom of the shoes that kept the soldier standing firm are like your faith that will keep you standing strong on the evil day. God wants you to be certain you are saved because that confidence will help you withstand even the most intense attack. The aged apostle John wrote to first-century Christ-followers: "I write these things to you who believe in the name of the Son of God so that you may know that you have eternal life" (1 John 5:13 NIV). Knowing that you are in Christ will give you a firm footing so that you can stand strong in your faith and witness.

Wear the first three pieces of armor all the time. Why? They are connected to your identity in Christ. The next three pieces you "take up" to help you stand firm when you are fighting a spiritual battle.

The Shield of Faith

Guess what Satan likes to go after when you find yourself in the heat of the battle? He goes after your *faith*. If the Accuser of the brethren can get you to doubt your faith when all hell is breaking loose against you, then you may temporarily lose your footing. The psalmist Asaph expresses this thought when he says, "But as for me, my feet had almost slipped; I had nearly lost my foothold" (Psalm 73:2 NIV).

What is the shield of faith? Paul is referring to the large Roman shields of the first century. They were often covered with leather, which could be soaked in water so the fiery darts would not harm the warrior in battle. Called a *scutum*, this large, curved, rectangular shield was approximately four feet tall and two and a half feet wide. "This size allowed a soldier to hide his entire body behind it for protection from arrows, javelins, and sword blows. The curved shape helped deflect incoming projectiles."[57] The Roman legion had a unique way of defeating the enemy with their scutum: the soldiers stood side by side to form a wall with their shields, which protected the army against the flaming darts of the enemy. The wall formed by these interlocked shields was called a *testudo*, meaning "tortoise" in Latin, because the wall of protection resembled a turtle's shell.[58]

What can we learn from this? Faith not only enables you to stand strong in the battle, but faith also brings Christ-followers together to stand strong as one. God does not call us to faith alone; He also provides courageous brothers and sisters to stand with us "in the evil day, and having done all, to stand." You are a ***Soldier***, so knowing how to suit up and be prepared for battle is vital.

> **God provides courageous brothers and sisters to stand with us "in the evil day."**

How can you "take up" this shield of faith? Choose to believe in God no matter what comes your way. Hebrews 11:1 reminds us that faith is believing even when you cannot see the outcome. Faith is trusting God to deliver what He has promised us in His Word. As you **Go After Jesus** and find yourself in an intense battle, make sure you have spent time with the Lord in prayer and in His Word so your trust in God is strong enough to get you through the battle.

The Helmet of Salvation

How does a helmet protect a soldier? The Roman soldier's helmet was called the *galea*. This crucial piece of armor was typically made of iron or bronze and often included cheek guards and a neck guard. Sometimes these helmets had added features for officers of rank, including a crest of horsehair or feathers. These stunning helmets not only protected the soldier but also intimidated the enemy.[59] What is the main purpose of a helmet in a battle? It protects a soldier's head from objects coming toward him. If the enemy can take out your head, you're dead! The same is true in a spiritual conquest. If Satan can throw sinister thoughts that penetrate your mind, or even worse, find their way inside the framework of your thought life, then he has a foothold in your life.

{ If the enemy can take out your head, you're dead! }

Satan's initial strategy is to keep you away from God's salvation *before* you come to Christ; then he changes his strategy to cause you to doubt your salvation *after* you choose to **Go After Jesus**. How can you "take up" this piece of equipment so your mind is protected from Satan's arrows? First, determine to think like Jesus. Paul calls this having the mind of Christ: "Let this mind be in you which was also in Christ Jesus" (Philippians 2:5).

How can you have the mind of Christ when you struggle daily to do God's will and view life from His perspective? The struggle is real, but every time you listen to God's Word and apply it to your life, God shapes your mind to think more and more like Jesus. Paul tells us that when we change the way we think, our minds are being renewed, which leads to a transformed life far different from our old, worldly life. (See Romans 12:1–2.)

The second step is to learn to take captive the bad thoughts that come your way every day. Here was Paul's strategy for deflecting the enemy's evil thoughts that kept coming at him: "We demolish arguments and every pretension that sets itself up against the knowledge of God, and we take captive every thought to make it obedient to Christ" (2 Corinthians 10:5 NIV).

Renew your mind daily in God's Word, and reject thoughts that are not from God.

As you **Go After Jesus**, you can put on the helmet of salvation by doing these two things: Renewing your mind daily in God's Word and rejecting thoughts that are not from God. How can you know a thought is not from God? It takes time, but a renewed mind filled with God's Word will be able to discern what is from God and what is from the enemy. For example, if you feel guilty over a past sin you already confessed, you can immediately recognize that thought is not from God, because the Word of God tells you are already forgiven and cleansed from all unrighteousness (1 John 1:9).

The Sword of the Spirit

The sword is the only explicit offensive weapon mentioned in Ephesians 6. (There is one other offensive weapon . . . so keep reading). Paul identifies the sword's significance clearly: "the sword of the Spirit, *which is the word of God*" (v. 17, emphasis added).

The Roman soldier typically had access to two types of swords: the *gladius* and the *spatha*. The most used sword was the gladius, an essential sidearm used by legionnaires, generals, and emperors. This versatile, short sword, often eighteen to twenty-four inches long, was often used in battle because of its strength and flexibility.

The gladius was created as a weapon that could easily penetrate the enemy's armor.[60] The spatha was much longer than the gladius; it came into usage much later, starting in the late first century AD and being much more widely used in the late second and early third century. This sword was much more effective for the cavalry because it provided a longer reach to strike the opponent.[61]

When the apostle Paul was writing to the church at Ephesus about the armor of God, which sword did he mean? Paul uses the Greek word *machaira*, which referred to a small sword.[62] This would have pointed the reader toward the gladius. Using this historical and cultural backdrop, we can draw this application: God's Word is like the gladius, sharp, quick, effective, and precise.

{ Use God's Word as an offensive weapon to defeat the enemy's advances. }

As you **Go After Jesus**, you will need to use God's Word as an offensive weapon to defeat the enemy's advances. Another insight related to this weapon is the Greek word for *word*: *rema*. *Rema* refers to a spoken word. This is different from the other Greek word, *logos,* which refers to the concept of wisdom in general.[63]

Rema is a spoken word used for a specific situation. When Satan comes after you with a specific temptation, you will need a specific verse to defeat that type of temptation. If Satan tempts you with lust, use a Bible verse that deals with overcoming lust, such as 2 Timothy 2:22: "Flee the evil desires of youth and pursue righteousness, faith, love and peace, along with those who call on the Lord out of a pure heart."

What if the enemy comes after you with the temptation of bitterness? Paul gives us this instruction about bitterness in Ephesians 4:31: "Get rid of all bitterness, rage and anger, brawling and slander, along with every form of malice" (NIV). Bitterness is the opposite of forgiveness. Bitterness is chewing on an offense until it rots and poisons you. It will lead to all the other sins mentioned in Ephesians 4:31. When the enemy tempts you to hold a grudge against someone who has deeply hurt you, pray about that matter until God heals the hurt. As you wait for healing, put Ephesians 4:32 into practice: "Be kind and compassionate to one another, forgiving each other, just as Christ God forgave you" (NIV).

The Secret Weapon

You also have a bonus weapon that many people do not realize is part of the armor of God. Paul lists six pieces of armor in Ephesians 6: The belt of truth, the breastplate of righteousness, the gospel shoes of peace, the shield of faith, the helmet of salvation, and the sword of the Spirit (the Word of God). But there is one more weapon that empowers all the other weapons. Are you ready for it? *Prayer*!

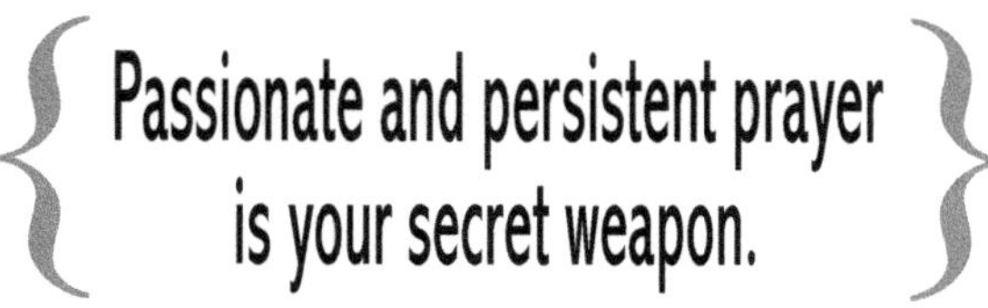
Passionate and persistent prayer
is your secret weapon.

After Paul describes the six pieces of armor in Ephesians 6, he says, "*Praying* always with all prayer and supplication in the Spirit, being watchful to this end with all perseverance and supplication for all the saints" (v. 18, emphasis added). I call this secret weapon the *P3* weapon, *Passionate and Persistent Prayer.* Your daily prayer life is the relational force that strengthens and empowers you to stand strong during your daily spiritual battles.

Maximize Your Prayer Life

How do we unleash this secret spiritual weapon? First, pray *persistently.* Paul says we should pray "always . . . with all perseverance" (v. 18). How is it possible to pray always? Paul means to always be in the spirit of prayer. Start your day off with a special time of prayer, then keep your prayer life going throughout the day. Whisper a prayer for someone in need, thank God for your daily meals, and offer up a prayer for the injured person when you hear an ambulance go by.

Second, pray *comprehensively.* Paul tells us to pray "with all prayer ... for all the saints" (v. 18). Develop a robust prayer life that covers many needs in the world around you. One strategy I use is a prayer list on my phone on my *To Do* app. This organizes my prayers and keeps my mind from wandering during my prayer time. Be comprehensive in your prayer coverage: Pray for those in authority, such as the president and key elected leaders, pray for your pastor and local church, pray for the members in your family, pray for your community, and pray for other areas of concern God brings to your attention. Praying in this fashion will help your prayers cover the all-encompassing needs in the world around you.

Third, pray *personally*. Paul says our prayer life should include *"supplications"* (v. 18). Supplications are earnest, specific petitions or requests. God knows what your needs are, but He wants you to mention them by name. One of the reasons God created prayer is that He desires a living and intimate relationship with you. He wants you to ask Him for things; just like a dad or mom wants their children to approach them with a need they not only *can* meet, but also have the *desire* to meet out of a heart of love.

{ **The Spirit helps us offer up powerful, bold, and effective prayers.** }

Fourth, pray with *assistance*. Paul also tells us to pray "in the Spirit" (v. 18). What does that mean? To pray in the Spirit means we have a prayer partner who desires to help us offer up powerful, bold, and effective prayers. The Holy Spirit, who lives inside each Christ-follower, prays for us in our weakness and helps us to pray in a way that lines up with God's will (Romans 8:26-27). When you pray, remember you have the assistance of the Holy Spirit, who is not only praying *for you* but who will also pray with you as you pray to the Father "in the Spirit."

Fifth, pray with *expectation*. As you pray, be "watchful" (v. 18). The Greek word for watchful means to pray in an alert, attentive, and ready way.[64] When Jesus asked Peter, James, and John to pray with Him in the garden of Gethsemane, He found them sleeping three times when they should have been praying. Jesus spoke directly to Peter and told him the importance of "watching" and praying so he could avert the temptations that were going to come his way (Matthew 26:36-46).

One way to stay engaged while praying is to maintain a sense of expectation. If you believe God has something special in store for you, pray with expectation. If you understand that temptations and trials are heading your way, pray with watchfulness. The secret weapon of prayer is underutilized by too many Christ-followers. If we better understood the power and the potential unleashed through prayer, I think we would pray not just more often, but also with a sense of anticipation and watchfullness as we seek the face of our heavenly Father.

> **{ You are fighting a battle in a war that has already been won. }**

As you **Go After Jesus**, do not forget to put on the full armor of God. God has graciously given you this armor so that in the evil day, "having done all," you can stand firm in your faith. You are fighting a battle in a war that, from eternity's perspective, has already been won. Jesus won the war when he died and rose again. You are not fighting *for* victory; you are fighting *from* victory. So, stand strong. "Let nothing move you. Always give yourself fully to the work of the Lord, because you know that your labor in the Lord is not in vain" (1 Corinthians 15:58 NIV).

CHAPTER 16 RECAP

Go After Jesus Principle #16

As you **Go After Jesus**, take up the full armor of God so you can stand firm in the day of battle.
Read: Ephesians 4:31-32, 1 Peter 5:8

Key Takeaways

Be aware of the spiritual battle going on around you. But also be encouraged because God has graciously provided you with everything you need to be successful in the war.

Put on the armor of God every morning. God's armor is the only way you can stand strong when temptation and trials come your way.

Cultivate a fervent prayer life. Persistently and comprehensively pray for the needs around you, believing God can do the impossible in the challenging situations you face daily.

Reflection

What evidence do you see of the intense spiritual battle going on around you?

Of all the pieces of armor covered in this chapter, which ones are you most likely to forget about? What new habit could help you remember them?

Who stands with you (and prays for you) as you fight spiritual battles?

Looking Ahead

Chapter 17: My War Stories

CHAPTER 17

My War Stories

> "Finally, my brethren, be strong in the Lord and in the power of His might. Put on the whole armor of God, that you may be able to stand against the wiles of the devil."
> Ephesians 6:10–11

My mind raced, my heart pounded, and my anxiety rose to new heights. I had just received the most unusual message in my inbox: "Leave my servant alone." What in the world was this about? As I read the scathing and threatening message, fear washed over me like a tidal wave.

As my heart rate increased, I asked myself, "What is this message all about?" I had gone to the local Starbucks to enjoy a latte as I studied for my upcoming Sunday sermon, and there I encountered a strange-looking man. That is not unusual in the weird, small city of Asheville, North Carolina. Sipping my latte, I initiated a conversation with this young man, who looked like he was in his early twenties. After we chatted a bit about what was on his mind (he wanted to talk about legalizing marijuana), I gave him my business card and invited him to church for the upcoming Sunday.

Within twenty-four hours of inviting this man to church, something bizarre happened: His "master" took offense and rebuked me for trying to share Christ with his personal slave. "Leave my servant alone!" I did not know that such servant/slave relationships still existed in America. I was heartbroken to discover this young man was involved in some type of sick relationship that had a dark and sinister spiritual backdrop. As I researched this dark "master" who messaged me, I found out he was involved in witchcraft. He claimed to be a warlock. His social media page was full of images of witches and warlocks. Talk about something so bizarre it makes the hairs on your neck stand up.

After I prayed and processed the encounter, I realized this truth: I am in a spiritual battle, and I need to be prayed up and armored up every time I share Jesus with someone who does not yet know Him. In this chapter, I will share with you some real-life stories that may help you handle difficult spiritual attacks when they come your way. This chapter is not intended to scare you but to prepare you.

{ **We need to be prayed up and armored up whenever we share Jesus with someone.** }

How did I handle the warlock master situation? Since this was a new experience, I did the only thing I knew to do: *Pray!* Prayer should be our first line of defense and offense. As discussed in the previous chapter, prayer is the secret weapon that activates and empowers your spiritual armor so you can stand strong in the day of battle.

Another battle strategy is *seeking wise counsel.* As you **Go After Jesus**, do not go through life alone. You were meant for community, and with community comes support and backup. After my bizarre encounter at Starbucks that day, I reached out to some trusted, godly leaders who helped me walk through that attack. Wise counselors can help you see the situation from God's perspective. Scripture reminds us that "in the multitude of counselors there is safety" (Proverbs 11:14).

How did this story turn out? Thankfully, the warlock master never came after me. I do not know what happened after he sent that email, but it appears he turned his attention to other sinister things. Remember, God fights our battles for us. For example, when the children of Israel faced their worst fears as Pharaoh and his army drew near to attack them, they were terrified. The Israelites were at an impasse, the Red Sea in front of them and Pharaoh closing in behind them. When they needed some reassurance, Moses gave them this word of hope: "The Lord will fight for you. Just stay calm" (Exodus 14:14 NLT).

I encourage you to memorize that verse in preparation for your next spiritual attack. Sometimes the best response is simply to pray and wait. Pray to God and wait on Him to act on your behalf.

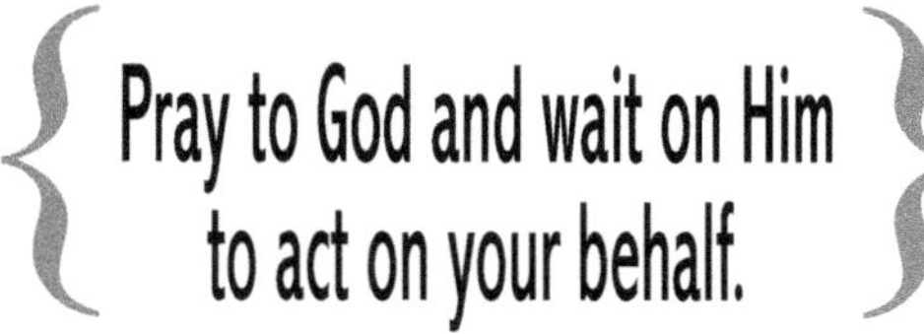

Many victories in our ongoing spiritual conflicts are brought about because of passionate prayer and waiting for God to move. If God is fighting for you, you can rest assured He is going to bring about His greater purposes in the situation.

Church Hurt

Here is the story behind another one of my spiritual scars. One of the worst battles I ever faced was not from the world but from the church. Out of respect for the body of Christ, I will not use the names of the people involved, and I will leave out some details.

Over the last three decades, I have served on staff at nine churches. My first staff position began when I was eighteen years old. I am sure I made a ton of mistakes in my early ministry days; and thankfully, most of the people were gracious, as I was young and had a lot to learn. Of all the churches I served, one incident stands out as a battle story.

The church's mission was to reach those who were far from God, and we did whatever we could to connect with people who needed salvation. Satan seems to work the hardest against you when you are taking members out of his kingdom of darkness. When people accept Christ, two things occur: The angels in heaven rejoice, and Satan and his angels are angry because another soul has been redeemed from their kingdom of darkness.

Back to my story. In my early twenties, I was serving the church with a red-hot passion to reach people. But another pastor at the church wanted the church for himself. He missed his former role of lead pastor at another church and planned to knock me out of my role as the lead pastor of this church. Sadly, he worked this plan tirelessly in a subtle, clandestine way. I was so naïve that I did not notice what was happening behind the scenes; I found out later from fellow staff members what was taking place. One of the other pastor's best friends told me the dark truth about how I was being pushed out of my leadership role.

The other pastor used his gift for connection and communication to spread lies and slander about me to the other pastors and key leaders. Things became so toxic for me and my family that we decided it was best to hand over the church and walk away. I left a church I started with a broken heart, a knife in my back, and nothing to show for it but heartache and heartbreak.

{ A big part of our healing process is learning to forgive those who hurt us. }

As I reflected on this painful ministry experience, I realized there were mistakes made on both sides, and I have owned my part in this episode. The hard lesson in any church conflict is this: Most of the time, the blame is shared between both parties. Seldom is one side 100 percent at fault. The key is to own your part of the blame. I have done that, and I have left the rest at the foot of the cross.

How did I work through my church hurt? First, I took about six months away from ministry to find restoration and healing. A big part of my healing process was learning to forgive those who had hurt me. By the grace of God, I have forgiven the other pastor along with the other leaders who rallied around him. Forgiveness is so beautiful. When you forgive someone, you lay the offense (on both sides) at the foot of the cross. You let Jesus deal with any correction that needs to take place, and you walk away free from that heavy burden.

Promises for the Soldier in Battle

Here is a sacred secret about suffering: Some of my greatest spiritual treasures have come from darkness and suffering. Jesus has a mysterious way of turning our *worst scars* into our *brightest stars*. Because of those battles, I have grown so much as a follower of Jesus. Like Jacob in the Bible, who wrestled with the Angel of the Lord, I also walk with a humble limp. As you **Go After Jesus**, you are growing to become more like Jesus. He takes the present you have and develops it into the best future version of you, so you can accomplish His will for your life.

{ **Jesus has a mysterious way of turning our worst scars into our brightest stars!** }

You are a spiritual ***Soldier*** for the Kingdom of God. It's not a matter of *if* you will face battles, but *when*. When you are engaged in spiritual warfare, embrace this truth: You are not alone. Jesus told His disciples that as they went out making disciples, they could rest assured in two things. We can rest in them, too. First, you are operating in His authority, not your own. Second, Jesus is with you wherever you go (Matthew 28:20).

If I know God is for me and goes with me, I do not have to fear who may come against me. Let that truth rest deep within your soul: You are never alone. In your present battles, Jesus is with you, and if He is with you, He will help you fight your way to the other side of your struggle.

Battle Builds Character

Something special happens to battle-tested Christ-followers. Paul tells us, "We also glory in tribulations, knowing that tribulation produces perseverance; and perseverance, character; and character, hope. Now hope does not disappoint, because the love of God has been poured out in our hearts by the Holy Spirit who was given to us" (Romans 5:3-5).

As you **Go After Jesus** as a ***Soldier***, you are starting to look like Jesus, in your *character*. *Hope* is something everyone desires. Paul tells us that when we go through severe trials because of our faith, God is doing something in us. Trials produce *perseverance*, the ability to hang in there when the going gets tough. A spiritual ***Soldier*** needs grit and tenacity so he can stand strong in the day of battle.

{ If you have faithfully persevered and focused on Jesus, your character will resemble His. }

Perseverance also develops something in your life: *character*. When you have been battle-tested, you are different on the other side of your struggle. If you have faithfully persevered and focused on Jesus, your character will develop to resemble Him. The fruit of the Spirit will grow in your life, and you will become more loving, joyful, patient, and kind, even toward those who are difficult to love. Others will see the goodness of God in your life.

Your life will also be overflowing with *faithfulness*, and people will be able to count on you because of your Christlike character. In tense situations, you will have gentleness, a form of meekness. *Meekness* is not *weakness*; it is power under control. Earlier, we talked about the fruit of the Spirit, one fruit with nine flavors. The last flavor listed is the hardest to develop: Self-control. When the Spirit is leading your life, you have given up your control. Jesus now reigns on the throne of your heart, which enables you to follow His plans and purposes for your life (Galatians 5:24-25).

CHAPTER 17 RECAP

Go After Jesus Principle #17

Every spiritual ***Soldier*** has a few battle stories to share.
You are not alone because Jesus goes with you.
Exodus 14:14, Romans 5:3-5, Galatians 5:22-25

Key Takeaways

Get prayed up before you enter the battle. When I received the message from the warlock master, I needed to spend time in prayer about that situation. Prayer gives you the courage, protection, and coverage you need before, during, and after a spiritual battle.

Trust is a must for every soldier. As you **Go After Jesus**, learn to trust your Savior. Jesus gives you the necessary guidance and grace for each day's battles.

God is doing a work in you as you go through each trial. The hurt of a trial is never wasted if you keep your focus on Jesus. When the spiritual attacks become intense, remember that God is helping your character to develop. In the heat of the conflict, that which does not look like Jesus is getting refined by the fire.

Reflection

How could you prepare for an encounter like mine, confronted with evil up close and personal?

Are you carrying around any church hurt, experiences with other Christ-followers that have left you bruised and bleeding? What first step can you take toward healing?

In what ways has God turned one of your worst scars into a bright star?

Looking Ahead

Part 6: The Lover
Chapter 18: Jesus, Our Model of Love

Part Six

The Lover

I long to fully devote my mind, heart, and soul to Jesus.

The Seeker: I want to ***discover*** the awe-inspiring truth of who Jesus really is.
The Disciple: I am ***determined*** to follow Jesus wherever He leads.
The Friend: I ***desire*** to enjoy the richness of daily, intimate time with Jesus.
The Fisherman: I ***aspire*** to bring others into the Kingdom of God.
The Soldier: I ***aim*** to stand boldly for Jesus in life's battles.
The Lover: I ***long*** to fully devote my mind, heart, and soul to Jesus.

CHAPTER 18

Jesus, Our Model of Love

"Now before the Feast of the Passover, when Jesus knew that His hour had come that He should depart from this world to the Father, having loved His own who were in the world, He loved them to the end."
John 13:1

Love is powerful. It will move you to action you would otherwise not take. The worst of times brings out the worst in those who operate from hate, but the worst of times will bring out the best in those who live with a love for God and others. People are like herbal tea bags; their true colors, flavors, and aroma bleed out in hot water.

Dietrich Bonhoeffer was motivated by intense love for God and others. His love moved him to take actions that eventually cost him everything, including his life. He knew firsthand about the tyranny of evil and that if he did not act, Adolph Hitler's malevolent reign would continue unchecked. Somebody had to do something and do it immediately; otherwise, the worst would continue to happen. More and more Jews would perish under Hitler's satanic reign of hate and terror.

Bonhoeffer had considerable influence as a German theologian and as a local pastor. His deep commitment to his faith and to the gospel motivated him to join the resistance movement to stop Hitler's power. While many people left Germany to escape Hitler's reign of terror, Bonhoeffer stayed. When others crumbled under fear and the threat of impending death, Bonhoeffer did what true leaders do: he took strategic steps to produce lasting change.

In 1943, Bonhoeffer was caught and arrested by the Nazi soldiers. Despite being in dire prison conditions, he continued to write, teach, and inspire others. His body was confined, but his words were free and powerful. His prison writings encouraged others to hold on to their faith, to be willing to sacrifice for the greater good, and to do their part to oppose evil.[65]

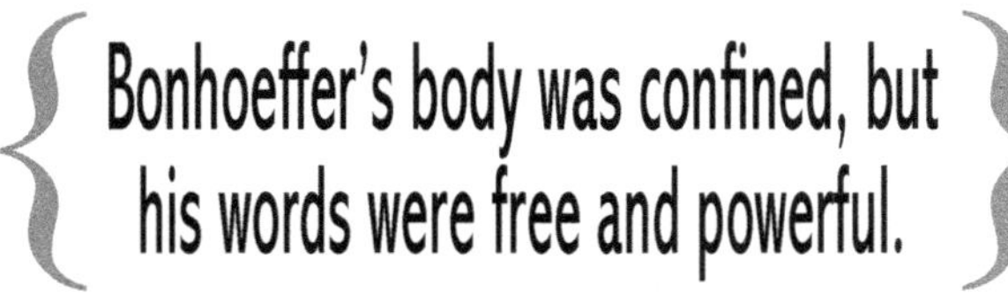
Bonhoeffer's body was confined, but
his words were free and powerful.

I wish Bonhoeffer's story ended well, but he was executed in April 1945, just weeks before the end of World War II. What motivated Bonhoeffer to embrace such self-sacrifice? What led him to stay when others fled? Why did he continue to encourage others even when his life was about to be brutally taken by the hands of evil men? What inspires some to take a sacrificial stand while others flee in fear?

Love

You have chosen to **Go After Jesus**. You started as a ***Seeker*** and have now grown into understanding your identity as a ***Disciple***, a ***Friend***, a ***Fisherman***, and a ***Soldier***. Now, it is time to learn how to fully devote your heart, mind, and soul to Jesus as a ***Lover***.

The Call to Love Jesus Above All

Do you want to be a ***Lover*** of Jesus? Do you desire to follow Him with passion and purpose? Do you want to be led by a greater and bigger vision than anything you could imagine? If you said, "Yes," to these questions, you will devour these next three chapters as I lay out the path to growing in your love for Jesus and for others.

Jesus was helping His disciples understand who He really was. Not just another spiritual leader like John the Baptist, Elijah, or any of the other Old Testament prophets. When Jesus asked the Twelve who they thought He was, Peter spoke for the entire group: "You are the Christ, the Son of the living God" (Matthew 16:16).

Jesus told Peter he was not bright enough to come up with this revelation of the nature of Jesus on his own. Rather, this came straight from God the Father (v. 17).

In the context of Peter's confession of faith, Jesus taught the Twelve about how to fully **Go After Jesus**:

> "If anyone desires to come after Me, let him deny himself, and take up his cross, and follow Me. For whoever desires to save his life will lose it, but whoever loses his life for My sake will find it. For what profit is it to a man if he gains the whole world, and loses his own soul? Or what will a man give in exchange for his soul?" (Matthew 16:24-26)

The Lover's Sacrifice

Love will move you to give up everything for the sake of the one your soul desires. Jesus was asking His twelve disciples to recognize who they were in Christ (their identity) and what they were willing to do for the sake of the gospel (their sacrifice and ministry).

The ***Lover*** is willing to lay down his or her life for the sake of Christ. Before you can truly live for something, you must be willing to die for it. You cannot fully live out your identity in Christ until you have laid yourself on the altar as a living sacrifice.

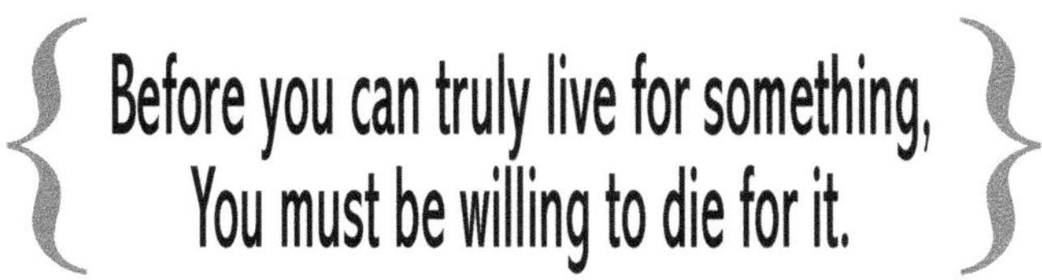
Before you can truly live for something,
You must be willing to die for it.

Lovers Seek the Other Person's Well-Being

Jesus carefully crafted His words to His disciples as He prepared them for His soon-to-be departure from the earth: "If anyone desires to come after Me, let him *deny* himself" (Matthew 16:24, emphasis added). The ***Lover*** is so motivated by wanting what is best for the one they love; they are willing to put themselves last. Love moves you to seek the well-being of your loved one above yourself.

When Lori and I met, I wanted to do whatever was necessary to demonstrate my growing love for her. After our first date, I drove an hour one way to take her back to her apartment. This meant I only had a few hours' sleep because I had to work the morning shift. The next day, I was dead tired from the lack of sleep, but I did not care. Why? Because I was crazy in love with this young lady, willing to travel to the moon and back if it meant spending another minute with her. Play the beat: "I would walk 500 miles, and I would walk 500 more ...!"[66]

What does Jesus mean by "denying" ourselves so we can follow Him? To deny yourself means you put aside any ambitions, goals, or desires that conflict with God's will for your life. Paul told the church at Philippi, "Let nothing be done through selfish ambition or conceit, but in lowliness of mind let each esteem others better than himself. Let each of you look out not only for his own interests, but also for the interests of others" (Philippians 2:3–4).

{ God asks you to give up something only because He has something better waiting for you. }

The ***Lover*** who desires to **Go After Jesus** is willing to lay aside his rights, privileges, and dreams to pursue the greater dream of seeking first the King and His Kingdom. Why would God call you to deny yourself? Why not make following Him easy? God only asks you to give up something because He has something better waiting for you.

Lovers Are Willing to Sacrifice Their Lives

God asks the ***Lover*** to leave the lesser loves of this world to pursue a higher love. Jesus asks you to lay down the temporary so you can take up the eternal. Against the backdrop of eternity, everything you possess apart from Christ is only a temporary treasure that will eventually fall apart. The ***Lover*** is willing to deny himself because the sacrifice is worth the cost. As the missionary Jim Elliot once said, "He is no fool who gives what he cannot keep to gain what he cannot lose."[67] Many people wear a cross on a necklace as a religious symbol. When the first-century Christ-followers saw a cross, they thought of a tragic, excruciating death on a wooden pole in public disgrace. Today, an electric chair might be an equivalent symbol. "If you want to come after me . . . deny yourself . . . and be willing to go to the electric chair."

> **Jesus asks you to lay down the temporary so you can take up the eternal.**

How many of us would sign up for death on a cross? In modern churches, I do not think many hands would be raised. Why did Jesus use such a grotesque symbol in His teaching? He was headed to a cross, so using one as an illustration may be one reason. In essence, Jesus is saying, "I am going to die for you. Are you willing to die for me?" Jesus laid down his life for you. Are you willing to do the same should that be the consequence of following Jesus in a hostile world?

In the Gospel of John, Jesus echoes this sacrificial call: "My command is this: Love each other as I have loved you. Greater love has no one than this: to lay down one's life for one's friends" (John 15:12-13 NIV). What are ***Lovers*** willing to do? They give all their heart, all their soul, and yes, even their life for the sake of the one they love.

A Classic Sacrificial Love Story

One of the most famous stories in English literature is the love story of Romeo and Juliet. Shakespeare masterfully crafts a story about two lovers who are forbidden to see each other because their noble families are embroiled in a bitter feud. Romeo and Juliet get married in secret, hoping their surprise union will end the feud. Their clandestine marriage only makes matters worse, though, resulting in Romeo killing Juliet's cousin, Tybalt, in a duel.

The friar (minister) who married them devised a plan with Juliet that would allow the lovers to be together again. Juliet would take a potion that will make her appear dead for forty-two hours, and then Romeo will go to her family's tomb, take her away, and the two will live happily ever after.

Just one problem: Romeo did not know Juliet was alive. Desperate to be with Juliet even in death, Romeo takes a poisonous potion, which causes him to die right beside his lover. In tragic irony, Juliet awakens moments after Romeo's death, which causes Juliet such heartbreak and grief that she chooses to die too by stabbing herself with Romeo's dagger. When the news reaches Romeo and Juliet's families, they reconcile and end the feud.[68] This story makes me sad. Why were these two lovers kept apart? May I give you some good news on the tail of this heart-wrenching story about Romeo and Juliet? Jesus died for you so that you can live for Him! Jesus died physically, so you can live eternally. He sacrificed Himself so you could be with Him forever. He paid the ultimate sacrifice because of His great love for you.

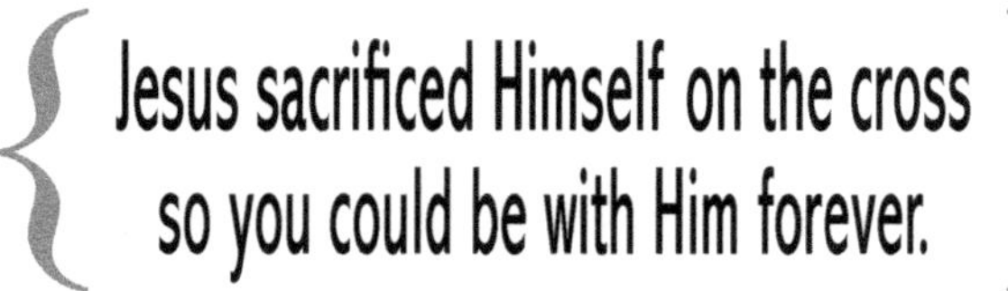

Jesus sacrificed Himself on the cross
so you could be with Him forever.

Paul describes a picture of the Greatest Lover: "But God demonstrates His own love toward us, in that while we were still sinners, Christ died for us" (Romans 5:8). Jesus drank from a cup, the cup of God's wrath, to redeem all those who would become His spiritual brides. Drinking from this cup resulted in His death. Does that remind you of Romeo drinking the cup full of poison to be with Juliet?

The gospel message is much better, though. Romeo and Juliet perished, but Jesus came back to life again because He is God; and He will eventually take us to live with Him forever. As Christ-followers, we do not have a tragic, fictional love story ending; we have a sacrificial, real-life love story that continues forever.

True Lovers Walk Together

As true ***Lovers*** of Jesus, we choose to deny ourselves and take up our cross. But what's next? After giving us two hard things to do, Jesus gives us something we can look forward to: "And follow Me." As you **Go After Jesus**, the greatest delight of your life will be following Jesus. You *get to* do life with Jesus. You have the privilege of walking with Jesus just like Adam and Eve walked with God in the Garden of Eden.

> Following Jesus looks different for every Christ-follower.

What does it look like to follow Jesus in your everyday life? Following Jesus looks different for every Christ-follower because God has a unique plan for each of His children. We all are so very different from one another, with different birthplaces, family backgrounds, and socio-economic experiences. We all have unique stories. Your personality and your passions are uniquely different from anyone else living today. With so much diversity, how can we all follow Jesus in the same direction, with unity?

Just like the sun shines on the earth at different times and in different light patterns, our lives will look vastly different, but we are all living in the light of the Lord. Despite such diversity among disciples, there are some core, universal principles of following Jesus for all Christ-followers of all times.

What Does a Lover of Jesus Look Like?

Lover Principle #1: Go where He calls you to go.

First, the call to love Jesus is to *go* wherever He tells you to go. Throughout the entire exciting narrative of Scripture, God is calling people to *go* to new places. God called Abraham to leave his homeland in Haran and *go* to a land that God would show him. Abraham left the familiar behind to pursue God's plan for his life (Genesis 12:1-3). When Moses was eighty years old, God called him to leave Midian and *go* back to Egypt so he could lead the Israelites out of bondage and into God's promised land (Exodus 4:18-20).

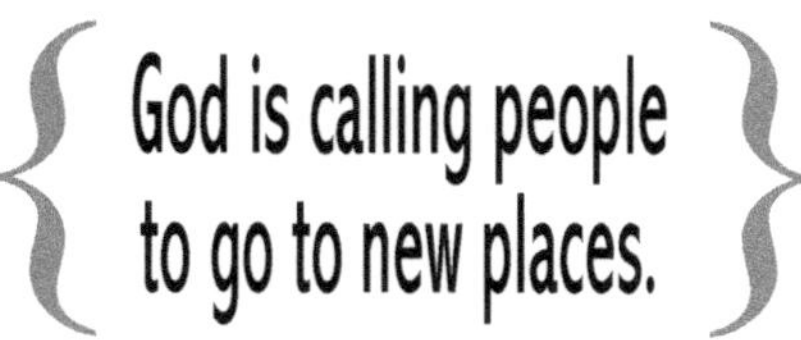
God is calling people
to go to new places.

Peter, along with the other disciples (the Twelve minus Judas), spread the gospel to areas outside Jerusalem. Jesus told them to leave the comforts of home and *go* to places that were uncomfortable and even unknown. (See Acts 1:8.) The apostle Paul left his hometown in Tarsus to spread the good news about Jesus and to start new churches in Asia Minor.[69] Before He returned to heaven, Jesus called those who loved Him to "make disciples of all the nations" (Matthew 28:19). This assignment was given not only to the apostles; it is also given to every Christ-follower. To **Go After Jesus** is to go wherever Jesus calls you to go. To follow Jesus is to go where He leads. As you go, Jesus goes with you. He promised His disciples, and He promises us, "I am with you always, *even* to the end of the age" (Matthew 28:20).

Lover Principle #2: Be the hands and feet of Jesus.

The second universal aspect of loving Jesus is to be His hands and feet in the world. Paul told the congregation at Ephesus that Christ-followers share these seven things as a church: one body, one Spirit, one hope, one Lord, one faith, one baptism, one God the Father who is above all and works in and through us all (Ephesians 4:4-6). These seven connectors unite all Christ-followers. But within the beautiful tapestry of unity, we also have diversity. Each of us has at least one spiritual gift, a grace gift used to build up the church. (See Ephesians 4:7–16.)

What does it mean to be the hands and feet of Jesus? You do your part in serving others. As you **Go After Jesus** as the ***Lover***, you serve the local church by using your gifts, talents, and abilities to help it grow. The result of everyone doing their part is the "growth of the body for the edifying of itself in love" (Ephesians 4:16). The church will be built up in love, and that is what ***Lovers*** of Jesus do: Love one another and build up other members of the body of Christ.

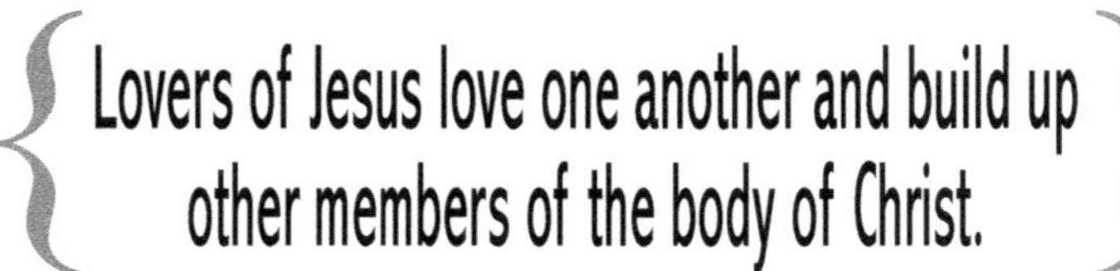
Lovers of Jesus love one another and build up
other members of the body of Christ.

Lover Principle #3: Become more like Jesus.

The third universal aspect of loving Jesus is that the closer we walk *with* Jesus, the more we become *like* Jesus. Some biblical scholars call this aspect of spiritual growth *sanctification*. Sanctification is the process of becoming more like Jesus as you grow in grace and as you study the Scriptures. Paul told the Christ-followers in Rome to present their bodies as "a living sacrifice" to God, which means God wants you to give all of yourself to Him (Romans 12:1 NIV). Being a living sacrifice means you identify as a ***Lover*** of God, you give all of yourself to the One who gave all of Himself to you on the cross.

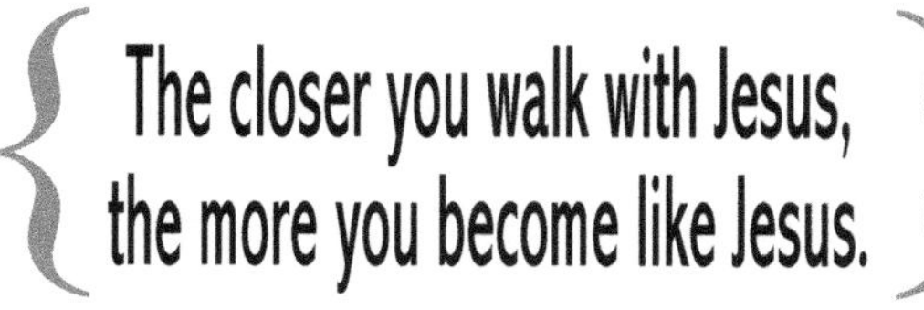
The closer you walk with Jesus,
the more you become like Jesus.

The church at Corinth was messed up in many ways; sexual immorality was rampant within the church, division was common, and everyone had their favorite preacher. Paul gave them another truth that reveals the process of spiritual growth within all Christ-followers as they become more like Him: "We all, with unveiled face, beholding as in a mirror the glory of the Lord, are being transformed into the same image from glory to glory, just as by the Spirit of the Lord" (2 Corinthians 3:18). We are being "transformed" to look more like Jesus as we follow Him in our daily lives.

As you **Go After Jesus** as a ***Lover***, something amazing happens: You find that Jesus is living His life through you. The Person of the Holy Spirit lives within you, and as you let the Spirit lead you, God is working in and through you in your daily life. Paul explained this process of God living in and through us: "I have been crucified with Christ; it is no longer I who live, but Christ lives in me; and the life which I now live in the flesh I live by faith in the Son of God, who loved me and gave Himself for me" (Galatians 2:20).

CHAPTER 18 RECAP

Go After Jesus Principle #18

As you Go After Jesus, you will become a Lover of Jesus, who is the ultimate model of perfect love and devotion.
Read: Ephesians, John 13:1, John 15:12 13, Galatians 2:20

Key Takeaways

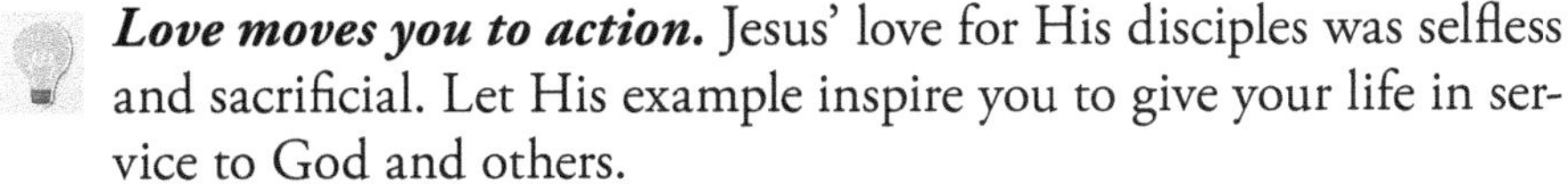

Love moves you to action. Jesus' love for His disciples was selfless and sacrificial. Let His example inspire you to give your life in service to God and others.

Great love leads to great sacrifice. You cannot fully love someone and stay the same. If you truly love Jesus with your entire self, you will deny yourself, take up your cross, and follow Him.

Love changes you from the inside out. The process of sanctification is the work of grace after you become a follower of Jesus. The closer you follow Jesus, the more you become like Him in your character and your actions.

Reflection

How are you demonstrating your love for Jesus daily?

Is God asking you to lay aside anything—ambitions, goals, or desires that conflict with His will? What might be keeping you from obeying His request?

How does loving Jesus look different for you than it does for other Christ-followers you know?

Looking Ahead

Chapter 19: Love Is . . . ?

CHAPTER 19

Love Is . . .

"Love is patient, love is kind. It does not envy, it does not boast, it is not proud. It does not dishonor others, it is not self-seeking, it is not easily angered, it keeps no record of wrongs. Love does not delight in evil but rejoices with the truth. It always protects, always trusts, always hopes, always perseveres. Love never fails."
1 Corinthians 13:4–8 (NIV)

If someone asked you to define the essence of love, how would you respond? So many people have tried to define love, but their understanding does not move anyone to live a life of love. When you think of the essence of true love, what comes to mind first? What examples or experiences have shaped your view of what love is and what love does?

When I think about true love, love that is unconditional and unrelenting, one that is sacrificial and expressive, I think about my mom. My mother, Janice Brown, is the proud mom of six children, four boys and two girls. I came as the last of the six, an unplanned, surprise gift for my parents. By the time I made my debut, most of my siblings were teenagers; a few were leaving the nest (moving out). This meant I was treated almost like an only child since the others were spreading their wings and flying off to college or to their new adult lives.

My parents never had a lot of money, but they always had a lot of love. My dad worked almost sixty hours per week to provide for our one-income household. He taught me the value of a strong work ethic while my mom taught me how to love God, love others, and simply love life. I am so blessed to say I have never felt unloved by my parents. They protected me from harm, they have provided for me even when they did not have much, and they loved me even when I was not feeling loved by outsiders.

Has someone in your life shown you unconditional love? If not, I pray that God will send someone into your life where you can see love in action. The apostle Paul helps all of us, including those of us who have not had a good example of love, understand what true love is. Many people call 1 Corinthians 13 "the love chapter" because it describes what true love is and what it does in and through a person's life.

Three Kinds of Love

Before I break down what love is, I will define what love is *not*. Apart from God, people experience three kinds of love. The first is *pseudo love*, a counterfeit, temporary love. Some people will offer you friendship only to use you to accomplish their goals and ambitions, and then discard you when they get out of you what they needed. How many of you have felt discarded by someone after you have helped them? This is an example of pseudo love, attention showered on you by someone because they want to use you to accomplish their goals.

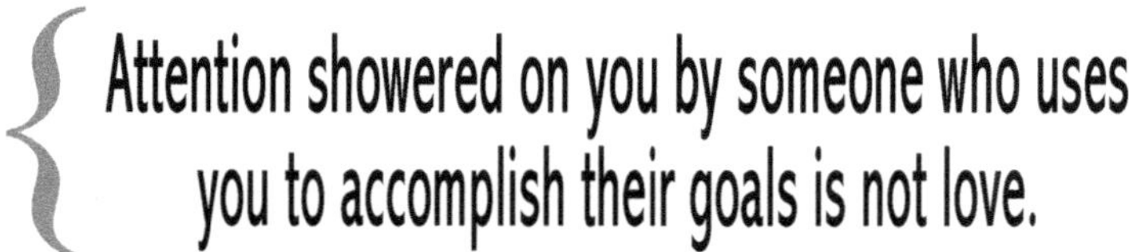

Attention showered on you by someone who uses
you to accomplish their goals is not love.

The second kind of love is *superficial love*. It is circumstantial, based on conditions that can change. A husband may walk out of a marriage because he does not feel passionate about his wife anymore. A girl may break up with her boyfriend because she is no longer attracted to him, or he simply is "not much fun". This is superficial, conditional love; feelings that change when something or someone more attractive comes along.

Superficial love prompts people to think or even say, "I love you *because* . . ." and "I'll love you *if* . . ." I love you because you are beautiful. I love you because you are so great with my children. I will love you if you promise to always be there for me.

I will love you if you will ____________________(fill in the blank). Superficial love will not survive the storms of life.

The third type of love is *constant love;* it can survive, even thrive and grow, through the fiercest storms of life. This love is unconditional. It is not based on how good you are or what you do; it is based on the choice to love and care for someone, no matter what. Constant love is the only kind God offers us because it is an integral part of His nature; human relationships, however, are only rarely based on this love.

True love is so rare that we should consider ourselves blessed if another human being demonstrates this kind of love for us. What would it be like to have someone love you no matter what you do? Is it possible to be loved even during those times and seasons when you are very difficult to love? The answer is an emphatic yes! Thankfully, as you **Go After Jesus,** you can discover and even walk in this type of love. How? God gave us instructions on how to give and receive constant love.

Agape love is the unconditional and sacrificial love that comes from God.

What Is Constant Love?

In 1 Corinthians 13, Paul introduces us to God's constant love, true love, called *agape.* Agape love is the unconditional and sacrificial love that comes from God.[70] It is a conscious choice that results in actions, attitudes, and behaviors that truly benefit the recipient of this amazing love. Next, I will unpack the scriptures to discover what love is and does.

True love treats others better than they deserve. Paul begins with this description: "Love is patient, love is kind" (1 Corinthians 13:4 NIV). Love does not give up on people because it is patient. Love is willing to keep on fighting another day because the person is worth the struggle.

I am so glad God treats us this way: He does not give up on us despite our behavior, even on our worst days. Instead, He is patient with us. Philippians 1:6 states, "He who has begun a good work in you will complete it until the day of Jesus Christ."

**Love does not give up on people.
It treats others with dignity and respect.**

True love is kind. This means love has good manners. It treats others with dignity and respect. You treat them the way you want to be treated. You approach others with a smile and a courteous greeting. I am so glad God is kind to us. He is never gruff. John 17:23 tells us God the Father loved Jesus' disciples the same way He loves Jesus!

Can you fathom that you are loved with the same love the Father has for Jesus? How does the Father love Jesus? The Father loves Jesus with an eternal, all-consuming love; it is larger than the universe, more expansive than the cosmos, deeper than the ocean, and powerful enough to light up the largest city forever. This is our Father's love for us.

First John 3:1 says it like this: "See what great love the Father has lavished on us, that we should be called children of God! And that is what we are!" (NIV). What is true love? True love treats us far better than we deserve. It treats us with kindness and compassion, which flows out of our new heart, given to us when we were adopted into God's very own family. (See Ezekiel 36:26.)

True love desires God's best for others. Not only is true love patient and kind, but it also "does not envy, it does not boast, it is not proud" (1 Corinthians 13:4). Since love is all about what is best for others, it does not want to take away; instead, it wants to give. Envy is wanting what others have. True love is outward-focused, so it does not want to take from others; it wants to add to others. It desires God's absolute best for the one who is loved. Therefore, if someone is more of a taker than a giver, they are not walking in true love.

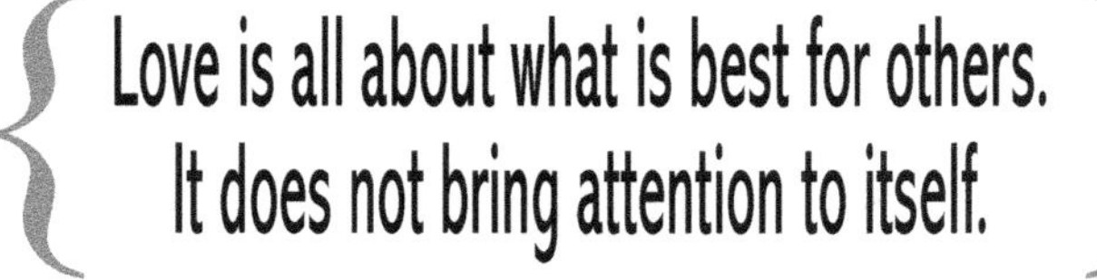
Love is all about what is best for others.
It does not bring attention to itself.

True love does not boast. Since love is not inward-focused, it does not bring attention to itself. Boasting is self-focused, but if you love someone with agape-like love, you will highlight God's blessing in their lives, not focus the spotlight on yourself.

True love is not proud. A prideful person is all about himself. The root of pride is *insecurity.* An insecure person often finds it challenging to build up someone else since they need to be built up themselves. You cannot give what you do not have. True love happens when a person can give out of the overflow of their relationship with Christ. A broken person's heart is fragmented. A depressed person's love is unstable. True love is the by-product of a person who is secure in Christ and can give out of the abundance of the love they have received from Christ. *True love honors others.* Paul writes, "It does not dishonor others," because true love wants to give, not take away (1 Corinthians 13:5).

How would you answer this heart-probing question: Are people better off after they met you than before they knew you? Because true love changes a person, other people should be transformed after they encounter the love of Jesus at work in and through you.

When people encountered Jesus while He was on Earth, one thing was true: They could not remain as they were. They had a choice. Either they responded to Jesus with a complete life change, or they ran in the opposite direction. Having seen the Light of the World, some chose to love darkness rather than the light because their deeds were evil. (See John 3:19.) The bottom line is that no one can experience the love of God and stay the same.

{ Love shows others respect and desires others to thrive. }

What does it look like to honor someone you love? It means you show them respect and desire them to thrive. You build others up with your words; you never put them down. Honoring someone means you always act in their best interests; you do not prioritize your pursuits at their expense. You extend the love of Christ to that person because they have been made in the image of God. As you honor them, you honor your Creator.

True love is not selfish. Recently, a couple started attending the church I pastor for an interesting reason. Friends at their previous church turned out not to be friends after all. Why? These so-called friends were friendly to this couple only because they wanted to recruit them for their business, which had a multi-level marketing (MLM) structure. An MLM works something like this: The more people who join your business, the more you can earn from their earnings. Once this couple decided they no longer wanted to pursue being part of the business, the so-called friends no longer wanted a relationship with them.

Have you had a similar experience? Are some people friendly to you only if they think they can get something from you? They will be your best friend when you are meeting a need or desire they have, but as soon as you do not scratch their itch, you are discarded like yesterday's newspaper. Paul lets us in on this beautiful truth: True love is not selfish because it is focused on the other person's well-being.

True love has a long fuse. Paul says love is "not easily angered" (1 Corinthians 13:5 NIV). If you love someone with agape-like love, you choose to *put up* with them instead of *giving up* on them. Love bears the weight of others' offenses, mistakes, and failures for a long time. It hangs in there when the going gets tough.

{ Love hangs in there when the going gets tough. }

I love each of my six children with all my heart, but I am going to be transparent. Sometimes it is hard to love them. On certain days and in certain moments, their behavior pushes all my buttons. But guess what? Because of my unconditional love for them, I love them no matter what they say and no matter what they do. I make the choice to love them on their good days as well as their challenging ones.

True love has so much compassion and empathy toward others that it chooses not to react in anger when it would be easy to do so. I often say to my children, "I love you always, I love you forever, and I love you no matter what!" As you **Go After Jesus**, you are called to walk in a new kind of love, one far different from the world's inferior types of love. Jesus offers a sacrificial love, one that is willing to devote an entire life for the sake of others. Jesus calls this a "greater love." (See John 15:12-13.)

True love keeps no record of wrongs. Has someone held a grudge against you for something you did? Were they unable to let go of that hurt? Most, if not all of us, have had this happen. But true love forgives completely and chooses not to hold the past against someone. Paul says God's love "keeps no record of wrongs" (1 Corinthians 13:5 NIV). Love knows how to forgive and move past the past.

Love knows how to forgive and move past the past.

Cars have a big front windshield but a small rear-view mirror. Why? Drivers spend most of their time looking ahead to where they are going rather than looking behind at where they have been. True love works the same way. When you believe the best about another person and you have high hopes of what God will do in their life, you choose to look to what is ahead, not what is behind.

When you disagree with a loved one, do not hold what has been forgiven in the past against them in the present. Paul advises us on how to maintain loving relationships with one another in the church: "Bear with each other and forgive one another if any of you has a grievance against someone. Forgive as the Lord forgave you" (Colossians 3:13 NIV). In other words, forgive in the same manner as Jesus has forgiven you. How did Jesus forgive you? Did He hold your past against you? No. In the same way, we are to forgive others because of our great love for them.

True love brings out the best. Love actively seeks to bring out the best in other people. Paul lists another characteristic of love: It "does not delight in evil, but rejoices with the truth" (1 Corinthians 13:6 NIV). Love takes no delight in sin, shame, or scandal. Anything that promotes sin cannot be called true love. Rather, love is always fueled by that which is true. In fact, truth and love work in tandem.

The more truth grows, the more love grows; and the more love grows, the more truth can prosper. Love "always protects, always trusts, and always hopes" (1 Corinthians 13:7 NIV). True love has a persevering nature, which is why it should last a lifetime. Since love always protects, it is willing to stand up for someone else. It is trusting, but not naïve. It is always hopeful, which means it focuses more on another person's potential than on their failures.

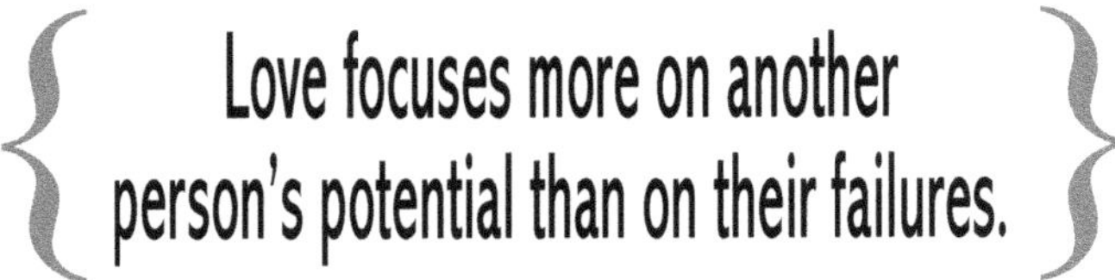

This is the way God's love works toward us and in us. He loves us just the way we are, but He loves us too much to let us stay that way. True love changes someone from the inside out. Once you have encountered the love of God, a tidal wave of grace leaves you forever changed and transformed by that grace.

True love lasts forever. Has someone ever said they loved you, but now they are no longer in your life? Did they love you with unconditional love, or was it some other type of love? God's agape love endures. When God loves you, He loves you forever.

Paul finishes this stunning love chapter with two final descriptions of true love: It always perseveres. Love never fails" (1 Corinthians 13:7-8 NIV). People may fail you, but true love never will. Only God is always loving, so you can count on Him never to fail you. The writer of the book of Hebrews gives us this promise from God: "Never will I leave you; never will I forsake you" (Hebrews 13:5 NIV). David conveyed this same truth in one of his psalms: "Though my father and mother forsake me, the Lord will receive me" (Psalm 27:10 NIV).

Here's good news as you **Go After Jesus** as a ***Lover***: You are loved more than you will ever know. In turn, you are called to live out the love you have received so the world can see that Jesus is still alive, living through you. Love is all about treating others better than what they deserve because of the power of God's grace at work in your life.

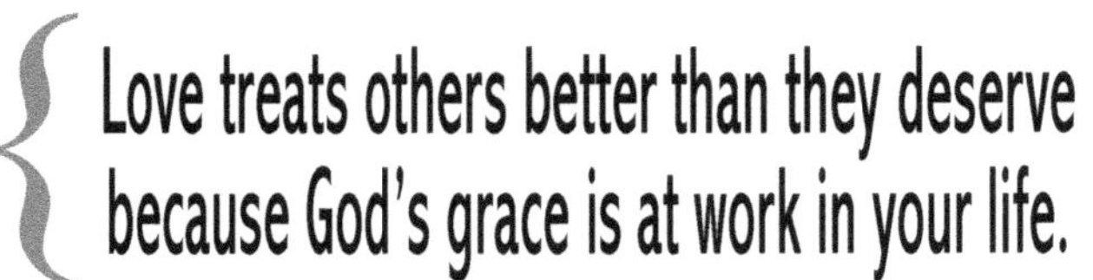

Love treats others better than they deserve
because God's grace is at work in your life.

What have we learned about love in this chapter? Love is all about wanting God's best for everyone you meet because you have the heart of Christ for others. Love is all about honoring others because honor is the culture of the Kingdom of God. Love is all about forgiving others when they have wronged you, because you also have been forgiven, and the forgiven forgive. So, throw away that list of grudges and wrongs, and choose to walk in the forgiveness true love brings. True love also always looks for the best in others and brings out God's redemptive potential in their lives. Finally, true love never sees any person or situation as hopeless because love sees others through the eyes of faith, focusing not on what is but on what can be and what should be.

CHAPTER 19 RECAP

Go After Jesus Principle #19

True love goes beyond feelings; it is the choice to love others like Jesus loves us, with relentless passion and unwavering grace.
1 Corinthians 13:4-8, John 17:23, 1 John 3:1

Key Takeaways

True love is unconditional. It will enable you to become outward-focused, patient, and kind, always seeking the best in others and for others without envy or pride.

True love forgives. It will help you keep no record of wrongs, forgive others, and focus on the future rather than dwelling on past hurts.

True love endures. It will enable you to protect, trust, hope, and persevere. True love, God's agape love, never fails and never gives up on others.

Reflection

Who stands out in your mind as a model of true love? What characteristics of love does that person consistently demonstrate?

What about God's constant love for you is difficult to accept? How does God's love fill you with joy and praise?

What aspects of true love do you demonstrate? What characteristics does the Holy Spirit need to cultivate in you?

Looking Ahead

Chapter 20: The Greatest Love

CHAPTER 20

The Greatest Love

Jesus said, "Greater love has no one than this:
to lay down one's life for one's friends."
John 15:13 (NIV)

William Borden had so much going for him. His family was well known due to their business successes in the early 1900s, and he was the heir to the Borden family fortune. William's options seemed unlimited. He could go wherever he wanted after high school graduation. With his family's status and prestige, he could marry just about anyone he desired. He could become the next president of his parents' company. With a life full of exciting possibilities, what choices would he make?

William eventually did something that shocked his family and still amazes historians. During his travels through Asia, the Middle East, and Europe, he became burdened for the lost. His heart was especially moved for Muslims who desperately needed to know the truth about Jesus Christ, so he wrote a letter telling his parents he planned to prepare for the mission field. Shortly after making that decision, he wrote two words in the back of his Bible: "No Reserves."

William attended Yale University and became one of the leaders of a campus prayer movement there. He then studied at Princeton Theological Seminary. Despite his family's immense wealth and all the opportunities available to a young man in his twenties, William continued to prepare for and pursue his dream of reaching Muslim people for Christ.

After he completed his studies at Princeton, William felt the call to reach the Kansu people, a Muslim group in China. Before he moved to China, William sailed to Egypt to study Arabic so he would be ready for missionary work in China. However, after William arrived in Cairo, the unthinkable happened. He contracted spinal meningitis. Within a month, twenty-five-year-old William was dead.

This story may seem to be a sad tale of a wasted life, unrealized potential, and a tragic ending to a young man's bright future. However, William's death is not the end of his story. At the funeral, the speaker read what William wrote in the back of his Bible. In addition to "No Reserves," he added these two phrases: "No Retreats" and "No Regrets." The "No Regrets" phrase was dated just before his death.[71]

{ William Borden's motto: No Reserves, No Retreats, and No Regrets. }

William's story has inspired countless young people to dedicate their lives to the mission field, no matter the cost. William's life was not wasted; he died in faith, and his faith continues to inspire people to follow God's call for their lives. His life is a testimony demonstrating the highest level of following Jesus: Laying down your life for the sake of your greater love for the Lord Jesus Christ.

Your Life Matters

In this summary, I will bring together all six identities of going after Jesus throughout your lifetime. Let this truth sink deep into your heart: ***your life matters to God.*** You are here on Earth for a reason. God has custom-designed you for a purpose. He arranged the exact time of your birth in the exact place on planet Earth where you can fulfill God's call on your life. As Paul preached to the Greek philosophers and intellectuals at the Areopagus in Athens (Mars Hill), he gave them this incredible truth: "From one man he [God] made all the nations, that they should inhabit the whole earth; and he marked out their appointed times in history and the boundaries of their lands" (Acts 17:26 NIV).

Think deeply about that verse for a few moments. God's plan is so purposeful that He "marked out" the "appointed times" and "boundaries" for each person who ever walked on planet Earth. In Psalm 139, David gives us the same truth: God was at work in us even when we were in our mother's womb (vv. 13–16). Friend, you are not here by *accident*; you are here by divine *providence*. God does not work by human *coincidence*, but by divine *providence*!

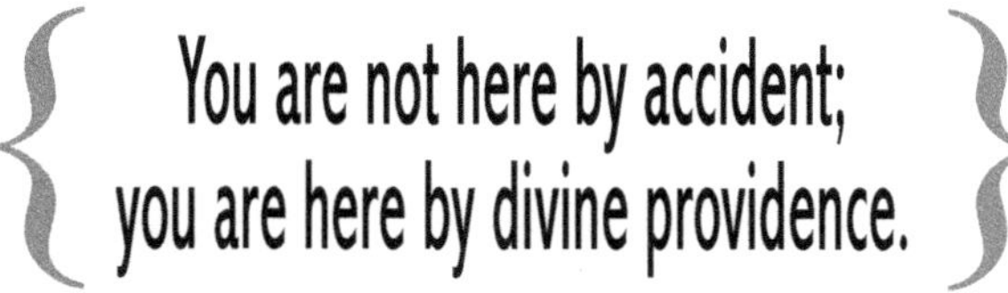
You are not here by accident;
you are here by divine providence.

Your Move, Do Not Waste Your Life

Your life is too short to waste. I discovered that when I was fifteen years old. As a teenager, I prayed a prayer that forever changed the trajectory of my life: "Lord, help me to realize how short my life really is. Teach me to number my days." God answered that prayer quickly. From that moment on, I have been living like someone whose days are numbered. I guess you could say that from that moment on, I had an "old soul," who understands life is way too short.

Live like someone whose days are numbered.

Guess what? Your days are also numbered. The psalmist prayed: "Teach us to number our days, that we may gain a heart of wisdom" (Psalm 90:12 NIV). Reflecting on his own suffering and sickness, Job reveals: "A person's days are determined; you [God] have decreed the number of his months and have set limits he cannot exceed (Job 14:5 NIV).

If your days are numbered and their limit is determined, how should you be living? What would happen if you surrendered all your plans to the plans and purposes of God? How would your life change the world around you? Who would be in heaven because of your ministry? How many people could you impact with the message of the gospel in your lifetime?

Your Life as a Blank Check to God

Around the same time I prayed the life-altering prayer about God helping me to realize the brevity of my life, I also did something else: I wrote God a check. I told God that my life was a *blank* check, and He could write whatever He wanted on it. "God, I am willing to *go* wherever You want me to go. I am willing to *do* whatever You want me to do. No limitations. No restrictions. At any cost. God, I am fully Yours. Amen."

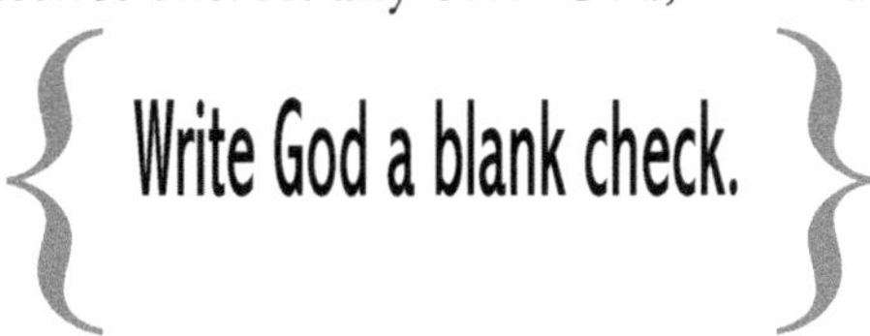

As you **Go After Jesus,** you eventually reach the point where you are willing to lay down your life out of love; not out of obligation, not because you must, but because you get to. The greatest offering you can give to Jesus is yourself! What do you have to lose? Jesus said, "Whoever seeks to save his life will lose it, and whoever loses his life will preserve it" (Luke 17:33). Laying down your life for Jesus now means living with Him forever.

The Greatest Love Is Sacrificial Surrender

You may know John 3:16, but do you know what 1 John 3:16 says? John 3:16 speaks of God's love for us, but 1 John 3:16 ties God's love for us to our response to Jesus' sacrificial love: "This is how we know what love is: Jesus Christ laid down his life for us. And we ought to lay down our lives for our brothers and sisters" (NIV). God loves you so much that He gave . . . how did God give?

The Father gave the greatest gift in human history to a world that had great needs, the need for forgiveness, salvation, and restoration. Jesus Christ came to Earth to make the greatest sacrifice on your behalf. He paid a debt He did not owe because you owed a debt you could not pay. Why did Jesus do that? Out of love for you. Friend, Jesus loves you that much!

His sacrificial and redemptive love should move you to do the same: give your life for others out of love for Jesus.

The call to **Go After Jesus** is the call to be a ***Lover***, a lover of God who, in turn, loves others! What does this look like? How can you give your life to others out of your love for Jesus?

> **Give your life for others out of your love for Jesus.**

The answer is both simple and complex. (Yes, I know that is a paradox.) The simple response is one word: *surrender*. When you surrender your life to Jesus, you begin to live a life of love for God and others. The complex part is that surrender will look different for every follower of Jesus.

For some Christ-followers, it is lived out daily as you spend time with Jesus, serve others, and build up the local church using your spiritual gifts. For others, this decision may take them to the foreign mission field, serving a group that God laid on their hearts to reach with the gospel.

For a few, it may mean giving their very life for the sake of the gospel in a sacrificial way. According to some researchers, around 70 million Christ-followers have been martyred for their faith since the time of Jesus.[72] In modern times, it is estimated that on average, 90,000 Christians are killed every year because of their faith.[73] I do not know about you, but those numbers alarm me. Would I lay down my life for the sake of the gospel? I pray that I would. I believe God gives each person the grace needed for each situation they face. I also pray that neither you nor I must face the ultimate decision to lay down our lives for the sake of the gospel, but should the good Lord call us to do so, may we be found faithful even unto death!

Your Purpose: The Six Identities

What is God's objective for your life? God's greatest purpose is for you to accept Jesus as your Lord and Savior, to be adopted into His family, and to live out His plan for your life. In **Go After Jesus**, you discovered what following Jesus looks like. First, you find who Jesus is as a ***Seeker***. Seeking after Jesus is a journey that does *not* end after you become a Christ-follower; it continues for the rest of your life, so never stop seeking to know Jesus better.

Second, you follow Jesus as His ***Disciple***. Jesus said, "Follow Me" (Matthew 4:19 NIV). Following Jesus is the *delight* of every disciple. As you pursue Jesus, you become His disciple, learning His ways and walking in His purposes for your life. As a student of the Savior, you never stop learning more about your Lord every day that He gives you this side of eternity.

Third, as you follow Jesus daily, you grow in intimacy with Him as His ***Friend***. A friend of Jesus enjoys special privileges others miss out on, knowing God in a profound and personal way, learning the secrets of God often hidden from others, and experiencing heightened levels of joy, peace, and purpose in their daily life. Your relationship grows each day as you commit to spend time in His Word and connect with other Christ-followers in authentic community.

{ Spend time in God's Word and connect with other Christ-followers. }

Fourth, as you grow in your friendship with God, you develop a new passion: introducing your friends to your new best friend! You begin to "catch men" for Jesus as a ***Fisherman***. You are now part of a higher and greater purpose than yourself. You are now living for the King and His Kingdom. Your aspiration is to love God and to love people. As your love for God grows, your desire to reach people who are lost will also grow. One of the greatest expressions of love for your neighbors is guiding them into a saving faith in Jesus Christ.

Fifth, when you start bringing people to Christ, you encounter spiritual warfare. Satan is threatened when you help rescue people from his kingdom of death and darkness. He hates it when you participate in God's rescue mission to lead people out of darkness and into His glorious light! As you **Go After Jesus**, you hear the call to battle, the call to be a courageous ***Soldier*** for the cause of Christ. In this world, you will have trouble, but you also realize Jesus has already overcome the world (John 16:33). You learn to soldier up and gear up, as you prepare to stand strong in the day of battle (Ephesians 6:10-18).

The sixth identity of a Christ-follower is complete devotion as the ***Lover*** of Jesus. He taught His disciples this about being a ***Lover***: "Greater love has no one than this: to lay down one's life for one's friends" (John 15:13). Jesus asks you to give your entire self to Him since He gave His entire self for you. If Jesus asked you to lay down your life for the sake of the gospel, would you be willing to do that?

I'm Rooting for You!

Reading the book is just part of the adventure of a lifetime. Your decision to **Go After Jesus** is all of grace, not of works. This book is not an attempt to teach you ways to gain God's favor; His favor is found through Christ alone. This book is about your identity as a follower of Jesus. The emphasis is not on the *Do*, but on the *Who*. The *Do flows out of the Who*. In other words, your daily actions flow out of your identity in Jesus Christ.

Every long journey begins with a single step. If you have decided to **Go After Jesus,** now it is your turn to live it out in your daily walk with God. I wish you all of God's richest blessings as you grow in the grace and knowledge of our Lord Jesus Christ (2 Peter 3:18).

Let's **Go After Jesus**,
Dr. Timothy Brown

CHAPTER 20 RECAP

Go After Jesus Principle #20

You are not willing to die for Jesus until you are first willing to live for Jesus. The call to **Go After Jesus** is the call to be a sacrificial Lover, willing to lay down your life for the sake of the gospel.
John 15:13, 1 John 3:16, Philippians 2:3–4

Key Takeaways

Sacrificial love defines true discipleship. Just like Jesus laid down His life for you, you should be willing to lay down your life for Him; whether this means a life fully surrendered to doing God's will or giving your very life for the sake of the gospel.

Live with No Reserves, No Retreats, and No Regrets. Let William Borden's motto challenge you to fully **Go After Jesus** by living boldly for Christ, holding nothing back.

Your life matters to God. Remember your six identities as you **Go After Jesus.** You are a ***Seeker***, a ***Disciple***, a ***Friend***, a ***Fisherman***, a ***Soldier***, and a ***Lover***.

Reflection

What do you admire most about William Borden's love for Jesus? How can you cultivate that trait?

Are you willing to write God a blank check? If so, take a paper check, write your commitment on it, and keep it in your Bible as a reminder.

What identity best describes you now, ***Seeker, Disciple, Friend, Fisherman, Soldier,*** or ***Lover***? What can you do today that will move you forward toward the next identity?

About the Author

Family Life: Dr. Timothy Brown is married to the love of his life—Lori Brown. Together, they currently have six children (3 boys and 3 girls). Timothy has served as the Lead Pastor of Radiant Church since 2016, which is located in the Asheville, North Carolina area.

Mission: Timothy's life mission is to Encourage, Equip, and Empower people to live out the destiny that God has for their life. He has a heart for helping every Christian reach their full redemptive potential in Christ.

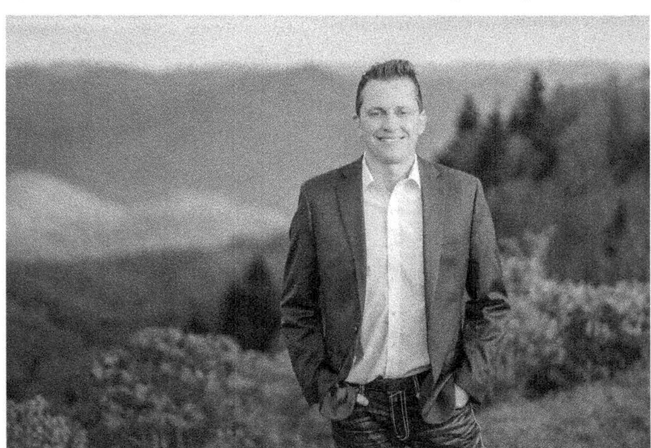

Education: Timothy is a lifelong learner and has advanced degrees in ministry and preaching, including a Doctor of Ministry Degree in Preaching from Columbia International University.

Hobbies: Timothy enjoys pleasant conversations over coffee at the local coffeehouses. He also enjoys a lively game of basketball, whether it is pickup basketball or watching an NBA game on TV.

Contact: Connect with Timothy at www.DrTimothyBrown.org. You can also find him on social under the handle @drtimothybrownministries on Facebook, YouTube, and Instagram.

Resources: Dr. Timothy is creating and launching new books, devotionals, and other helpful resources. Find these discipleship tools at www.DrTimothyBrown.org.

Endnotes

1. Jon Bloom, "Your Emotions Are a Gauge, Not a Guide," *Desiring God,* August 3, 2012, https://www.desiringgod.org/articles/your-emotions-are-a-gauge-not-a-guide.

2. Jamie Smart, "Are Your Feelings Always a Reliable Guide?" *Uplift*, accessed December 21, 2024, https://upliftconnect.com/are-your-feelings-always-a-reliable-guide/.

3. Hillsdale College Online Courses Blog, "Julian the Apostate's Attempt to Restore Roman Paganism," accessed January 11, 2025, https://onlinecoursesblog.hillsdale.edu/julian-the-apostates-attempt-to-restore-roman-paganism/.

4. "Hypocrite," *Merriam-Webster Dictionary*, accessed December 21, 2024, https://www.merriam-webster.com/words-at-play/hypocrite-meaning-origin.

5. Qtd. in Eugene Peterson, *A Long Obedience in the Same Direction.* 20th Anniversary Edition (Downers Grove, Ill: InterVarsity Press, 2021), epigraph for chap. 1. Kindle

6. Chris Opfer, "What If Earth Changed Its Orbit?" *HowStuffWorks*, updated June 9, 2023, https://science.howstuffworks.com/science-vs-myth/what-if/what-if-earth-changed-its-orbit.htm.

7. "What Is Koinonia?" *Got Question*s, accessed June 29, 2021, https://www.gotquestions.org/koinonia.html.

8. Chad Harrington, "Everything You Need to Know About the ACTS Prayer Model, *Him Publications,* accessed December 21, 2024, https://himpublications.com/blog/acts-prayer-model/.

9. John Piper, "What Is Worship?" *Desiring God,* April 29, 2016, audio transcript, https://www.desiringgod.org/interviews/what-is-worship.

10. “What Does It Mean That the Holy Spirit Is Our Paraclete?” *Got Questions,* accessed December 21, 2024, https://www.gotquestions.org/paraclete-Holy-Spirit.html.

11. Bethany Verrett, “What Does It Mean to Be Holy?” *Bible Study Tools*, updated September 5, 2023, https://www.biblestudytools.com/bible-study/topical-studies/what-does-it-mean-to-be-holy.html.

12 “Spiritual Gifts Survey,” LifeWay, Lifeway Christian Resources, accessed December 21, 2024, https://s3.amazonaws.com/bhpub/edoc/DOC-Spiritual-Gifts-Survey.pdf.

13. Jeff Carver, “Discover Your Calling,” *Spiritual Gift Test,* accessed December 21, 2024, https://spiritualgiftstest.com/.

14. “Sea of Galilee,” *Bible Places*, accessed June 13, 2022, https://www.bibleplaces.com/seagalilee/.

15. Tom Schad, “What We Know About the Kobe Bryant Helicopter Crash, One Year Later,” *USA Today*, January 25, 2021, https://www.usatoday.com/in-depth/sports/nba/lakers/2021/01/25/kobe-bryant-what-we-know-helicopter-crash-one-year-later/4239967001/ (accessed June 21, 2025).

16. “G533 - aparneomai – Strong’s Greek Lexicon (nlt).” Blue Letter Bible. Accessed Jan 1, 2025. https://www.blueletterbible.org/lexicon/g533/nlt/mgnt/0-1/.

17. “How Many Prophecies Did Jesus Fulfill?” *Got Questions*, accessed on June 12, 2023, https://www.gotquestions.org/prophecies-of-Jesus.html.

18. University of Hong Kong, “Honorary Degree of Doctor of Social Sciences: Jacqueline Pullinger,” accessed January 11, 2025, https://www4.hku.hk/hongrads/graduates/honorary-degree-of-doctor-of-social-sciences-jacqueline-pullinger.

19. Jackie Pullinger and Andrew Quicke, *Chasing the Dragon* (London: John Murray, 2012).

20. “Apprentice,” *Merriam-Webster Dictionary*, accessed December 21, 2024, https://www.merriam-webster.com/dictionary/apprentice.

21. Veera Korhonen, publisher, “How Often Do You Attend Church or Synagogue—At Least Once a Week, Almost Every Week, About Once

a Month, Seldom, or Never?" *Statista*, July 5, 2024, https://www.statista.com/statistics/245491/church-attendance-of-americans/.

22. "Frequency of Prayer," Religious Landscape Study, *Pew Research*, accessed December 21, 2024, https://www.pewresearch.org/religion/religious-landscape-study/frequency-of-prayer/.

23. Source unknown, adapted from "One Day at a Time," *Bible.org*, accessed December 21, 2024, https://bible.org/illustration/one-day-time.

24. J. I. Packer and Carolyn Nystrom, *Abiding in Christ*, LifeGuide Bible Studies, (Lisle, Illinois: IVP, 2009), 5.

25. Corrie ten Boom, *The Hiding Place,* 35th Anniversary Edition (Grand Rapids: Baker, 2006), chap. 12. Kindle.

26. Max Lucado, *God Thinks You're Wonderful* (Nashville: Thomas Nelson, 2003), 10–14, 20.

27. "Happy," *Merriam-Webster Dictionary*, accessed December 21, 2024, https://www.merriam-webster.com/dictionary/happy.

28. Meg Bucher, "The Beauty of Seeking Both Joy and Happiness in Christ," https://www.biblestudytools.com/bible-study/topical-studies/the-beauty-of-seeking-both-joy-and-happiness-in-christ.html.

29. Qtd. in Connie Stemmie, "You Are the Average of the Five People Quote: 5 Lessons," *Develop Good Habits*, August 30, 2023, https://www.developgoodhabits.com/five-people/.

30. "What Is the Favor of God, and How Can I Get It?" *Got Questions,* accessed December 21, 2024, https://www.gotquestions.org/favor-of-God.html.

31. For more of Joseph's story, read Genesis 37–50.

32. Rick Warren, *The Purpose Driven Life* (Zondervan, 2002), p. 149.

33. Al Fadi, "I Wanted to Die for Allah. Now I Live for Jesus," *Christianity Today*, January/February 2023, https://www.christianitytoday.com/ct/2023/januaryfebruary/al-fadi-muslim-holy-warrior-saudi-arabia-allah-jesus.html.

34. For more details on biblical fishing, see "Fishing in the Bible and the Ancient Near East," The Wiki Bible Project, last edited December 9, 2007, http://thewikibible.pbworks.com/w/page/22174694/Fishing%20in%20the%20Bible%20and%20the%20Ancient%20Near%20East.

35. Some attribute this quote to President Theodore Roosevelt. "Theodore Roosevelt Quotes," *Theodore Roosevelt Center*, accessed December 21, 2024, https://www.theodorerooseveltcenter.org/Learn-About-TR/TR-Quotes?page=112.

36. Dave Ferguson, "5 Ways to B.L.E.S.S. Your Neighbors," edited transcript of a message given at the Verge Conference, accessed December 21, 2024, https://s3.amazonaws.com/media.cloversites.com/58/58ca5f3b-3a08-47d8-8c92-2bb67c222414/documents/5-Ways-To-BLESS-Your-Neighbors-Ferguson.pdf.

37. Dave Ferguson, "5 Ways to B.L.E.S.S. Your Neighbors."

38. SmallCircle, accessed January 11, 2025, https://www.smallcircle.com/.

39. The Navigators, "Disciplemaking," accessed January 11, 2025, https://www.navigators.org/disciplemaking/

40. YouVersion, "Bible Reading Plans," accessed January 11, 2025, https://www.bible.com/reading-plans.

41. Pittwater Online News, "Mark Twain, J.F. Archibald, and Henry Lawson in Narrabeen, 1895," accessed January 11, 2025, https://www.pittwateronlinenews.com/Mark-Twain-JF-Archibald-Henry-Lawson-Narrabeen1895.php.

42. John MacArthur, "The Story of the Calm: Part 2," Grace to You, accessed January 11, 2025, https://www.gty.org/library/sermons-library/42-108/The-Story-of-the-Calm-Part-2

43. "Sea of Galilee," *Bible Places*, accessed June 13, 2022, https://www.bibleplaces.com/seagalilee/.

44. For an example, see Acts 13:16–41.

45. "The Miraculous Catch of Fish and the Calling of Peter—Acting in Faith," The Spiritual Family, The Work, accessed December 21, 2024, https://www.thework-fso.org/faith-and-life/the-miraculous-catch-of-fish-and-the-calling-of-peter-acting-in-faith-1.

46. See John 6:1–14.

47. James Miller, "Built to Sail," Illustration Exchange, posted September 22, 2018, https://illustrationexchange.com/illustrations?category=631.

48. “Medal of Honor: Captain Florent Groberg,” U.S. Army, Medal of Honor Recipients, accessed January 11, 2025, https://www.army.mil/medalofhonor/groberg/.

49. “Boot Camp,” *Today’s Military*, accessed December 21, 2024, https://www.todaysmilitary.com/joining-eligibility/boot-camp.

50. Barb Raveling, “Spiritual Attack: 10 Tips for Spiritual Warfare,” excerpt from podcast, July 30, 2020, https://barbraveling.com/spiritual-attack/.

51. Don Stewart, “When Does Satan Spiritually Attack the Believer?” *Blue Letter Bible*, https://www.blueletterbible.org/faq/don_stewart/don_stewart_95.cfm.

52. Don Stewart, “When Does Satan Spiritually Attack the Believer?”

53. *Spiritual Attacks*. Scribd, https://www.scribd.com/document/715746398/spiritual-attacks, accessed January 11, 2025.

54. *NKJV Study Bible, Full-Color Edition*, digital version. Copyright ©1997, 2007 by Thomas Nelson, Inc. Accessed January 11, 2025.

55. Ibid.

56. Family Times, “Victory Illustration,” accessed January 11, 2025, https://www.family-times.net/illustration/Victory/200230/

57. Steven P. Wickstrom, “(4) The Shield of Faith” *Group Bible Study*, accessed December 21, 2024, https://www.groupbiblestudy.com/post/4-the-shield-of-faith.

58. “What Is the Shield of Faith?” *Got Questions*, accessed December 21, 2024, https://www.gotquestions.org/shield-of-faith.html.

59. “Roman Helmet,” *History Cooperative*, accessed January 11, 2025, https://historycooperative.org/roman-helmet/?utm_source=chatgpt.com.

60. “What Is the Difference Between a Gladius and Spatha?” *Coloring Folder*, accessed January 11, 2025, https://coloringfolder.com/what-is-the-difference-between-a-gladius-and-spatha/.

61. “The Roman Spatha: Its Use and Evolution,” *Classics World*, accessed January 11, 2025, https://classicsworld.wordpress.com/2024/05/08/the-roman-spatha-its-use-and-evolution/.

62. G3162 – *machaira*. Blue Letter Bible. Accessed December 21, 2024. https://www.blueletterbible.org/lexicon/g3162/kjv/tr/0-1/.

63. "G4487 - rēma – Strong's Greek Lexicon (kjv)." Blue Letter Bible. Accessed Dec 21, 2024. https://www.blueletterbible.org/lexicon/g4487/kjv/tr/0-1/.

64. "G69 - agrypneō – Strong's Greek Lexicon (kjv)." *Blue Letter Bible*. Accessed Dec 21, 2024. https://www.blueletterbible.org/lexicon/g69/kjv/tr/0-1/.

65. Encyclopaedia Britannica, "Dietrich Bonhoeffer: Ethical and Religious Thought," accessed January 11, 2025, https://www.britannica.com/biography/Dietrich-Bonhoeffer/Ethical-and-religious-thought.

66. "I'm Gonna Be (500 Miles)," written by Craig and Charlie Reid, released by The Proclaimers in 1988. Chipping Norton Recording Studios, England.

67. Justin Taylor, "They Were No Fools: The Martyrdom of Jim Elliot and Four Other Missionaries," *The Gospel Coalition*, January 8, 2016, https://www.thegospelcoalition.org/blogs/justin-taylor/they-were-no-fools-60-years-ago-today-the-martyrdom-of-jim-elliot-and-four-other-missionaries/.

68. Read William Shakespeare's "Romeo and Juliet": https://folger-main-site-assets.s3.amazonaws.com/uploads/2022/11/romeo-and-juliet_PDF_FolgerShakespeare.pdf.

69. Acts 9–28 describe the life and missionary journeys of Paul.

70. "Love-Agape (Greek Word Study)," *Precept Austin*, updated July 7, 2023, (accessed June 21, 2025).

71. "Missionary William Whiting Borden," *Ligonier Ministries*, accessed January 11, 2025, https://learn.ligonier.org/articles/missionary-william-whiting-borden.

72. Cath Martin, "'70 Million Christians' Martyred for Their Faith Since Jesus Walked the Earth," *Christian Today*, June 25, 2014, https://www.christiantoday.com/article/70-million-christians-martyred-faith-since-jesus-walked-earth/38403.htm.

73. Dr. Todd M. Johnson, "Christian Martyrdom: Who? Why? How?," blog post, Gordon-Conwell Theological Seminary, December 18, 2019.

www.ingramcontent.com/pod-product-compliance
Lightning Source LLC
Chambersburg PA
CBHW051513120626
46551CB00012B/900
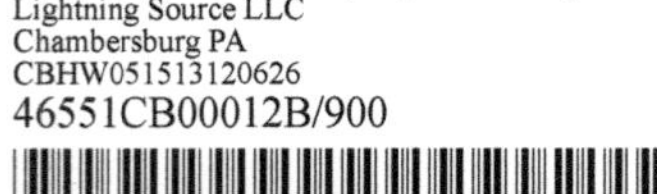
9798999822802